# Multinationals and Global Consumers

*The AIB Southeast Asia Series*

Series Editor: **T. S. Chan**, Lingnan University, Hong Kong

The Academy of International Business Southeast Asia Region (AIB-SEAR) series publishes books which aim to inform and inspire academics, researchers and practitioners with an interest in further advancing knowledge and understanding of international business and multinational company behavior from and within the Southeast Asia Region.

Political changes and financial issues have been at the forefront of international business for several years, yet one trend is clear: the focus of global business is now on Asia. The growth of Asian economies in recent years, in particular China and several other ASEAN countries, has been based on the manufacture and export of goods around the world, especially large quantities of consumer goods being exported to Western Europe and North America. The AIB-SEAR series examines these international links which are essential to the expanding Southeast Asia economies. Moreover, these Asian countries have emerged as viable and important consumer markets, creating tremendous potential for multinational firms as growth destinations. The focus of the AIB-SEAR book series is on the continuous evolution of international business.

*Title includes:*

T. S. Chan and Geng Cui (*editors*)
MULTINATIONALS AND GLOBAL CONSUMERS
Tension, Potential and Competition

**The AIB Southeast Asia Series**
**Series Standing Order ISBN 978–1–137–30726–2 (hardback)**
(*outside North America only*)

You can receive future titles in this series as they are published by placing a standing order. Please contact your bookseller or, in case of difficulty, write to us at the address below with your name and address, the title of the series and the ISBN quoted above.

Customer Services Department, Macmillan Distribution Ltd, Houndmills, Basingstoke, Hampshire RG21 6XS, England

# Multinationals and Global Consumers

## Tension, Potential and Competition

Edited by

T. S. Chan
*Lingnan University, Hong Kong*

Geng Cui
*Lingnan University, Hong Kong*

First published 2013 by
PALGRAVE MACMILLAN

Palgrave Macmillan in the UK is an imprint of Macmillan Publishers Limited,
registered in England, company number 785998, of Houndmills, Basingstoke,
Hampshire RG21 6XS.

Palgrave Macmillan in the US is a division of St Martin's Press LLC,
175 Fifth Avenue, New York, NY 10010.

Palgrave Macmillan is the global academic imprint of the above companies
and has companies and representatives throughout the world.

Palgrave® and Macmillan® are registered trademarks in the United States,
the United Kingdom, Europe and other countries.

ISBN 978–1–137–30728–6

This book is printed on paper suitable for recycling and made from fully
managed and sustained forest sources. Logging, pulping and manufacturing
processes are expected to conform to the environmental regulations of the
country of origin.

A catalogue record for this book is available from the British Library.

A catalog record for this book is available from the Library of Congress.

# Contents

# Figures and Tables

## Figures

## Tables

# Preface

The Academy of International Business Southeast Asia Region (AIB-SEAR) has forged a collaborative link with Palgrave Macmillan by publishing a new series. The first volume of this series, with most of the chapters based upon selected papers presented at the AIB-SEAR 2012 Conference, is organized around the theme "Multinationals and Global Consumers: Tension, Potential and Competition." This theme has two distinct components: the strategy of multinational firms in advancing global markets among developed and emerging countries for business and market development, and the ultimate target group of multinational firms – global consumers.

Political changes and financial issues have been at the forefront of international business for the last several years, yet one trend is clear: the focus of global business is now on Asia. The growth of Asian economies, in particular those of China and several other ASEAN countries, has been based on the manufacture and export of goods around the world, especially the large quantities of consumer goods being exported to Western Europe and North America. Moreover, these Asian countries have emerged as viable and important consumer markets, creating tremendous potential for multinational firms as growth destinations.

Using the United States–China trade relationship as an example, the emergence of global consumers has led to a new phase in the cycle of globalization for multinational business activities. Since the early years of China's Open Door Policy, low-end consumer products were made in Chinese factories based on labor cost advantages, with finished goods being sent to the United States for consumption by American consumers. Nowadays, premium product parts (e.g., furniture bases) produced in Chinese factories are being sent to the United States to be assembled with other components. Subsequently, the finished products (e.g., expensive couches) are then sent back to China to be sold to a growing middle class with strong purchasing power and preference for luxurious imports. Such is the cycle of globalization, pushing multinational firms into necessary partnerships and alliances that imply tension, potential and competition, with opportunities for both tremendous upside and profoundly negative consequences.

The book is organized around a schematic theme of international business research in Asia. The nature of the contributions is diverse in many ways and the book is divided into three parts: Multinationals and Organizational Management, International Business and FDI, and Marketing and Consumer Behavior. This diversity also reflects different managerial issues, theoretical perspectives, methodological approaches and industrial settings. This first volume goes beyond mere acknowledgement of the various challenges to international business to offer appropriately informed and insightful conclusions/suggestions in a local and indigenous context. More importantly, it also discusses issues of growth-seeking firms from emerging countries that embrace the pathway of internationalization, often with favorable outcomes, but at other times with unsuccessful results.

While the world pays close attention to Asian consumer markets and, in particular, Chinese consumers, how marketing and consumer behavior interact in the local context is paramount to the success of market penetration. Other key areas for marketing research in Asia covered in this book include the promotion of brands and perception of country of origin issues, as well as how consumers respond to service failures and counterfeit products. In addition, the accounts of multinationals from emerging countries posit interesting considerations because they highlight the difficulties that these firms face, both at home and abroad, while competing with multinationals from the developed world.

While the selected chapters are limited in scope, they highlight some of the more pressing issues under the rapid pace of economic progress and intensifying global competition. Finally, given the rapidly changing global business environment, the book's discussion of issues, trends and challenges pertaining to international business in transition and developing economies is especially relevant and timely. Even though the globalized world is becoming "flat," no matter where in the world a multinational firm is based, regardless of whether a firm is buying or selling in Asia, obtaining a better understanding of the ways in which Asian strategies are being formulated and executed is critical to the success of all firms.

*T. S. Chan, Chapter Chair*
*AIB-SEAR*

# Contributors

**Joseph Aiyeku** is Professor of Marketing in the Department of Marketing and Decision Sciences at Bertolon School of Business, Salem State University, USA, where he teaches global marketing, marketing management, consumer behavior, sales management, retailing and sport marketing at both graduate and undergraduate levels. He has published and presented over 60 articles in various journals and conferences worldwide. He is a co-editor of three books, including *The Dynamic of Marketing in Africa*. He specializes in macro-marketing, marketing and development, global consumer buying behavior and entrepreneurship in the developing countries. He is Visiting Professor of Marketing at Ramkhamhaeng University in Thailand, where he supervises PhD students' dissertations in global marketing. He was also a LEADS scholar for the National University Commission in Nigeria as well as a visiting professor in the Faculty of Business, University of Lagos. He serves on the editorial board of several journals.

**Bradley R. Barnes** is Associate Dean for Internationalization and Professor of International Management and Marketing at Sheffield University Management School, UK. Prior to that he was the Hong Kong Alumni Endowed Chair in International Management at Kent Business School. He has a PhD from the University of Leeds. He has over ten years' international marketing exposure working with companies to physically promote their products and services in Europe, the Middle East and the Far East. He has published in a range of practitioner and academic journals, including *Journal of International Business Studies, Journal of International Marketing, International Business Review, International Marketing Review, Industrial Marketing Management, Journal of Business-to-Business Marketing, European Journal of Marketing, Journal of Marketing Management* and *International Journal of Advertising*. Currently his research focuses on international business relationships and he is developing a research center that is primarily engaged with Chinese business.

**T. S. Chan** is Associate Vice President (Academic Quality Assurance) and Shun Hing Chair Professor of Marketing at Lingnan University,

Hong Kong. He received his DBA from Indiana University Bloomington, and BBA and MBA degrees from the University of Wisconsin at Madison. As an active researcher, he has published/edited 10 books and over 100 articles and papers in the areas of international marketing strategies, cross-cultural consumer behavior, joint venture decisions and marketing education. He serves on the editorial board of five international journals. He is also Chair of the Southeast Asia Regional Chapter of the Academy of International Business. He consults widely for universities, corporations and government agencies in Hong Kong and abroad. His areas of consulting include strategic marketing planning, effective selling, leadership and human relations, and intercultural communication.

**Shao-Chi Chang** received his PhD in finance from the State University of New York at Buffalo, USA. He is Professor of Finance at National Cheng-Kung University, Taiwan. His major research interests focus on corporate financial strategy and value creation, and he has published several articles on these topics in leading journals.

**Sheng-Syan Chen** received his PhD in finance from the State University of New York at Buffalo, USA. He is Professor of Finance at the College of Management, National Taiwan University, Taiwan. His major research interests focus on corporate finance and investments, and he has published more than 15 articles on these topics in leading finance journals.

**Xudong Chen** is Professor and Director of the Institute of Global Business at the School of Management, Zhejiang University, Hangzhou, China. She received bachelor's and master's degrees in economics from Hangzhou University, China, and Indiana University at Bloomington, Indiana, USA, respectively. Her research interests include transnational business activities of SMEs, growth of SMEs and government policy, corporate social responsibility and firm performance, and firm growth in China's private sector.

**Maggie Y. Chu** is a doctoral student at the Chinese University of Hong Kong. She has strong interests in doing consumer behavior research, particularly on issues pertaining to consumption failure, choice freedom and the influence of affect in evaluative judgments. Her dissertation looks at the situation where an unfavorable consumption outcome is led by a series of decisions. More specifically, she investigates how choice freedom over these decisions mitigates the impact of the unfavorable outcome.

**Geng Cui** is Professor, Department of Marketing and International Business, Lingnan University, Hong Kong. He received his education at Peking University (BA), Cornell University (MPS) and the University of Connecticut (PhD), and taught at two US universities before joining Lingnan University in 2000. His research interests include consumer behavior and marketing in China, foreign direct investment strategies and performance, and quantitative models in marketing. His work has appeared in leading academic journals such as *Management Science, Journal of International Business Studies, Journal of Management Information Systems, International Journal of Electronic Commerce, Journal of International Marketing* and *Journal of World Business*, and he has won several research awards. He is a leading scholar on Chinese consumer research, which has been widely cited and adopted for marketing practice and teaching. He has been a consultant to local and overseas organizations on China's business and marketing strategies.

**Chaoqun Duan** is a manager in the general affairs division, Agricultural Bank of China, Ningbo, China. She received her master's degree in business administration from Zhejiang University and a bachelor's degree in international trade from Zhejiang Gongshang University, Hangzhou, China. During her master's studies she went to Babson College, USA, and EMLYON Business School, France, for a joint Global Entrepreneurship Program. Her research interests focus on strategic alliances of SMEs and international entrepreneurship.

**Dirk Holtbrügge** is Professor and Head of International Management at the School of Business and Economics, University of Erlangen-Nürnberg, Germany. He received his doctorate from the University of Dortmund, Germany. In September 2012 he was listed in a research-related ranking of the newspaper *Handelsblatt* as one of the top-100 professors of business administration in Germany, Austria and German-speaking Switzerland. His main research interests are in the areas of international management, human resource management and management in emerging markets. He has published 7 books, 8 edited volumes and more than 70 articles in refereed journals such as *Academy of Management Learning & Education, Human Resource Management, International Business Review, International Journal of Cross Cultural Management, International Journal of Emerging Markets, Journal of International Business*

*Studies, Journal of International Management, Management International Review* and *Thunderbird International Business Review*. He is also a member of the editorial boards of *Journal for East-European Management Studies* and *Management International Review*. He has large experience in executive education and works as a consultant for firms in Germany and abroad.

**Shengsheng Huang** received his PhD from Rutgers University. He is Assistant Professor of Management at University of Houston-Victoria, USA. His current research interests include strategies and technology diffusion of multinational corporations, and Chinese-related phenomena such as guanxi, the Chinese automobile industry and China outward foreign direct investment.

**Wiboon Kittilaksanawong** is Associate Professor in the Faculty of Management, Nagoya University of Commerce and Business, Japan. He received his PhD from National Taiwan University. He was a visiting scholar at the Chinese University of Hong Kong. He has almost 12 years of work experience in multinational and Thai enterprises. He also has teaching experience at Zhejiang University and Zhejiang Gongshang University, China. He was a principal investigator of a research project "The Role of Entrepreneurship Capital, Strategic Orientation and Institutional Environment in the International Entrepreneurship of Worldwide Private Enterprises from China's Zhejiang Province," funded by Zhejiang Provincial Natural Science Foundation of China. His research interests include global business and strategy, business strategies in emerging markets and international entrepreneurship.

**Heidi Kreppel** received her doctorate from the University of Erlangen-Nürnberg, Germany. Her research interests include the internationalization of firms from emerging markets. She has published several articles in edited volumes and in journals such as *International Journal of Emerging Markets* and *Journal of Global Marketing*.

**Jung-Ho Lai** received her PhD from the Institute of International Business, National Cheng-Kung University, and is Associate Professor at National Taipei College of Business, Taiwan. Her academic interests are primarily in the fields of corporate governance and international business management, and she has numerous publications in conference proceedings and journal, such as *Financial Management* and *Journal of International Management*.

**Zejian Li** received his PhD in economics from Kyoto University and is Associate Professor of Asian Economy in the Faculty of Economics, Osaka Sangyo University, Japan. He is also a project researcher at Manufacturing Management Research Center, University of Tokyo. He has authored numerous articles on strategy, marketing, innovation and the automotive industry of BRIC countries, published in both Japanese and English (e.g., Routledge International Studies in Business History). His current research focuses on the rise of independent automobile makers in China.

**Greg Mahony** is Assistant Professor in Economics at the University of Canberra, Australia. Since completing a master's of economics at the University of Sydney, he has taught at a number of universities in the UK and Australia, as well as in China and Singapore. He has published in the areas of the Australian economy, foreign direct investment and the knowledge economy. His current research interests include services trade and investment in the Asia Pacific region, institutions, social norms and regulatory regimes, and institutions and service provision. He is currently supervising doctoral research students in the areas of social capital and agricultural development in Vietnam and financial development and openness in Malaysia.

**Shige Makino** is Professor of Management in the Department of Management and Outstanding Fellow of the Faculty of Business Administration, the Chinese University of Hong Kong. He served as chairman of the department from 2007 to 2013. He is an Academy of International Business (AIB) Fellow and has served as a vice president of the AIB. He is also a past-president of the Association of Japanese Business Studies. He has a remarkable publication record, is widely cited and was ranked by *International Journal of Business* as one of the 20 most prolific academics in international strategic management research. He has won numerous awards for both research and teaching, including the Haynes Prize for the Most Promising Scholar from the Academy of International Business in 2002. He focuses on studying strategies for international market expansion and management.

**Ling Peng** is Associate Professor, Department of Marketing and International Business, Lingnan University, Hong Kong. She received her PhD from the University of Alberta. Her research, addressing the psychometric theories of measurement issues in marketing, has appeared in *Journal of Product Innovation Management*, *International*

*Journal of Market Research, Journal of Marketing Management* and *Journal of Global Marketing*, among others. Her current research focuses on new product and innovation management, e-commerce and social media.

**Patrick S. Poon** is Associate Professor in the Department of Marketing and International Business, Lingnan University, Hong Kong. He received his master's of engineering and technology management and PhD (technology management and marketing) from the University of Queensland. His research interests include technology management, cross-cultural consumer studies, services marketing, knowledge management and social marketing. He has published in various international refereed journals, such as *Journal of Consumer Marketing, Journal of Marketing Management, Psychology & Marketing, European Journal of Marketing* and *International Marketing Review*.

**Bilal Rafi** completed his bachelor of philosophy with first-class honours at the University of Canberra, Australia. His thesis was related to the analysis of the economic policies of the ASEAN. In 2011 he was awarded the University of Canberra Medal for his academic achievements. He is also actively involved in teaching in the Faculty of Business, Government and Law, University of Canberra, and works as an economic analyst for a private consultancy that provides strategic advice to clients, producing original empirical research. He is currently a doctoral candidate at the University of Canberra. His research interests include spatial economics, growth theory, inequality and labour economics.

**Chris Sadleir** is Assistant Professor in Government at the University of Canberra, Australia. He holds a PhD in public sector management from the University of Canberra, for which he researched the emergence of foreign direct investment governance and regulation in Australia. His research practice explores adaptations in government capacity and structures to change, including responding to pressures for economic openness and stronger regional ties in Asia. Research students working with him are exploring these issues in the context of Indonesia.

**Saraphat Somboon** is Senior Lecturer in Managerial Accounting in the Department of Managerial Accounting, Kasetsart University, Thailand, where he teaches a range of accounting courses, including advanced managerial accounting, strategic managerial accounting, control management and problems in auditing at both undergraduate and graduate levels. He is Visiting Professor of Accounting at the Asian University.

He specializes in management control systems and managerial accounting, especially in the context of cultural differences. He is a certified public accountant in Thailand and a member of the Thai Federation of Accounting Professions.

**Lisa C. Wan** is Assistant Professor in the School of Hotel and Tourism Management, the Chinese University of Hong Kong. She received her PhD in marketing from the same university. Her research interests include services marketing, cross-cultural consumer behavior and consumer decision-making. She has published in major international academic journals, such as *Journal of Consumer Research, Journal of International Marketing, International Journal of Hospitality Management, Journal of Business Research* and *Journal of International Consumer Marketing*.

**Yue Wang** received his PhD in management from the University of Melbourne, Australia. He is Associate Professor of International Business in the Department of Marketing and Management, Macquarie University, Australia. His previous positions include a senior lectureship in the School of Management, University of New South Wales, and a number of visiting positions at Nagoya City University and Doshisha University in Japan, Shanghai Jiaotong University in China and the Korean University Business School. His current research interests focus on alliance strategies of multinational enterprises in China and internationalization strategies of emerging-market multinationals. His recent publications appear in journals such as *Management International Review, Journal of International Management, Journal of Business Research, Asia Pacific Journal of Management* and *Thunderbird International Business Review*.

**Lianxi Zhou** is Professor of Marketing and International Business at Brock University, Canada. He is also Chair Professor at Shaoxing University, China. He has a PhD in marketing from Concordia University, Canada. He has published extensively in leading marketing and international business journals, including *Journal of International Business Studies, Journal of the Academy of Marketing Science, Journal of Business Venturing, Journal of International Marketing, Journal of World Business, European Journal of Marketing, Industrial Marketing Management* and *Journal of Business Research*. Currently he is undertaking several government-funded research projects. His research interests are mainly in the areas of strategic marketing and international entrepreneurship.

# 1
# International Business Research in Asia

*Shige Makino, T. S. Chan and Geng Cui*

## Research on Asian firms

Makino and Yiu (2013) have conducted a systematic literature search of Asian firm strategies published in eight top-tier management journals: *Academy of Management Journal* (AMJ), *Academy of Management Review* (AMR), *Administrative Science Quarterly* (ASQ), *Journal of International Business Studies* (JIBS), *Journal of Management* (JoM), *Journal of Management Studies* (JMS), *Organizational Science* (OrgSci) and *Strategic Management Journal* (SMJ). There were 228 articles published between 1980 and 2011, and among the abovementioned eight journals, JIBS and SMJ published 71% of the research on Asian firm strategies with 94 and 69 articles, respectively. In addition, JMS published 19 articles, AMJ and OrgSci each published 18, AMR and ASQ each published 4 and JoM published 2.

With respect to country focus, among the 12 Asian countries, Japan is ranked first as the subject of 98 articles, accounting for almost 40% of the total articles published. China is ranked second as the subject of 76 articles (31%). Taken together, Japan and China account for 71% of the Asian country samples. Studies on Korea, Taiwan and India are growing, with 17, 13 and 13 articles, respectively, followed by 9 articles on Singapore and 7 on Hong Kong. The topics are all related to international strategy: foreign market entry (20%), joint ventures (13%), multinational corporations (MNCs) (9%), corporate governance (9%), business groups (8%) and network-based strategy (7%). Therefore international business (IB) research on Asian firm strategies exhibits a rising trend. The topics of such research have covered a range of management issues that add significant value to the study of organizations and strategic management. The publication of these articles also suggests that researchers have conducted more robust and in-depth studies of the country-specific contexts that surround Asian firms and organizations.

One of Asia's strengths is its ability to provide unique research settings for international business researchers. It has one of the world's largest advanced economies (i.e., Japan), the two economies with the highest gross domestic product per capita (Singapore and Hong Kong), and the world's two largest emerging economies (China and India), along with a varied collection of less developed economies. In addition, Asian countries are characterized by distinctive business systems that are bounded by historical legacies, institutional embeddedness and sociocultural cohesiveness. Thus research on Asian economies and companies has important implications for theory development and practice in the international business field. Recent research suggests that many interesting phenomena in this region contradict conventional beliefs. Several such critical issues that researchers should address when conducting international business research in Asia are highlighted in the following examples.

## Three paradoxes in international business research

### Ownership advantage paradox

Ownership advantage has been identified as a key determinant of foreign direct investment (FDI) (Dunning 1981). Internalization theory suggests that companies with greater ownership or competitive advantage over local rivals are more likely to engage in FDI. In emerging economies, however, this is not always the case. Consider Google's exit from China. Google was struggling with censorship and shut down its China operations two years ago. Despite its advantages over the local competitor, it failed to sustain its business in China, whereas Baidu, a Chinese-run search engine company, enjoys a close relationship with the government and maintains the market leader position in China. This is a good example of conventional theory failing to explain FDI practice in emerging economies. The same can also be said of eBay's first entry into China, which ended in failure due to strong local competition from Taobao.com.

### Risk–return paradox

Within the framework of asset pricing theory, large exposure to risk factors should be associated with higher expected returns in that risk and return are positively associated. An examination of the mean and standard deviation of return on sales (ROS) for Japanese subsidiaries in Asia revealed a clear positive association between the two. In this example, China provides a high-risk, high-return environment for Japanese firms. However, the story changes when the performance of local (indigenous) firms is examined. With the exception of a few countries, a moderate negative relationship was observed between the mean and standard deviation of ROS. In this example, China provides a low-risk, high-return environment to local (indigenous) firms. Thus the asset-pricing model is unable to explain a cross-section of expected returns in Asia. One reason for this is that Asian nations have unique institutional environments that influence foreign and domestic firms in different ways, but the specific factors and mechanisms of such influences have yet to be identified.

### Paradox in the flying geese hypothesis

The flying geese hypothesis, proposed by Japanese scholar Kaname Akamatsu (1962), suggests that less developed Asian nations will follow the growth path of advanced economies in a wild-geese flying pattern. Underlying this hypothesis is the assumption that the growth of advanced economies in Asia (e.g., Japan) is a driving force for the growth of less developed Asian economies. However, while the advanced economies have experienced slower growth, some emerging economies, particularly China, have become the world's fastest-growing markets. The viability of MNCs hinges on their success in these emerging economies, such that the growth of advanced economies is no longer a driving force in the growth of emerging economies but rather is conditioned, by and highly dependent on, the emergent economies' growth.

These examples illustrate some of the ways in which conventional wisdom cannot precisely explain today's international business practices in Asia. Thus unconventional perspectives are needed to examine these issues. In this regard, the following approaches to conducting research on Asian firms and organizations have been proposed: i) multilevel, ii) historical and iii) variance-based.

## Three perspectives for international business research in Asia

### A multilevel perspective

Multilevel analysis has become popular in international business research, in part because scholars have recognized that separating micro- and macro-issues is increasingly irrelevant. Multilevel research is a useful approach to examining the multiple causes or consequences of behavior at and across different levels. For example, employees' job satisfaction cannot be comprehensively understood once separated from broader institutional and social contexts, such as labor laws and national culture. Another reason for the increasing popularity of multilevel research is that a single-level analysis often creates misleading implications for practice.

Multilevel thinking has important implications for theory development. Organizational management theories in international business research explain variations in the behavior and performance of individuals and organizations. It is important to understand that such variations come from both within- and between-country variations. This means that both the within- and the between-country variations in observed behavior and performance must be explained. If the focus remains exclusively on within-country variations, ignoring the "country context" or between-country variations, researchers risk producing findings that are undercontextualized. To understand complex practices in Asian business, one must understand the unique country contexts.

Makino, Isobe and Chan (2004) conducted a variance component analysis on a panel of data on the performance of more than 5,000 Japanese subsidiaries in 80 countries and 160 industries over ten years, and found that country differences explain 5.5% of the total performance variation (see Table 1.1). One interesting finding is that country effects are stronger than parent-firm effects, and as strong as industry effects in emerging economies, which suggests that country differences can be considered to be an additional factor in explaining performance variations, and that their effects are greater in emerging economies. They also examined how much the regional differences within a host country can explain the performance variations of Japanese subsidiaries in the US and China, and found that regional differences mattered more in China than in the US, indicating that China provides more discontinuous and heterogeneous environments for Japanese firms compared with the US (Chan, Makino and Isobe, 2010).

One general implication of these findings is that locations, including countries and subnational regions, matter more in emerging economies than in advanced economies. In conventional strategic management theories, such industrial organization (IO) and the resource-based view (RBV), researchers have examined why company performance varies between industries and among firms, but these conventional studies have paid little attention to how much county context matters and why. In this regard, international business scholars have a great opportunity

*Table 1.1* Variance component analysis of performance of Japanese subsidiaries

| Variables | Estimate | % variance explained |
|---|---|---|
| Year | 0.06 | 0.1 |
| Foreign subsidiary | 20.90 | 31.4 |
| Parent firm | 7.17 | 10.8 |
| Host country | 3.67 | 5.5 |
| Industry | 4.61 | 6.9 |
| Error | 30.21 | 45.3 |
| Total | 66.6 | 100.0 |

*Source*: Makino et al. (2004).

to develop alternative theories that can complement those based on IO and RBV.

## Attention to history

History is important in understanding the complex nature of international business practices. A country's institutions evolve in a path-dependent manner with cross-country relations developing as a consequence of a variety of historical events. As Jones et al. (2006) note, however, "IB researchers have tended to treat history in a stylized fashion with little concern for the complexities of particular historical situations." For instance, many researchers have used "distance" variables to capture the cultural, administrative, geographic and institutional differences between countries. However, this popular stream of distance research may provide misleading implications for international business practices if historical factors are not considered. Such research focuses on distance in culture, administrative practices, geographic proximity or economic development between home and host countries. Ghemawat's (2001) CAGE model (referring to cultural, administrative, geographic and economic distances among countries) is one of the frameworks that examine how distance affects the flow of economic activity across borders. The basic premise underlying this stream of research suggests that distance makes international exchanges and interactions difficult and costly.

However, distance research has several critical weaknesses. First, it focuses on the static comparison of location-specific attributes that reside independently within countries and overlooks the effects of relational factors that have been historically developed between countries (Makino and Tsang, 2011). For example, Vietnam has diverse historical links with a number of other countries as a consequence of occupation, colonization and war. It was under the direct rule of, or paying tribute to, successive Chinese dynasties (111 BC to the early nineteenth century), colonized by France (1880s to 1954) and then unified as the Socialist Republic of Vietnam and supported by the former Soviet Union (1975–). It engaged in the Sino-Vietnamese War (1979) with China. If distance research is conducted, France and Vietnam would have a large cultural and geographical distance. However, France has been one of the major investors in Vietnam due to the previous colony–colonizer relationship. In contrast, despite the fact that China and Vietnam have a very small cultural and geographical distance, they do not have a meaningful trade relationship due to the previous war. Thus historical ties provide an additional factor that affects FDI decisions in Vietnam beyond what has been captured by the effect of conventional distance variables. Understanding a country's effect on international business requires a historical understanding of that country and its international relations.

**Attention to variance**

Finally, variances in the phenomena of interest, rather than the average effect, demand greater attention from researchers. One often assumes that observed events will follow a normal distribution as the sample size grows, and that average values tend to represent the most essential characteristics of the sample. The values that deviate from the average are usually considered to be non-essential or noise. Ironically, most practitioners are interested in how to excel against rivals rather than how to become the average company. Hence a simple comparison of average values across samples may not provide meaningful implications for practice. For example, assume a distribution of firm performance in two countries, A and B. Country A has a lower average than Country B, but it also has exceptionally high performers. Country A is more successful than Country B in terms of the average performance of its firms. However, one may also suggest that Country B is successful because it hosts its own group of exceptionally good firms.

In this example the amount of variance contains critical information about the business environments in each country. Most large sample studies, particularly those that use regression analysis, merely show the "average tendencies" of the sample, which masks the complex nature of the data. Thus the examination of variance provides additional implications for international business research in Asia. A recent study looked into the patterns of performance distribution of Japanese subsidiaries across countries (Makino 2012). While the overall observed distributions followed a bell-shaped curve, a close look at the data revealed that there are four distinct performance distribution patterns: one for advanced economies, one for transitional economies and two for emerging economies. In the advanced economy model, the performance distribution had a bell-shaped structure with a high peak. In the transitional economy model, the performance distribution had a bell-shaped structure with two lower peaks. As for the emerging economies, the performance distribution had a bell-shaped structure with a very low peak and the curve was skewed to the left, leaving a greater proportion on the positive side of performance. Another model for emerging economies had an unclear, bell-shaped structure compared with the other models. These patterns suggest that the transitional and emerging economy models tend to have longer tails, greater skewedness and lower peaks compared with the models for advanced economies. The underlying factors of the variant performance distributions among different country groups warrant systematic investigation.

## About this book and its chapters

Research on Asia and Asian firms can potentially make a tremendous contribution to international business theory development and practice. Scholars must develop stronger theoretical foundations to explain why countries and their institutional factors matter. There is a great opportunity for international business scholars to develop alternative theories of strategic management to complement IO and RBV. International business scholars are in an ideal position to provide useful insights into the practice of international business in Asia. Meanwhile, practitioners must recognize that international business skills are becoming more important than ever due to the rise of emerging economies. They must develop robust strategies to handle the complex local environments in these countries.

This book is the first in a series, and both represent an effort by the Southeast Asia Regional Chapter of the Academy of International Business (AIB) to address these challenges in international business research and take advantage of the opportunities afforded by the rise of Asian economies and companies. They address some of the issues raised above and also showcase the international business research on and from Asia. This volume offers a collection of chapters, some of which were presented at the 2012 AIB Southeast Asia Regional Chapter

Conference in Xiamen, China. These contributions touch on several areas of international business research, with an emphasis on Asia, and are organized into three sections.

## Multinationals and organizational management

Strategic alliance is one of the primary vehicles for firms to acquire complementary resources, enhance competitiveness and expand in overseas markets. How various factors underlying the agent costs of such alliances affect the performance of firms remains understudied. In an empirical study testing the agency costs in strategic alliances, Lai, Chen and Chang (Chapter 2) examine the role of corporate governance mechanisms in explaining the valuation effect of alliance investments. After analyzing the data from 1,743 announcements of interfirm cooperative investments, they find that board meetings, managerial ownership and managerial equity-based compensation have significantly positive effects on alliance outcomes. Furthermore, board meetings and incentive plans exert a more pronounced influence on cross-border (vs. domestic) and unrelated (vs. related) alliances. However, board size, proportion of outside directors and anti-takeover protection are not significant in explaining alliance valuation effects, likely due to the counteractive effects. Thus if the executives take advantage of alliances for self-serving purposes rather than for alliance value creation, both firms in the alliance may not reap the benefits of the alliance. Firms are advised to monitor the "observable" governance mechanism of a foreign partner and uncover its "invisible" commitment to the alliance to help mitigate the liability of foreignness that confronts MNCs when undertaking overseas alliance investments.

A transition economy is one that is shifting from central planning toward a more liberalized market economy with increased entrepreneurship activities. Such entrepreneurship activities of small and medium-sized enterprises (SMEs) represent an important driving force in the economic development of transition economies. Kittilaksanawong, Chen and Duan (Chapter 3) explore the factors driving alliance formation in the transitional economy of China. Based on in-depth interviews with SMEs and intermediary organizations in China's Zhejiang province, one of the country's most developed private economies, the case studies illustrate the role of the Zhejiang local government and others in facilitating the formation of SME alliances in the province. Through extensive case studies and theoretical discussions, they develop propositions that highlight the unique characteristics of alliance formation in transition economy SMEs, particularly the moderating role of intermediary organizations. The selected case studies of Chinese SMEs illustrate how these firms formulate and implement their strategies (i.e., strategic alliances) to take advantage of opportunities and overcome a variety of challenges in their internationalization efforts.

Although many foreign firms have pursued management localization in emerging economies such as China, the effect of such a strategy on subsidiary performance has received little attention. Cui, Chan and Huang (Chapter 4) study the effect of management localization on the performance of foreign subsidiaries in China. Drawing from the RBV, they propose that management localization serves as a means to acquire local managerial resources for MNCs and that its effect on subsidiary performance depends on several key contextual variables. Based on a survey of foreign invested enterprises in China, they find that the degree of management localization alone does not improve subsidiary performance, whereas local resource dependency, headquarters support and the participation of local managers significantly moderate the effect of management localization on subsidiary performance. The findings have meaningful implications for human resource management in multinational subsidiaries in overseas markets.

In an empirical investigation of domestic and MNCs in Thailand, Saraphat and Aiyeku (Chapter 5) focus on the cross-country differences in budgetary characteristics and managerial effectiveness. Specifically, they examine the role of budgetary characteristics (budgetary participation, budget goal difficulty, budget goal clarity, budgetary evaluation (general and punitive), budgetary feedback, and budgetary slack) on managerial effectiveness. They also consider procedural fairness and budgetary motivation in assessing managerial effectiveness for both domestic companies and US MNCs in Thailand. The results reveal that budget goal clarity and budgetary motivation have the greatest effects on the managerial effectiveness of national companies, while budgetary participation and procedural fairness are the most influential determinants of managerial effectiveness for multinational counterparts.

### International business and foreign direct investment

At the nexus of international entrepreneurship research, young international firms are claimed to possess "learning advantages of newness", enabling them to flourish abroad. Zhou, Barnes and Chan (Chapter 6) draw on evidence from case studies of 11 companies in China to explore the significance of network dynamics and upgrading in providing the learning advantages for young entrepreneurial firms to achieve early and rapid internationalization. Specifically, they report the changing nature of the network dynamics associated with young internationalizing firms in China, as they search for learning advantages by mobilizing different types of external business and social networks. Based on the findings from the case studies, they propose a theoretical framework to illustrate how Chinese entrepreneurs build on such network dynamics, involving a combination of domestic agents, overseas Chinese merchants and international distributors, to rapidly upgrade their absorptive capacity to enjoy the learning advantages during the initial stages of internationalization.

An increasing number of emerging market firms are joining the global competition for consumers. To understand how these firms compete internationally, given their inherent disadvantages in brand recognition and proprietary technology, existing studies have emphasized the positive role of social capital in their internationalization process. Based on a case study of Chinese automakers' dramatic rise and fall in the Russian market from 2004 to 2009, Li and Wang (Chapter 7) posit that social capital can be a double-edged sword for emerging market firms' international expansion, and that over-reliance on social capital may inhibit these firms' internationalization after their initial entry into global markets. They also emphasize the contingency value of social capital in the different stages of a firm's internationalization process and call for more rigorous studies of the effect of social capital on firm internationalization.

The role of institutions has attracted increasing attention in the fields of international business and strategic management. Mahony, Rafi and Sadleir (Chapter 8) examine the effect of MNC strategy, institutions and state capacity on the inward FDI of Association of Southeast Asian Nations (ASEAN) countries. They posit that states' institutional capacity, specifically bureaucratic capacity, is a central mediating factor for management decisions regarding entry mode, and they explore the dimensions of the capacities and capabilities of the ASEAN states to assess the extent to which they are associated with inward FDI. They draw on approaches from public administration and political science to reconceptualize this problem and empirically test the relationship between bureaucratic capacity and inward FDI of ASEAN countries.

### Marketing and consumer behavior

As MNCs expand in marketplaces around the world, they provide competitive offerings to indigenous consumers in terms of product quality, but often lag behind in shoring up the quality of services. Thus service failure and the following recovery efforts may present significant challenges for MNCs and domestic firms alike. Meanwhile, consumers from different countries and cultures may exhibit distinctive perceptions of and reactions to service failures. In their critical review of cross-cultural research on consumer responses to service failure, Wan and Chu (Chapter 9) review the key concepts used in cross-cultural research on service failure and recovery, examining how Asian and Western consumers react to service failures and service recovery, and providing future directions for cross-cultural service failure research, especially regarding the role of power distance, prevention vs. promotion focus, and consumers' emotional reactions to service failures.

The purchase of counterfeit products is an ongoing, worldwide problem, despite global initiatives and international treaties to address the issue. One potential obstacle in the fight against this problem is the lack of understanding of consumers' motivations for engaging in such purchases. Peng, Wan and Poon (Chapter 10) examine the role of self-discrepancy in consumer responses to counterfeit products. They attempt to advance the theoretical understanding of consumer responses to counterfeits by examining how consumers' self-discrepancy influences their attitudes and purchase intentions toward counterfeits. Their results indicate that self-discrepancy has a positive effect on consumer responses to counterfeits, and that there are cross-cultural and cross-category differences in this effect. These findings have important implications for both academic researchers and marketing managers.

As MNCs from emerging economies expand overseas, they often face the challenges of liability of foreignness and the lack of strong brand reputation. Kreppel and Holtbrügge (Chapter 11) examine the perceptions of Chinese and Indian brand personalities in Germany. Based on Aaker's brand personality scale, they analyze the similarities and differences in German consumers' perceptions of the brand personalities of two laptop brands from China and India. The results of a survey of 654 German consumers reveal significantly higher values for the Chinese laptop in terms of "competence" and "ruggedness", and show that the perceived personality of Chinese and Indian brands is influenced by demographic and psychographic factors. The authors draw implications that may help Chinese and Indian companies with regard to their market segmentation and marketing-mix strategies in overseas markets.

Note: The first part of this introduction is partially adapted from the keynote speech by Prof. Shige Makino at the opening plenary session of the AIB Southeast Asia Regional Chapter Conference in Xiamen, China, December 4–6, 2012.

## References

Akamatsu, K. (1962) A historical pattern of economic growth in developing countries. *Journal of Developing Economies*, 1(1): 3–25.

Chan, C. M., Makino, S., and Isobe, T. (2010) Does sub-national region matter? Foreign affiliate performance in the U.S. and China. *Strategic Management Journal*, 31(11): 1226–1243.

Dunning, J. H. (1981) *International Production and the Multinational Enterprise*. London: Allen and Unwin.

Ghemawat, P. (2001) Distance still matters: The hard reality of global expansion. *Harvard Business Review*, 79(8): 137–147.

Jones, G. and Khanna, T. (2006) Bringing history (back) into international business. *Journal of International Business Studies*, 37(4): 453–468.

Makino, S. (2012) Corporate performance around the world. Unpublished working paper, Chinese University of Hong Kong.

Makino, S., Isobe, T., and Chan, C. M. (2004) Does country matter? *Strategic Management Journal*, 25(10): 1027–1043.

Makino, S. and Tsang, E. W. (2011) Historical ties and foreign direct investment: An exploratory study. *Journal of International Business Studies*, 42(4): 545–557.

Makino, S. and Yiu, D. W. (2013) A survey of strategic behaviour and firm performance in Asia. In Redding, G. and Witt, M., editors, *Oxford Handbook of Asian Business Systems*, Oxford University Press.

# Part I

# Multinationals and Organizational Management

# 2
# A Test of Agency Costs in Strategic Alliances

*Jung-Ho Lai, Sheng-Syan Chen and Shao-Chi Chang*

## Introduction

The incidence rate of strategic alliances has accelerated in recent decades, and alliances have become one of the most important entry modes into foreign markets (Hergert and Morris, 1988; Glaister and Buckley, 1996; Nielsen, 2007). Earlier studies show that multinationals use alliances to enter the markets of countries that enforce restrictive conditions on foreign investments (Hood and Young, 1979). Later research shows an increase in firms voluntarily entering into alliances in response to changing, unpredictable, globalized competition. By participating in cooperative ventures, multinationals stabilize the flow of needed resources, smooth global operations and increase the speed at which they can enter new markets (Lavie and Miller, 2008). The fewer resource commitments required in alliances further allow firms to more flexibly hedge uncertainty in overseas investments, compared with alternative entry modes, such as mergers and acquisitions and wholly owned greenfields (Brouthers, Brouthers, and Werner, 2008). However, despite the purported advantages underlying alliances, empirical evidence shows that there are as many enterprises that succeed in their alliance engagements as those that fail to do so (e.g., Das, Sen and Sengupta, 1998; Ren, Gray and Kim, 2009). The presence of a mixture of outcomes suggests that realization of the purported advantages of alliances depends on how the associated costs are controlled.

While the bulk of studies extensively analyze factors that influence alliance performance, most investigate how the characteristics of transactions or environments influence the valuation effect of alliances. Specifically, these studies are based on transaction-level analysis and apply, for example, transaction cost economics (e.g., Reuer and Ragozzino, 2006) or investigate environmental-level factors by applying, for example, industrial organization economics (e.g., Hymer, 1976; Caves and Mehra, 1986). Given the extant studies' inconclusive findings, researchers highlight the need to use a multilevel perspective to revisit this issue (e.g., Reuer and Ragozzino, 2006). This study responds to this call by exploring whether the corporate governance mechanism is a salient factor that affects alliance outcomes. This is an organization-level concern that has not previously been considered. Based on agency theory, how corporate governance mechanisms address the associated costs and affect the value creation of a firm's alliance investments is examined.

Akin to acquisitions and internationalization, in which the overinvestment problem has been identified (Carpenter and Sanders, 2004), alliances function as a way for firms to expand business and undertake investments; they may therefore similarly suffer from management's distortion of firm capital for personal use (Reuer and Ragozzino, 2006). Given the notion that an effective governance system alleviates agency hazards (Jensen, 1993), this study takes a detailed look at the influences that various governance mechanisms may exert on the valuation effects of alliances. These influences are addressed by considering the board of directors, managerial incentive plans and the external takeover market, all of which are mechanisms that exert separate and uniquely important governance effects on alliance outcomes.

The next section reviews the literature on agency behavior and corporate governance, and proposes several testable hypotheses. An outline of the sample selection and methodology follows. The empirical findings are presented, and the chapter concludes with a discussion of the findings and their implications.

## Literature review and hypothesis development

### Agency problems in alliances

The notion that a separation of ownership and control may cause a transfer of wealth from shareholders to managers is emerging in alliance studies (Keown, Laux, and Martin, 2005; Pangarkar, 2007). Due to the disparate objectives and risk preferences between managers and shareholders, managers may reach alliance decisions that are not as shareholder-oriented as the conventional alliance literature suggests.

Subsequently, the variety of agency problems in alliances that emerge from prior studies is discussed in detail.

## Overinvestment

Agency theory states that managers may be tempted to undertake value-diminishing investments to overexpand corporate business beyond the optimal size for two reasons: their compensation may depend on the size of assets under managerial discretion and their power increases with the resources under their control (Jensen, 1986, 1993). Alliances pave the way for corporate investments and expansions, and some empirical studies support the presence of uneconomic overinvestment in alliances. By employing the event-study approach, Keown et al. (2005) and Min and Prather (2001) show that managers take advantage of cooperative investments to overexpand firms. Chang and Chen (2002) find that a higher debt ratio is associated with better performance among alliances or joint ventures. Unless the market believes that a project is worthwhile, external funds are unavailable or prohibitively expensive (Jensen, 1986). The significant disciplinary role of debt therefore governs the overinvestment hazard of alliance investments.

## Risk reduction

Diversification theory argues that unlike shareholders who can diversify personal investment risk through portfolio allocation, managers have difficulty hedging the risk of their central concern – compensation and employment (Amihud and Lev, 1999). The alliance literature documents that exposure to personal risk may lure managers to undertake uneconomic alliances that enable them to mitigate undiversified risk at the cost of lower returns. Ozcan and Eisenhardt (2009) observe from the wireless gaming industry that firms may form multiple alliance ties to manage industry uncertainty, although these alliances are not easily maintained due to little subsequent attention and limited resources. Pangarkar (2007) finds managerial myopic investment behavior in alliances, whereby managers prefer low-risk, short-term projects that represent the non-value maximizing use of capital to hedge personal risk. Finally, managers may discard short-term costly investments with long-term benefits because they do not expect to remain in the firm and share the resulting rewards (Graber, 2003).

## Competition avoidance

Managers may undertake unwise alliance decisions for reasons of competition avoidance or defensiveness rather than shareholder wealth maximization (Porter and Fuller, 1986). Agency theory suggests that without proper motivation, managers may be reluctant to engage in creative activities involving new technologies because such activities take time and effort to learn and manage (Aggarwal and Samwick, 2006). Thus instead of pursuing innovation or seeking product improvement, some managers prefer to cooperate with rival firms to reduce competition in the product market that results in welfare loss (Santos and Eisenhardt, 2009).

### Corporate governance and alliance performance

The potential agency problems underlying alliance activities highlight the importance of well-functioning corporate governance mechanisms that discipline managers so that they act in the shareholders' interests. This section examines the governance effects of the board of directors, incentive-alignment instruments and market for corporate control. The observations are directed toward the characteristics of an alliance, which are important in determining the effectiveness of governance mechanisms in alliance investments.

*Board of directors*

**Board size**

Previous research on the monitoring role played by the board argues that large boards tend to be ineffective monitors of management. A large board is likely to have severe communication and coordination difficulties due to the number of interactions among group members (Coles, Daniel and Naveen, 2008). Moreover, large board membership is also subject to a lack of cohesion and participation in addition to having a free-riding problem (Jensen, 1993). In contrast, a small board is more likely to effectively monitor and discipline management because it is more cohesive and tends to facilitate discussion among members, promote debate and prevent social loafing (Boone, Field, Karpoff and Raheja, 2007).

The monitoring efficiency of small boards is critical in a firm's alliance investments, as the transitional environment highlights the importance of the board response, which must be prompt. As previous research indicates, alliances are prevalent in changing competitive environments because they provide organizational flexibility and allow for the rapid repositioning of strategies (Brouthers et al., 2008). While an environmental transition usually initiates strategic changes as a firm adapts to the evolving conditions, board monitoring should be immediate to provide opportune discipline (Goodstein, Gautam and Boeker, 1994). Thus the following prediction is made:

*Hypothesis 1–1a: The smaller the board size, the stronger its disciplinary effect, resulting in less self-serving alliance decisions made by managers.*

In addition to monitoring efficiency, a board's role as resource provider is important in assessing the implications of board size for alliances. The literature on resource dependence theory argues that a board functions as a corporate cooperative mechanism to form links with the external environment by virtue of its access to important information and critical resources that buffer firms against adverse environmental change (Hillman, Cannella and Paetzold, 2000). Presumably a large board can provide a great deal of expertise and intellectual insight that is less likely to be found in a small board (Coles et al., 2008). Thus a large board may seem appropriate in an uncertain environment where the requirement for success is ambiguous and sound judgment requires the consideration of various strategic alternatives (Sampson, 2005). As alliances are prevalent in competitive environments, a diverse knowledge set from more board members appears to be advantageous with regard to broadening the managerial schemata of alliance knowledge. With such aids, managers can derive more comprehensive, sophisticated thoughts and carefully navigate their alliance challenges, avoiding the confined thinking of a small board that generates limited innovation. The advisory advantage associated with a large board provides an alternative perspective on the relation between board size and alliance outcomes, which is stated as follows:

*Hypothesis 1–1b: The larger the board size, the more sophisticated the counsel provided by directors, resulting in managers making better alliance decisions.*

### Outside director proportion

A similar trade-off between monitoring and counsel advantages predicts different relations between board independence and alliance outcomes. With respect to board monitoring, the traditional agency theory suggests that board structure comprises mostly outside directors due to their independence from management and impartial decision-making (Boone et al., 2007). However, the contingency view of board governance maintains that the optimal board composition is determined by the specific business environment in which firms operate (Coles et al., 2008). In noisy environments in which corporate activities have low information transparency, outside directors incur information access problems that aggravate their supervision inefficiency (Coles et al., 2008). Thus independent outside monitoring appears to be suboptimal in an alliance situation, where information asymmetry may impede the transfer of alliance-specific information to outsider directors. Inside directors, however, possess critical information about corporate resources and the task environment, and thus can more accurately assess management endeavors when information availability for outsiders is limited (Sanders and Carpenter, 1998). Therefore the following is hypothesized:

> *Hypothesis 1–2a: A board comprising more outside directors incurs more severe information asymmetry associated with alliances, resulting in worse alliance outcomes.*

While an outsider-dominated board can be less efficient in monitoring informationally asymmetric alliance activities, it can be helpful in providing the external resources that contribute to alliance success. As resource dependence theory holds, outside directors act as corporate boundary spanners to extract resources from the environment through their ties to strategically related stakeholders (Hillman et al., 2000). Especially in alliances, managers can leverage outside directors' relational ties to increase a firm's access to compatible, resource-fitted partners. Outsiders' knowledge of the industries related to proposed partnerships can also be helpful as it provides insight into industry recipes, such as development opportunity and threat, and competitive dynamics (Kor and Misangyi, 2008). The advantage of outside directors in providing critical external resources to alliances leads to a competing hypothesis:

> *Hypothesis 1–2b: A board comprising more outside directors generates more external resources for alliance plans, which benefits strategy outcomes.*

### Meeting frequency

While board structure may have a salient influence on alliance performance, a well-structured board functions poorly if it does not meet frequently. Because the board must reside at the internal control apex to be in charge of advising and monitoring management, frequently held board meetings aid a board's decisions tremendously by displaying substantial, timely and relevant information (Vafeas, 1999). Previous empirical works document that active board meetings perform as signals of increased vigilance and diligence in the governance of top management (e.g., Payne, Benson, and Finegold, 2009). Thus meeting frequency may influence a board's effectiveness in both monitoring and advising managerial alliance engagements.

The importance of an active board in alliances is highlighted due to environmental concerns. Previous studies argue that boards should increase the frequency of meetings whenever a high level of supervision and control is required (Payne et al., 2009). Given that alliances, which are prevalent in changing environments, are more frequently undertaken than larger-scale investments, such as acquisitions, frequent board meetings are appropriate as they provide the intense, timely monitoring of management, whereas fewer board meetings may fail to attain the relevant discipline to react to the focal alliance situation. The advantage of an active board in administrating alliance activities can also be inferred from its ongoing counsel in addressing the evolving alliance scenarios. Alliance contracts are typically incomplete because an alliance is a dynamic process that emerges and evolves (Sampson, 2005). The changing alliance context, not initially specified, sheds light on the importance of frequently held board meetings in advising and guiding future progress. The above discussion leads to the following hypothesis:

*Hypothesis 1–3: The number of board meetings positively influences alliance outcomes.*

### Incentive Alignment of Management
#### Managerial equity-based compensation

Agency scholars argue that equity-based compensation can align the interests of executives and shareholders by curbing executive opportunisms and discouraging risk aversion (Kang, Kumar, and Lee, 2006). When managers are compensated with shares and shares options, they increase their wealth sensitivity to firm performance, and thus are more diligent with regard to their duties and strive not to waste resources on value-decreasing projects. Equity-based pay also discourages uneconomic risk hedging by inducing risk-averse executives to take risky but profitable projects on behalf of risk-neutral shareholders (Cho and Shen, 2007). Because alliance investments can be beset by managerial misappropriation and unproductive risk hedging, it follows from agency theory that equity-based pay guides managers to reach better alliance decisions.

In addition to actively incentivizing interest alignment to ease the difficulty of monitoring alliance activities, the superiority of equity-based pay can also be inferred from its inherent flexibility. Considering the dynamics inherent in an alliance and the need for ongoing structuring to adapt to evolving goals, an adjustable governance system would seem to be mandatory. Because incentive plans are inherently flexible and can be frequently and inexpensively adjusted to precisely target executives (Aggarwal and Samwick, 2006), this sets their governance effect better than that of the board mechanism, of which restructuring is comparatively costly and infrequent, such that it cannot react in a timely fashion. The flexibility unique to incentive plans leads to the following hypothesis:

> *Hypothesis 2–1: Managerial equity-based compensation positively influences alliance outcomes.*

### Managerial ownership

In contrast with equity-based pay, the stock fraction held by management addresses managerial incentive by considering time-specific material. Ofek and Yermack (2000) report that in a typical, large public firm, top management owns less than 5% of the company. This small ownership may elicit a hazard of shareholder–manager goal incompatibility, with managers bearing little financial costs for their misappropriation behavior. Jensen (1993) argues that the divergence between stockholder and management interests can be minimized when managerial stockholdings are substantial. As managers increase their stockholdings, they participate in a greater fraction of the benefits associated with value-increasing decisions, and suffer proportionately from actions that erode shareholder wealth.

However, the argument that managerial ownership should be large meets with difficulty. A high level of stock ownership by managers can lead to management entrenchment, which can destroy shareholder wealth (Morck, Shleifer and Vishny, 1988). When managerial ownership is in place, but at a low level, interest alignment boosts the positive relation between ownership and performance; beyond this optimum level, the relation disintegrates. Undisciplined by shareholders, entrenched managers become lax in their duties and performance deteriorates as executive stockholdings increase. The proposed non-linear relation between managerial ownership and alliance performance leads to the following hypothesis:

> *Hypothesis 2–2: The effect of managerial ownership on alliance outcomes is positive at low levels of managerial ownership and negative at high levels of managerial ownership.*

### Market for corporate control

Many researchers regard takeover threats and the market for corporate control as the major vehicles of external governance, by which bidders make offers to the shareholders of target firms to obtain corporate control and replace the existing poor-performing managers (Cremers and Nair, 2005). If managers fear a hostile takeover and resulting job loss, they will be diligent in their alliance engagements. The takeover threat thereby better secures shareholder benefits by ensuring that corporate resources are utilized efficiently. Fama and Jensen (1983) argue that the market for corporate control can play a disciplinary role in resolving the problem of imperfect management rewards. Cremers and Nair (2005) similarly show that takeover vulnerability provides external discipline, which supplements internal governance mechanisms. The complementary governance effect of takeover threats on other mechanisms highlights its importance in governing alliance investments. Therefore a positive takeover–performance relation is inferred in alliances, as stated below:

*Hypothesis 3: The power of the external takeover market positively influences a firm's alliance outcome.*

### The contingent significance of governance mechanisms

The above discussion pertains to the disciplinary effect of governance devices in general. However, if managerial self-serving is an important factor influencing alliance outcomes, it can be expected that the benefits of corporate governance mechanisms will be intensified in alliances suffering from more severe agency hazards. Thus this investigation is further extended to include governance effectiveness by considering this contingency scenario. In particular, the activity type (equity/non-equity) of an alliance, its location (domestic/international) and business relations with parent firms are put forth, as these generate disparate agency implications.

First, because agency theory presumes that managerial self-purpose is more readily served when investing in different industries, the severity of the agency threat can be moderated by the industry relatedness between a firm and its alliance activity. Empirical evidence shows that most unrelated investments detract from firm value (Jiraporn, Kim, Davidson and Singh, 2006; Amihud and Lev, 1999). However, managers can be prompted to engage in these investments, from which they can appropriate private benefits, including hedging personal employment risk, entrenching themselves (Shleifer and Vishny, 1989), increasing income or the opportunity for skimming (Bertrand and Mullainathan, 2001), and consuming perquisites from business enlargements (Jensen, 1986, 1993). Because a more significant agency hazard magnifies the disciplinary effects of governance mechanisms, the more severe agency problem residing in unrelated alliances can enhance the governance benefits that firms receive.

Next, a greater benefit to corporate governance is likely to occur when alliances occur outside a firm's home country. This inference can also be derived from agency theory, which posits that in the absence of full information, agents may reach a decision suboptimal to their principals when private benefits outweigh the associated costs. For domestic alliances, the overall capability of firms is relatively easy to assess because their financial condition, quality of management and other attributes relevant to alliance success are readily observable (Gomez-Mejia and Palich, 1997). As an alliance expands beyond the domestic market, it exposes firms to an environment with distinct market conditions, institutional regulations and societal norms that add to the information complexity that corporate interested parties must cope with and may be unable to comprehend (Carpenter and Sanders, 2004). Because information asymmetry is crucial to the development of managerial opportunistic behavior, overseas alliances in which information accessibility is especially problematic facilitate managerial misbehavior and thus require more discipline on the part of corporate governance.

Finally, the benefit of governance mechanisms may depend on whether equity is involved in alliances, as agency rationale usually states that managers who act in their own self-interest tend to invest beyond the optimal level to seek empire-building or entrenchment (Jensen, 1986; Shleifer and Vishny, 1989). Equity alliances typically involve a high level of capital investments, whereas non-equity alliances take a contractual form demanding little capital infusion. Thus the overinvestment problem, which has been documented in joint-venture studies (Chang and Chen, 2002), is more likely to be observed in equity alliances (Keown et al., 2005). This implies that corporate governance will exert a stronger influence on alliances of equity form.

The three factors contributing to the articulated agency hazard all point to the contingent importance of corporate governance. From here, the following contingency hypotheses are developed:

*Hypothesis 4: The influence that governance mechanisms exert on alliances is more pronounced when a firm and its alliance are located in different industries than when they are located in the same industry.*

*Hypothesis 5: The influence that governance mechanisms exert on alliances is more pronounced when alliances cross-national borders than when they take place domestically.*

*Hypothesis 6: The influence that governance mechanisms exert on alliances is more pronounced in equity alliances than in non-equity alliances.*

## Research design and methodology

### Sample

An initial sample of US firms undertaking strategic alliances was selected from the Acquisitions and Alliances database of the Securities Data Company (SDC) over the 2001–2007 period. Representative alliance activities (e.g., R&D, manufacturing and marketing) were included, as suggested by Shah and Swaminathan (2008), and supply relationships, which resemble arm's-length transactions rather than collaborative investments, were omitted. Alliance announcements made by financial institutions (Standard Industrial Classification code 60–69) were excluded from the sample.

The initial announcement dates are confirmed by the *Wall Street Journal* (WSJ) Index. The alliance announcements all meet the following criteria. First, they avoid any potential confounding effect on the measurement of the valuation effect – that is, the sample firms do not have other major announcements (e.g., earnings, dividends or other forms of capital investment) five days before or after the alliance announcement date. Second, the daily stock return information is available from the Center for Research in Securities Prices (CRSP) returns files. Third, the companies' financial information is available from the Compustat files. The final sample comprises 1,743 announcements of interfirm cooperative investments.

### The dependent variable

The standard event-study method is used to examine stock price responses to corporate alliance announcements, which serve as the dependent variable. In the literature, event-study methodology is used to measure alliance outcomes (Park, 2004). Following Brown and Warner (1985), the market model is used to obtain estimates of the expected returns. The market model depicts the return on a security as varying with the market portfolio return, which is adjusted for the security's risk factor. That is,

$$E(Rit|It - 1, Rmt) = \alpha i + \beta i Rmt,$$

where $E(R_{it}|I_{t-1}, R_{mt})$ is the expected return of the $i$th firm at time $t$, given the available information $(I_{t-1})$, and the return on the market portfolio $(R_{mt})$; $\beta_i$ measures the risk or sensitivity of the firm's return relative to the market portfolio; and $\alpha_i$ is the intercept. The abnormal stock returns for the alliance announcements are calculated as the residual from the actual return and an expected return generated by the market model, with parameters $\alpha_i$ and $\beta_i$ estimated over a period of 200 to 60 days before the initial announcements. Day 0 in event time is the date of the publication in which the company's initial alliance announcement appears. The two-day period (day –1, day 0) cumulative abnormal returns for each security are measured by the deviation of the security's realized return over the two-day period from an expected return generated by the market model. Daily stock return information is collected from the CRSP returns files. The value weighted NYSE\AMEX\Nasdaq Index is used to measure market returns.

### Independent variables

The independent variables of interest measure three dimensions of corporate governance: the board of directors, instruments of interest-alignment and anti-takeover provisions. The variables of board attributes include board size, the fraction of outside directors and meeting frequency. Board size is measured by the number of directors. The fraction of outside directors is measured by the ratio of outside to inside directors, where outside directors are those without an executive position in the firm either currently or in the past, and who are unrelated to an executive. Meeting frequency is the number of board meetings held annually. Data on these variables are obtained from the Investor Responsibility Research Center, Inc. (IRRC)'s directors and boards dataset for the year before the alliance announcement.

Measures of managerial incentives are constructed from Standard and Poor's ExecuComp database. The top management team (TMT) is used as the unit of analysis because prior research indicates that TMT members are often the conceptualizers of alliance strategies (Carpenter and Sanders, 2004; Cho and Shen, 2007). Equity-based compensation is defined as the percentage of the values of stock options and restricted stock grants in an executive's annual compensation package (Kang et al., 2006). Managerial ownership is measured as the percentage of common equity held by the TMT.

The proxy for external governance is collected from the IRRC's governance dataset. The number of anti-takeover provisions is used to measure the degree to which management is sheltered from the external control market (Cremers and Nair, 2005; Gompers, Ishii and Metrick, 2003).[1] The presence of anti-takeover provisions measures the power-sharing relationship between management and shareholders.

More anti-takeover bylaws indicate greater difficulty in removing opportunistic managers, whereas fewer takeover protections suggest better control over management from the external market.

### Control variables

This study also controls for other variables that could affect the valuation effects of alliance investments, following previous studies. Specifically, the study controls for the following variables, as assessed by their values one year preceding the alliance announcement: firm's profitability measured by return on assets (Glaister and Buckley, 1996), debt ratio proxied by long-term debt to total assets (Chang and Chen, 2002), and firm size assessed by natural logarithm of the firm's market value of common equity (Chang, Chen, and Lai, 2008). Moreover, year and industry dummies are included in this regression model. The sample period (2001–2007) spans both bear and bull markets. Thus yearly dummies are included in the regressions to control for the potential influences of different market conditions. Industry dummies are also included to control for the potential effects of industry-specific differences.

## Empirical analyses and results

Table 2.1 provides the descriptive statistics and bivariate correlation matrix. The average firm value change of alliance announcements is significantly positive with a mean value of 0.379% ($p < 0.001$), suggesting that firms generally benefit from their alliance investments. However, there is also significant heterogeneity in firms' gains from alliances. The standard deviation of announcement-period abnormal returns is 3.731%, and 55.31% of announcing firms exhibit positive announcement effects. Table 2.1 also shows that quite a few independent variables are significantly correlated with each other. To assess the potential problem of multicollinearity, the variance inflation factor in the regression analyses is recomputed. Multicollinearity does not appear to be a major problem because most independent variables have variance inflation factors below the 5.0 criterion proposed by Marquardt and Snee (1975).

### Major governance effects

Table 2.2 presents cross-sectional regression analyses of the announcement effect of alliance investments. Models 1, 2 and 3, respectively, assess the influence of the board of directors, interest-alignment mechanisms and the external takeover market. Model 1 shows that announcement-period abnormal returns associated with alliance

*Table 2.1* Descriptive statistics and Pearson correlation coefficients

| Variables | Mean | S.D. | 1. | 2. | 3. | 4. | 5. | 6. | 7. | 8. | 9. | 10. |
|---|---|---|---|---|---|---|---|---|---|---|---|---|
| 1. Cumulative abnormal | 0.379 | 3.731 | 1.000 | | | | | | | | | |
| 2. Board size | 9.784 | 2.581 | −0.075 | 1.000 | | | | | | | | |
| 3. Outside director proportion | 0.720 | 0.133 | −0.020 | 0.212 | 1.000 | | | | | | | |
| 4. Meeting frequency | 8.135 | 2.792 | 0.093 | 0.053 | 0.095 | 1.000 | | | | | | |
| 5. Managerial equity-based | 0.515 | 0.231 | 0.068 | 0.125 | 0.101 | 0.073 | 1.000 | | | | | |
| 6. Managerial ownership | 0.023 | 0.048 | 0.027 | −0.268 | −0.328 | −0.142 | −0.335 | 1.000 | | | | |
| 7. Anti-takeover protection | 8.944 | 2.229 | −0.019 | 0.021 | 0.003 | −0.067 | −0.121 | 0.016 | 1.000 | | | |
| 8. Profitability | 0.052 | 0.112 | −0.111 | 0.150 | 0.025 | −0.133 | −0.012 | 0.063 | 0.036 | 1.000 | | |
| 9. Debt ratio | 0.134 | 0.120 | 0.018 | 0.262 | 0.121 | 0.025 | −0.059 | −0.222 | 0.130 | −0.196 | 1.000 | |
| 10. Firm size | 8.932 | 1.800 | −0.063 | 0.553 | 0.171 | 0.153 | 0.090 | 0.009 | −0.119 | 0.221 | 0.044 | 1.000 |

If the absolute value of the correlation is greater than 0.059, the correlation is significant at the 0.01 level.

*Table 2.2*  Cross-sectional regressions of the announcement effects of alliances on governance mechanisms

| Variable/model | 1 | 2 | 3 | 4 |
|---|---|---|---|---|
| *Board governance* | | | | |
| Board size | −0.001 | | | −0.0004 |
| | (−1.32) | | | (−0.74) |
| Outside director | −0.005 | | | −0.001 |
| Proportion | (−0.77) | | | (−0.15) |
| Meeting frequency | 0.001*** | | | 0.001*** |
| | (3.34) | | | (3.49) |
| *Incentive mechanism* | | | | |
| Managerial equity-based | | 0.015*** | | 0.014*** |
| Compensation | | (3.57) | | (3.42) |
| Managerial ownership | | 0.080* | | 0.090* |
| | | (2.14) | | (2.25) |
| Squared term of | | −0.173 | | −0.199 |
| Managerial ownership | | (−0.84) | | (−0.95) |
| *External governance* | | | | |
| Anti-takeover protection | | | −0.0003 | −0.0001 |
| | | | (−0.61) | (−0.35) |
| *Controls* | | | | |
| Profitability | −0.028** | −0.034*** | −0.034*** | −0.028** |
| | (−3.16) | (−3.99) | (−3.91) | (−3.15) |
| Debt ratio | 0.012 | 0.016† | 0.010 | 0.017* |
| | (1.47) | (1.91) | (1.31) | (2.04) |
| Firm size | −0.001 | −0.001† | −0.001 | −0.001† |
| | (−0.98) | (−1.92) | (−1.55) | (−1.72) |
| Industry dummies | included | included | included | included |
| Yearly dummies | included | included | included | included |
| $R^2$/Adj-$R^2$ | 0.0404/0.0287 | 0.0415/0.0298 | 0.0332/0.0225 | 0.0488/0.0349 |
| *F*-statistic | 3.45*** | 3.55*** | 3.11*** | 3.52*** |
| No. of observations | 1.743 | 7.743 | 1.743 | 1.743 |

†$p < 0.10$; *$p < 0.05$; **$p < 0.01$; ***$p < 0.001$.
*t*-value is in parentheses.

announcements are insignificantly related to board size. This finding does not support either Hypothesis 1–1a, that a smaller board faces fewer bureaucratic problems and thus is more functional, or Hypothesis 1–1b, that a larger board serves management well by offering broader expertise. The insignificance of board size could thus be due to the counteractive effects of the above two concerns. As for board independence, outside director proportion is also insignificantly related to the announcement returns. This result suggests that the information cost borne by outside directors (Hypothesis 1–2a) is probably neutralized by the external resources and expertise they provide (Hypothesis 1–2b). Model 1 detects a significantly positive association between board meeting frequency and market response to the alliance announcement ($p < 0.001$). This supports hypotheses 1–3, that active boards are effective in supervising and advising management when making alliance investments (Payne et al., 2009).

Model 2 examines how managerial interest alignment affects the valuation of alliance investments. Morck et al. (1988) suggest a non-linear relation between management ownership and organizational outcomes, with firm performance first rising and then declining as management equity ownership increases. A positive ownership effect without a non-linear pattern is observed. The coefficient on the managerial ownership term is significantly positive ($p < 0.05$), but the coefficient on the squared managerial ownership term is insignificant. This finding is similar to that of Reuer and Ragozzino (2006) with the number of alliances formed by firms as the dependent variable.

Model 2 also shows that the coefficient on the incentive measure of managerial equity-based compensation is significantly positive ($p < 0.001$). This reveals that equity-based compensation plans give managers incentives to undertake alliances that are in the interests of shareholders. Therefore structuring the compensation contracts of executives so that their compensation is tied to shareholder wealth can align the interests of managers and shareholders (Aggarwal and Samwick, 2006; Kang et al., 2006). The overall findings in Model 2 provide general support for hypotheses 2–1 and 2–2, suggesting the importance of incentive plans in governing management's alliance decisions.

Model 3 addresses the disciplinary effect of the external takeover market. In contrast with Hypothesis 3, an insignificant relation is found between takeover vulnerability and a firm's gains from alliances, indicating that shareholders may not rely on external governance to prevent managers from pursuing ill-conceived initiatives. This finding contrasts with previous studies on other investment forms, such as acquisitions, in which takeover threat secures shareholder interests (Fama and Jensen, 1983; Masulis, Wang and Xie, 2007). The result can be due to the counteractive effect of takeover protection, whereby shelter from the takeover market mitigates the agency problem of managerial myopia in alliance investments (Graber, 2003).

In Model 4, all of the governance variables in models 1 through 3 are combined, and the results are similar. The abnormal returns associated with alliance announcements are still significantly and positively related to meeting frequency, managerial ownership and equity-based compensation, revealing the independent benefits of these corporate governance mechanisms.

## Moderating effects

Hypotheses 4, 5 and 6 propose the contingent significance of corporate governance, whereby governance mechanisms have stronger benefits when the agency hazard is more pronounced. This issue is addressed in Table 2.3 through the construction of three moderating dummy variables, which are then made to interact with each corporate

*Table 2.3*　Cross-sectional regressions of the announcement effects of alliances on governance mechanisms and interaction variables

| Variable/Moderator dummy | Diversification dummy | International dummy | Equity dummy |
|---|---|---|---|
| *Board governance* | | | |
| Board size | −0.0005 | −0.0004 | −0.0004 |
| | (−0.97) | (−0.86) | (−0.85) |
| Board size × moderator dummy | 0.001 | 0.000004 | −0.002 |
| | (0.91) | (0.01) | (−1.64) |
| Outside director proportion | −0.003 | −0.001 | −0.001 |
| | (−0.42) | (−0.08) | (−0.16) |
| Outside director proportion × moderator dummy | 0.029† | −0.007 | 0.001 |
| | (1.91) | (−0.50) | (0.05) |
| Meeting frequency | 0.001*** | 0.001** | 0.001*** |
| | (3.39) | (3.07) | (3.44) |
| Meeting frequency × moderator dummy | 0.001** | 0.001* | −0.001 |
| | (2.91) | (2.05) | (−0.54) |
| *Incentive mechanism* | | | |
| Managerial equity-based compensation | 0.014*** | 0.013** | 0.014** |
| | (3.35) | (2.97) | (3.21) |
| Managerial equity-based compensation × moderator dummy | 0.026** | 0.017* | 0.005 |
| | (3.07) | (2.08) | (0.44) |
| Managerial ownership | 0.059** | 0.053* | 0.062** |
| | (2.60) | (2.40) | (2.80) |
| Managerial ownership × moderator dummy | 0.124** | 0.124** | 0.170* |
| | (2.90) | (2.80) | (2.01) |
| *External governance* | | | |
| Anti-takeover protection | −0.0001 | −0.0001 | −0.00004 |
| | (−0.28) | (−0.29) | (−0.10) |
| Anti-takeover protection × moderator dummy | 0.001 | −0.0004 | −0.001 |
| | (0.83) | (−0.47) | (−1.08) |
| *Controls* | | | |
| Profitability | −0.027** | −0.027** | −0.027** |
| | | | (−3.13) |
| Debt ratio | 0.018* | 0.019* | 0.018* |
| | (2.12) | (2.23) | (2.15) |

*Table 2.3*   (Continued)

| Variable/Moderator dummy | Diversification dummy | International dummy | Equity dummy |
|---|---|---|---|
| Firm size | −0.001† | −0.003† | −0.001 |
| | (−1.66) | (−1.82) | (−1.60) |
| Industry dummies | included | included | included yearly |
| Dummies | included | included | included |
| | 0.0619/0.0455 | 0.0567/0.0402 | $R^2$/Adj-$R^2$ |
| | | | 0.0548/0.0382 |
| *F*-statistic | 3.77*** | 3.43*** | 3.31*** |
| No of observations | 1,743 | 1,743 | 1,743 |

†$p < 0.10$; *$p < 0.05$; **$p < 0.01$; ***$p < 0.001$.
*t*-value is in parentheses.

governance variable. Data on the moderating dummies are obtained from the SDC database.

The first model examines the moderating effect of industry related-ness between a firm and its alliance activity, where the diversification dummy equals one when the announcing firm has a four-digit SIC code different from that of its alliance, and zero otherwise. The interaction term between this moderating variable and each governance variable measures whether the governance effect is more important for alliance activities that reside outside a firm's core business. Corporate gover-nance contributes significantly more to firm performance when the alliance activity is affiliated with a different industry from that of the firm – specifically, the valuation effects of diversified alliances, compar-ison with focused alliances, increase with outside director proportion ($p < 0.10$), meeting frequency ($p < 0.01$), equity-based compensation ($p < 0.01$) and managerial ownership ($p < 0.01$). This evidence supports Hypothesis 4, that a firm's non-core alliance investments augment the benefits of governance. Note that the inclusion of interaction terms does not alter the main effects of meeting frequency ($p < 0.001$), equity-based compensation ($p < 0.001$), and managerial ownership ($p < 0.01$), which remain significantly positive.

The next model examines whether a firm's governance mechanisms and its alliance location interactively shape the alliance outcome. The international dummy equals one when the alliance takes place over-seas, and zero domestically. The higher the meeting frequency ($p < 0.05$), equity-based compensation ($p < 0.05$) and managerial ownership ($p < 0.01$) of a firm undertaking an international alliance, the better its stock-market reaction to the alliance announcement, compared with that of a domestic firm. The results are consistent with Hypothesis 5, that the benefits of corporate governance mechanisms are more significant in international than in domestic alliances. Similar to the first model, the coefficients on meeting frequency ($p < 0.01$), equity-based compensation ($p < 0.01$) and managerial ownership ($p < 0.05$) are still significantly positive after including the interaction variables.

The last regression model examines the interactions between governance mechanisms and equity participation in alliances, where the equity dummy is one when the alliance involves equity participation and zero when it is based on a contractual agreement. This interaction term measures whether the governance effect is more pronounced when the alliance investment involves significant capital expenditure. Unlike the results in the first two models, there are insignificant moderating effects of equity participation, except for the interaction term between managerial ownership and the equity dummy, which shows a significantly positive coefficient ($p < 0.05$). This suggests that corporate governance, in general, exerts equivalent effects on a firm's equity and non-equity alliances, which rules against Hypothesis 6.

Several robustness checks are conducted using two different window lengths to measure the stock price reaction to the announcement of an alliance: $(-1, +1)$ and $(-2, +2)$. The regression results are qualitatively similar, suggesting that the findings remain robust for different window lengths of announcement-period returns. Likewise, whether the results are subject to the potential bias of data skewness is analyzed. Each variable is normalized and the regression analyses are reperformed. The study's conclusions remain unchanged.

## Discussion and implications

### Board of directors

The empirical results exhibit a favorable valuation effect of board meeting frequency, which highlights the importance of both the monitoring and the advisory roles of the board (e.g., Payne et al., 2009; Vafeas, 1999). Frequent board meetings are helpful in keeping managers on task and enhancing the flow of information between inside and outside directors. As the board becomes more informed about the issues surrounding alliance undertakings, it can act decisively and discourage strategic initiatives that transfer wealth from shareholders to managers at opportune moments. It can also assist managers in acquiring promising alliance chances in a timely manner and in adaptively restructuring post-formation operations in alliances.

Furthermore, there is an insignificant relation between board size and alliance outcomes. While this finding fails to support Hypothesis 1–1a on the monitoring benefit associated with a small board, it may be a neutralized result from the counsel aids of a large board, as stated in Hypothesis 1–1b. As resource dependence theory argues, the diverse thought generated by a large board can improve the decision-making quality of management (Coles et al., 2008). This is particularly important for alliances that prevail in uncertain environments where precise judgment is difficult to attain (Sampson, 2005). A larger board may serve alliance decisions well by bringing a level of sophistication to the discussion of critical issues, such as which activities to undertake, where to reach compatible partners and how to arrange appropriate operations.

Taken together, the findings regarding the effects that the informed, comprehensive advice offered by large boards and the active monitoring/counsel achieved by frequent board meetings have on alliance outcomes can have important implications for international business research. Extant studies show that boards increasingly participate in firms' internationalization activities (e.g., Filatotchev and Wright, 2011). However, the studies only provide evidence regarding the relationship between board characteristics and the degree of a firm's internationalization (e.g., Chen, 2011; Rivas, 2012). Thus the issue of how the board mechanism contributes to a firm's internationalization process and strategic undertakings is left relatively unaddressed (Lai, Chen, and Chang, 2012). However, based on the research results, which show that board capital helps to alleviate difficulties faced in strategic undertakings, particularly in uncertain environments where the achievement of an optimal decision requires considerable deliberation, future research can now further this analysis.

### Interest alignment of management

Stockholdings and equity-based compensation are found to have favorable effects on directing management toward value maximization in alliances. Because incentive plans allow managers to discipline themselves by creating a convergence of interests (Kang et al., 2006), they avoid the imperfect agent monitoring caused by the information inaccessibility embedded in alliances. This finding is consistent with international business research, which finds that self-motivation reduces the managerial inclination to take advantage of the costly monitoring environments of cross-border investments (Carpenter and Sanders, 2004; Sanders and Carpenter, 1998). As the issue of agency has been identified in firms' internationalization processes (Carpenter and Sanders, 2004), future studies may further explore the governance effect of the interest alignment mechanism on firms' internationalization strategies (e.g., entry mode choice and subsidiary ownership strategies). A comparison of the governance effect between stockholdings and equity-based compensation may be of specific interest, as the findings indicate that these two mechanisms can have different interest-alignment effects.

## Contingent significance of the governance mechanism

A more significant governance benefit is observed when firms undertake alliances out of their own industries, indicating that an uneconomical expansion is more likely to occur in a non-core than in a core alliance activity. This result is consistent with Jiraporn et al. (2006), who argue that corporate diversification activities require a stronger governance system to deter executive opportunistic misbehavior. Moreover, corporate governance exerts a more pronounced influence on cross-border (vs. domestic) alliances, which supports prior international business research documenting the increased difficulty of managing international (vs. domestic) alliances in the collection of information. This leads to a greater resultant cause–effect ambiguity of managerial decisions and thus magnifies the effect of governance measures on disciplining managers (Carpenter and Sanders, 2004). This finding generally supports the notion that in the information-asymmetric international environment, potential managerial self-serving behavior and corresponding governance benefits increase. While this study does not explore what factors differentiate the effects of the governance mechanisms among various international alliances, the international business literature shows that cultural and geographical distance between contracting parties can be significant determinants, as they generally increase with the degree of information asymmetry. Makino also provides a refreshing viewpoint in his keynote speech during the 2012 Academy of International Business Southeast Asia Regional (AIBSEAR) conference, indicating that historical factors such as wars or a colony relationship between the host and home countries can be other salient factors because they greatly influence the information available to the entrant firms. Future studies can reconcile these perspectives to further the analysis of and gain additional insights into this issue.

## Practical implications

This study may also have valuable implications for practitioners who are interested in undertaking international alliances. In the international information-asymmetric environment, how to identify which potential partner will help to achieve the greatest value creation in a cross-border alliance remains a debatable issue despite the significant results presented in existing studies. A review of the related literature shows that strategic and organizational fit between partnering firms are important criteria, as they directly determine the extent of an alliance's synergistic potential (Douma, Bilderbeek, Idenburg and Looise, 2000; Nielsen, 2007). Another stream of research highlights the importance of building trust in international alliances, as it may alleviate the problems stemming from the issue of contract incompleteness inherent in international alliances (e.g., Madhok, 1995). This study contributes to this research area by revealing the effect of corporate governance, a previously unexplored salient determinant. The findings provide essential knowledge regarding whether executives taking advantage of alliances for self-serving purposes rather than for alliance value creation results in both firms suffering. Alliance value creation under such circumstances cannot be reasonably expected even when the partnering firms have achieved strategic and organizational fit and have built a trusting relationship (Reuer and Ragozzino, 2006). Finally, uncovering that the "observable" governance mechanism of a foreign partner helps to predict its "invisible" commitment toward the alliance platform and can mitigate the liability of foreignness that confronts multinational enterprises undertaking overseas alliance investments.

## Note

1. Gompers et al. (2003) classify 24 anti-takeover governance provisions into five categories to assess the degree of management entrenchment: i) tactics for delaying hostile bids; ii) voting rights; iii) director/officer protection; iv) other takeover defenses; and v) state takeover laws.

## References

Aggarwal, R. K., and Samwick, A. A. (2006) Empire-builders and shirkers: Investment, firm performance, and managerial incentives. *Journal of Corporate Finance*, 12(3): 489–515.

Amihud, Y., and Lev, B. (1999) Does corporate ownership structure affect its strategy towards diversification? *Strategic Management Journal*, 20(11): 1063–1069.

Bertrand, M., and Mullainathan, S. (2001) Are CEOs rewarded for luck? The ones without principals. *Quarterly Journal of Economics*, 116(3): 901–932.

Boone, A. L., Field, L. C., Karpoff, J. M., and Raheja, C. G. (2007) The determinants of corporate board size and composition: An empirical analysis. *Journal of Financial Economics*, 85(2): 66–101.

Brouthers, K. D., Brouthers, L. E., and Werner, S. (2008) Real options, international entry mode choice and performance. *Journal of Management Studies*, 45(5): 936–960.

Brown, S. J., and Warner, J. B. (1985) Using daily stock returns: The case of event studies. *Journal of Financial Economics*, 14(1): 3–31.

Carpenter, M. A., and Sanders, W. G. (2004) The effects of top management team pay and firm internationalization on MNC performance. *Journal of Management*, 30(4): 509–528.

Caves, R. E., and Mehra, S. K. (1986) Entry of foreign multinationals into US manufacturing industries. In M.E. Porter (Ed.). *Competition in Global Industries*, Harvard University Press: Boston, MA, pp. 449–481.

Chang, S. C., and Chen, S. S. (2002) The wealth effect of domestic joint ventures: Evidence from Taiwan. *Journal of Business Finance and Accounting*, 29(1) and (2): 201–222.

Chang, S. C., Chen, S. S., and Lai, J. H. (2008) The wealth effect of Japanese–US strategic alliances. *Financial Management*, 37(2): 271–301.

Chen, H.L. (2011) Does board independence influence the top management team? Evidence from strategic decisions toward internationalization. Corporate Governance: *An International Review*, 19(4): 334–350.

Cho, T. S., and Shen, W. (2007) Changes in executive compensation following an environmental shift: The role of top management team turnover. *Strategic Management Journal*, 28(7): 747–754.

Coles, J. L., Daniel, N. D., and Naveen, L. (2008) Boards: Does one size fit all? *Journal of Financial Economics*, 87(2): 329–356.

Cremers, K. J. M., and Nair, V. B. (2005) Governance mechanisms and equity prices. *Journal of Finance*, 60(6): 2859–2894.

Das, S., Sen, P. K., and Sengupta, S. (1998) Impact of strategic alliances on firm valuation. *Academy of Management Journal*, 41(1): 27–41.

Douma, M. U., Bilderbeek, J., Idenburg, P. J., and Looise, J. K. (2000) Strategic alliances: Managing the dynamics of fit. *Long Range Planning*, 33(4): 579–598.

Fama, E. F., and Jensen, M. C. (1983) Agency problems and residual claims. *Journal of Law and Economics*, 26(2): 327–349.

Filatotchev, I., and Wright, M. (2011) Agency perspectives on corporate governance of multinational enterprises. *Journal of Management Studies*, 48(2): 471–486.

Glaister, K., and Buckley, P. (1996) Strategic motives for international alliance formation. *Journal of Management Studies*, 33(3): 301–332.

Gomez-Mejia, L. R., and Palich, L. E. (1997) Cultural diversity and the performance of multinational firms. *Journal of International Business Studies*, 28(2): 309–335.

Gompers, P. A., Ishii, J. L., and Metrick, A. (2003) Corporate governance and equity prices. *Quarterly Journal of Economics*, 118(1): 107–155.

Goodstein, J., Gautam, K., and Boeker, W. (1994) The effects of board size and diversity on strategic change. *Strategic Management Journal*, 15(3): 241–250.

Graber, R. S. (2003) Management turnover and under-investment in R&D: An agency theory explanation for under-investment in research and development in some corporations. *Journal of Social Political and Economic Studies*, 28(3): 295–323.

Hergert, M., and D. Morris. (1988) Trends in Collaborative Agreements. In *Cooperative Strategies in International Business*, Farok Contractor and Peter Lorange (Eds.), Lexington Books: Lexington, MA, pp. 99–109.

Hillman, A. J., Cannella, A. A., and Paetzold, R. L. (2000) The resource dependence role of corporate directors: Strategic adaptation of board composition in response to environmental change. *Journal of Management Studies*, 37(2): 235–256.

Hood, N., and Young, S. (1979) *The Economics of Multinational Enterprise*. Longman Group Ltd, London.

Hymer, S. H. (1976) *The International Operations of National Firms: A Study of Direct Foreign Investment*. MIT Press: Cambridge, MA.

Jensen, M. C. (1986) Agency costs of free cash flow, corporate finance, and takeovers. *American Economic Review*, 76(2): 323–329.

Jensen, M. C. (1993) The modern industrial revolution, exit and the failure of internal control systems. *Journal of Finance*, 48(3): 831–880.

Jiraporn, P., Kim, Y. S., Davidson, W. N., and Singh, M. (2006) Corporate governance, shareholder rights and firm diversification: An empirical analysis. *Journal of Banking and Finance*, 30(3): 947–963.

Kang, S. H., Kumar, P., and Lee, H. (2006) Agency and corporate investment: The role of executive compensation and corporate governance. *Journal of Business*, 79(3): 1127–1147.

Keown, A. J., Laux, P., and Martin, J. D. (2005) The information content of corporate investment announcements: The case of joint ventures. *Research in Finance*, 22: 33–71.

Kor, Y. Y., and Misangyi, V. F. (2008) Outside directors' industry-specific experience and firms' liability of newness. *Strategic Management Journal*, 29(12): 1345–1355.

Lai, J. H., Chen, L. Y., and Chang, S. C. (2012) The board mechanism and entry mode choice. *Journal of International Management*, 18(4): 379–392.

Lavie, D., and Miller, S. R. (2008) Alliance portfolio internationalization and firm performance. *Organization Science*, 19(4): 623–646.

Madhok, A. (1995) Revisiting multinational firms' tolerance for joint ventures: A trust-based approach. *Journal of International Business Studies*, 26(1): 117–137.

Marquardt, D. W., and Snee, R. D. (1975) Ridge regression in practice. *The American Statistician*, 29(1): 3–20.

Masulis, R. W., Wang, C., and Xie, F. (2007) Corporate governance and acquirer returns. *Journal of Finance*, 62(4): 1851–1889.

Min, J. H., and Prather, L. J. (2001) Tobin's q, agency conflicts, and differential wealth effects of international joint ventures. *Global Finance Journal*, 12(2): 267–283.

Morck, R., Shleifer, A., and Vishny, R. W. (1988) Management ownership and market valuation: An empirical analysis. *Journal of Financial Economics*, 20(1/2): 293–315.

Nielsen, B. B. (2007) Determining international strategic alliance performance: A multidimensional approach. *International Business Review*, 16(3): 337–361.

Ofek, E., and Yermack, D. (2000) Taking stock: Equity-based compensation and the evolution of managerial ownership. *Journal of Finance*, 55(3): 1367–1384.

Ozcan, P., and Eisenhardt, K. M. (2009) Origin of alliance portfolios: Entrepreneurs, network strategies, and firm performance. *Academy of Management Journal*, 52(2): 246–279.

Pangarkar, N. (2007) Survival during a crisis: Alliances by Singapore firms. *British Journal of Management*, 18(3): 209–223.

Park, N. K. (2004) A guide to using event study methods in multi-country settings. *Strategic Management Journal*, 25(7): 655–668.

Payne, G. T., Benson, G. S., and Finegold, D. L. (2009) Corporate board attributes, team effectiveness and financial performance. *Journal of Management Studies*, 46(4): 704–731.

Porter, M. E., and Fuller, M. B. (1986) Coalitions and global strategy. *In Competition in Global Industries*, Porter M. E. (Ed.). Harvard Business School Press: Boston, MA.

Ren, H., Gray, B., and Kim, K. (2009) Performance of international joint ventures: What factors really make a difference and how? *Journal of Management*, 35(3): 805–832.

Reuer, J. J., and Ragozzino, R. (2006) Agency hazards and alliance portfolios. *Strategic Management Journal*, 27(1): 27–43.

Rivas, J. L. (2012) Diversity and internationalization: The case of boards and TMT's. *International Business Review*, 21(1): 1–12.

Sampson, R. C. (2005) Experience effects and collaborative returns in R&D alliances. *Strategic Management Journal*, 26(11): 1009–1031.

Sanders, W. G., and Carpenter, M. A. (1998) Internationalization and firm governance: The roles of CEO compensation, top team composition, and board structure. *Academy of Management Journal*, 41(2): 158–178.

Santos, F. M., and Eisenhardt, K. M. (2009) Constructing markets and shaping boundaries: Entrepreneurial agency in nascent fields. *Academy of Management Journal*, 52(4): 643–671.

Shah, R. H., and Swaminathan, V. (2008) Factors influencing partner selection in strategic alliances: The moderating role of alliance context. *Strategic Management Journal*, 29(5): 471–494.

Shleifer, A., and Vishny, R. W. (1989) Management entrenchment: The case of manager-specific investments. *Journal of Financial Economics*, 25(1): 123–139.

Vafeas, N. (1999) Board meeting frequency and firm performance. *Journal of Financial Economics*, 53(1): 113–142.

# 3

# What Drives the Strategic Alliance Formation of Transition Economy Small and Medium-Sized Enterprises?

## The Moderating Role of Intermediary Organizations

*Wiboon Kittilaksanawong, Xudong Chen and Chaoqun Duan*

## Introduction

Small and medium-sized enterprises (SMEs) are increasingly playing an important role in the economic development of many emerging economies, particularly as they gradually become more involved in global markets through various means of internationalization. While the institutional environments in these emerging economies have progressed significantly toward market economies in recent years, providing SMEs with many opportunities, there are still considerable challenges that constrain SMEs' performance and growth. Many are pushed abroad as the result of discrimination in the domestic market. Given that the governments in many emerging economies are more interested in supporting large domestic and multinational firms through a variety of investment incentives, these ventures are at a great disadvantage in seeking resources in the domestic market.

Case studies of Asian firms, specifically Chinese SMEs, illustrate how they formulate and implement their strategies (i.e., strategic alliances)

This study is supported by the Canada International Development Research Centre (IDRC, Project no. 106341-001) and the Zhejiang Provincial Natural Science Foundation of China (Project No. LY12G02011).

to take advantage of such opportunities and to overcome a variety of challenges in their internationalization efforts. In fact, international business research on the strategies of Asian firms has displayed a rising trend (Chan, Isobe and Makino, 2008; Chan, Makino and Isobe, 2010; Makino, Isobe and Chan, 2004). The results of this study are intended to add to the conventional wisdom explaining current international business practices in emergent Asia.

Strategic alliances have continued to attract the attention of scholars and practitioners. The literature has demonstrated the functions and advantages of alliance formation in entering new markets, increasing market power, acquiring and exchanging skills, pursuing strategic renewal, sharing risk and investment, gaining economies of scale and scope, reducing liabilities of foreignness, mitigating government or trade barriers and acquiring institutional legitimacy (e.g., Baum and Oliver, 1991; Contractor and Lorange, 1988; Eisenhardt and Schoonhoven, 1996; Mowery, Oxley and Silverman, 1996; Ring and Van de Ven, 1992). Although interest in the drivers of strategic partnering has revealed a significant number of benefits among the collaborative firms, the literature has not paid enough attention to investigating the strategic alliance-formation process in transition economies. In particular, the extant research has not explored how SMEs based in transition economies use strategic alliances to overcome various constraints and facilitate their internationalization (Luo and Tung, 2007). The available research on the internationalization of SMEs based in emerging economies has focused mostly on large firms. Therefore, how small entrepreneurial firms based in emerging economies, or transition economies in particular, employ strategic alliances to facilitate their internationalization reflects a gap in the literature.

A transition economy is one that is shifting from a centrally planned toward a more liberalized market economy with increased entrepreneurship (Ahlstrom and Bruton, 2010). Entrepreneurship is critical to the economic development of transition economies, such as China and Russia, as they move toward a market economy. Compared with their counterparts in developed economies, the governments in transition economies continue to exert significant influence on the development of entrepreneurship, although the market mechanisms in these economies play increasingly important roles. While transition economies have recently made significant progress toward market-oriented frameworks, the regulative environment in these economies remains unfriendly to entrepreneurs (Peng, 2003). Many SMEs are pushed abroad due to discrimination in the domestic market. In fact, the governments in many emerging economies seem to be more interested in supporting large domestic and multinational firms through a variety of investment incentives. For example, the Chinese government has continued to encourage large, state-owned enterprises to expand abroad (Child and Rodrigues, 2005). Some state banks are not allowed to lend to private SMEs, and the latter are prohibited from listing on the domestic stock exchange. As a result, these ventures are at a great disadvantage in seeking resources in the domestic market.

Employing China as the research context, this study investigates SMEs' strategic alliance formation in Zhejiang province, one of the country's most developed private economies. Deriving value from strategic alliances essentially requires that a company selects the right partners, develops a suitable alliance design, adapts the relationship as needed and manages the alliance termination appropriately (Reuer, 1999). This study is based on in-depth interviews with Shengzhou Necktie Logistics (SNL) and LH Pharmaceutical Intermediates (LHPI) about strategic alliance formation in the pursuit of international entrepreneurship, along with additional site visits to 28 other SMEs in the province during March and July 2011. Built on resource-based theory (Harrigan, 1988), transaction cost economics (Hennart and Reddy, 1997) and institutional theory (DiMaggio and Powell, 1983), it critically reveals the drivers and facilitators of SMEs' strategic alliance formations in China's Zhejiang province. Essentially, the case studies reveal the role of Zhejiang's local government and others in facilitating the formation of strategic alliances within the province. These case studies highlight the unique characteristics of the alliance formations between transition-economy SMEs.

## Strategic alliance formation of Shengzhou Necktie and LH Pharmaceutical Intermediates

SNL was incorporated in June, 2009 with a registered capital of RMB50 million. The company was formed by six independent core manufacturing companies: Babe Group, Zhejiang Yashilin Group, Maidilang Group, Shengzhou City Qiandai Necktie Weaving, Danlu Clothing and Shengzhou Yuelong Necktie Weaving. To further expand its existing necktie-manufacturing business, SNL subsequently collaborated with Zhejiang Quanshun Silk and Jiaxing Weiyu Silk through an equity participation joint venture. LHPI was founded in 2005 with a specialization in trading pharmaceutical intermediates. It employed its own sales and distribution network along with service-specific capability.

LHPI searched for and helped domestic pharmaceutical intermediaries to meet the required standards of international drug manufacturers.

## Drivers of alliance formation

When expanding internationally, strategic alliances can be an effective strategy for SMEs to overcome capability deficiencies (Lee, Lee and Pennings, 2001). Transaction cost economics has been the principal theoretical approach to understanding why and when strategic alliances are formed (Hennart, 1988). This theory emphasizes transaction cost efficiency as the primary motivation for firms to enter into a strategic alliance. However, the logic of transaction cost minimization does not always capture the many other strategic advantages inherent in an alliance, such as learning, fast market entry and legitimacy attainment. To capture these strategic advantages, scholars have increasingly used the resource-based view in determining alliance formation (Wernerfelt, 1984). According to the resource-based view, when firms are in a vulnerable strategic position, they enter into a strategic alliance to access the necessary resources provided by their alliance partners (Eisenhardt and Schoonhoven, 1996). Built on this view, alliance formation is driven by the logic of strategic resource needs and social resource opportunities. For example, entrepreneurial firms form alliances when entering into new markets, when there are many competitors or when there is a pioneering technology involved (Eisenhardt and Schoonhoven, 1996). Further, relatively well-connected firms tend to form strategic alliances. In particular, resource-rich firms are likely to attract more resources (Eisenhardt and Schoonhoven, 1996). Thus the social, symbolic and signaling characteristics of alliances may serve as a source of legitimacy for partnering firms. Legitimacy refers to a generalized perception that the actions of an entity are desirable and appropriate within socially constructed norms, values and beliefs (Zimmerman and Zeitz, 2002). Establishing legitimacy potentially enhances the flow of resources that are indispensable to the survival and prosperity of SMEs (Deeds, Mang, and Frandsen, 2004). This legitimacy is thus particularly crucial to SMEs as a strategic resource with the potential to yield economic and competitive benefits (Dacin, Oliver, and Roy, 2007).

In transition economies, as market competition increasingly develops, the competitive pressure in some domestic industries may escalate significantly. The level of such competitive pressure in an industry thus becomes an important determinant of SMEs' strategies and performance (Boter and Holmquist, 1996). Under these circumstances, and to avoid head-on competition with domestic incumbents, SMEs may look for a better market prospect abroad (Dawar and Frost, 1999). Strategic alliances are therefore a crucial strategy for many SMEs in the pursuit of their internationalization and to escape fierce domestic competition. Because SMEs in emerging economies are generally not more advantageous than their counterparts in developed economies in terms of innovative technologies, forming alliances with others allows SMEs to access the necessary resources for internationalization (Ahlstrom, Young, Chan and Bruton, 2004). When the market power of SMEs in their home country is eroding, forming partnerships with others also gives them the chance to learn from their partners to overcome hurdles and take advantage of new opportunities (i.e., internationalizing operations). Essentially, the internationalization of SMEs in emerging economies is not necessarily based on their possession of abundant strategic assets but rather these SMEs are more adept at leveraging their organizational learning capabilities (Mathews, 2006).

The above notion suggests that SMEs in emerging economies form strategic alliances due to the domestic competitive pressure and a lack of some critical resources. While these SMEs may not be able to afford to compete for tangible resources, a more recent study has demonstrated that they can overcome resource restrictions and latecomer disadvantages in the global market via a series of aggressive risk-taking strategic imperatives that compensate for such weaknesses (Luo and Tung, 2007). Essentially, the aspects of entrepreneurial orientation may well explain the internationalization behavior of these SMEs. Entrepreneurial orientation refers to the tendency to act spontaneously, the willingness to innovate and take risks, and the propensity to be aggressive toward competitors and proactive about market opportunities (Lumpkin and Dess, 1996). These beliefs and values contribute to the success of many SMEs in emerging economies (Scott, 1995).

Given the escalating competitive pressure, resource constraints and low levels of legitimacy in addition to the restricted financing alternatives encountered by many SMEs in emerging economies, the rules and regulations in these emerging economies are likely to have a more pronounced effect on the strategies and performance of SMEs than they do on other established or government-supported enterprises. In emerging economies, industry conditions and firm resources and capabilities are not the only drivers of strategic choices and SME performance. The formal and informal institutional constraints also determine how these SMEs should conduct their business (Peng, Wang and Jiang, 2008). Based on these theoretical perspectives, field surveys and in-depth interviews, this study highlights the drivers of transition-economy firms' alliance-formation processes, which include the acquisition of critical resources, operation cost sharing, operation risk reduction, increase in competitive potential and governmental preferential treatment. Their associated propositions are then derived as follows.

## Acquisition of critical resources

During the new international market development process, SNL and LHPI were faced with critical input resource bottlenecks. The cost of raw material inputs in necktie manufacturing was relatively high, accounting for 70–80% of the finished product. Further, SNL found it very difficult to successfully build up its own brand in the international market to become a main gateway through which foreign buyers could procure local necktie products. Building its own international brand or re-establishing itself as an exclusive supplier of necktie products required large-scale manufacturing capabilities, long-term capital and step-by-step development. Without a solid foundation, foreign buyers might become competitors, substituting local suppliers through their larger global networks. Strengthening the control of raw material input costs was critical to the survival of SNL and other necktie-manufacturing companies. Through strategic alliance with other firms featuring complementary resources, SNL was able to increase its procurement alternatives and establish through joint investment among partners its own sericulture bases, thereby solving the problem of input resource bottlenecks, high raw material costs and large long-term capital investment. LHPI and its alliance partners had a very clear division of labor to supply raw pharmaceutical intermediates to drug-manufacturing firms. The strategic partnership allowed LHPI to pool specialized talent firms together on a complementary basis, thereby increasing the international competitiveness of all of the collaborative partners.

## Operation cost-sharing

Finished products, associated production processes and raw material inputs in necktie manufacturing among firms were highly homogeneous. Likewise, these firms' logistical needs were very similar. Firms operating independently resulted in highly redundant processes involving the procurement of raw material inputs, production processes and finished product logistics. These firms found it very difficult to be competitive in terms of product pricing in the export market. Thus SNL was motivated to form strategic alliances with other necktie manufacturers to reduce manufacturing and logistics costs, and increase efficiency through economies of scale, thereby increasing its competitiveness in the export market. Through strategic alliances with other necktie-manufacturing firms, SNL was able not only to share its manufacturing facility and logistics costs but also to negotiate a larger-volume raw material input for a better price. LHPI and its alliance partners had a clearer division of labor and thus were not motivated to form manufacturing collaborations as SNL did. However, LHPI's cooperation with many other domestic suppliers of pharmaceutical intermediate inputs provided it with more sourcing alternatives, thereby increasing its negotiation power through these partners and generating subsequent cost reduction.

### Operation risk reduction

SNL's strategic partners were involved in both necktie manufacturing and raw silk supply (e.g., Zhejiang Quanshun Silk and Jiaxing Weiyu Silk). Not only did these companies provide complementary resources and capabilities but through the collaboration, SNL was also able to extend its raw material input base, thereby significantly sharing and reducing the risk of supply shortage in its manufacturing processes. The strategic collaboration also ensured that the partners would work together on R&D and the resolution of any technical problems. LHPI collaborated with other SMEs to procure pharmaceutical intermediates from them and further sold these intermediates to foreign buyers. These SMEs had a relatively limited capability to tolerate the risk and uncertainty prompted by market and technological changes. Therefore instead of expanding into an unfamiliar business domain, they tended to adhere to the current business domain and enhance their existing specialized skills. Further, by partnering with LHPI, they also reduced the risk and uncertainty associated with the specificity of their professional skills. Through strategic partnering, the collaborating partners shared market information, and through an exclusive sales agreement, LHPI and partners significantly reduced the overall uncertainty and risk generated by market and technological changes.

### Increase in competitive potential

Market shares suggest that necktie manufacturing in Shengzhou was still competitive in the international markets. However, this competitive advantage exhibited an escalating risk unless the cluster was to initiate significant industry transformations and upgrades. Importantly, the entry barrier of the tie industry was low because the manufacturing and products were very homogeneous and easily imitated. Foreign buyers had greater negotiation power because they consulted through a few large domestic selling agents and made a critical purchase decision based on lower prices. Otherwise, these foreign buyers also negotiated with many individual manufacturers for the lowest price, thereby increasing competition among manufacturers within the industry and driving down the overall price. By forming strategic alliances, tie manufacturers increased their communication to reduce vicious competition among them, thereby increasing their negotiation power with overseas buyers. LHPI and its strategic partners were not motivated to enter an alliance in the same way because the pharmaceutical intermediate industry is highly differentiated, with firms specializing in their respective areas of pharmaceutical intermediates, which are difficult for others to imitate. The competition among these intermediate manufacturers was relatively benign. Particularly if they could develop a new synthetic before the expiration of associated patents, their negotiation power with overseas buyers would be very strong. In this respect, therefore, SNL's strategic alliances were considered compulsory, whereas for LHPI, they were beneficial but less critical due to the specificity of professional expertise.

### Governmental preferential treatment

SMEs in Zhejiang province generally lack necessary resources, thus government incentives are particularly attractive and essential for their development. While necktie manufacturing in Shengzhou had gained a reputation in both domestic and overseas markets, the industry development model remained very traditional and family-oriented. To expedite the industry transformation and upgrading, Zhejiang's provincial and municipal governments paid increasingly significant attention to the establishment of the necktie industry association. The governments implemented platforms to enhance the communication between businesses and governments, such that the latter could provide effective, supportive policies that strengthened the cooperation among these clustered firms, thereby enhancing their overall competitiveness in international markets. The pharmaceutical intermediate manufacturers' motivation to gain such preferential treatment in this manner, however, was not strong enough to attract significant attention from the local government. Alliance formation for LHPI and other pharmaceutical intermediate manufacturers was therefore relatively flexible and dependent on the needs of individual firms, in addition to not being significantly driven by governmental policies.

*Proposition 1: A transition-economy SME will be more likely to enter a strategic alliance to i) acquire critical resources, ii) share operation costs, iii) reduce operation risks, iv) increase competitive potential, or v) gain governmental preferential treatment.*

## Role of intermediary organizations

SMEs, particularly those in many emerging economies, have increasingly experienced the rapid market and technological changes and highly competitive pressure. Because SMEs generally have limited resources and have not established many relationships with outside actors, this change may bring about significant risk and uncertainty that could harm their survival and growth. The dynamic market and technological changes require ventures to constantly deal with environmental volatility, increase development speed, and establish new markets and technologies (Katila and Shane, 2005; Li and Atuahene-Gima, 2001; Smith, Collins and Clark, 2005). Essentially, the literature has demonstrated that ties with service intermediaries, universities, research institutes, regional trade associations, technical assistance centers and other established firms have a positive effect on firm innovation (Zhang and Li, 2009; Baum, Calabrese and Silverman, 2000).

These market intermediaries relay information among transaction parties and provide a variety of support services (Akerlof, 1970; Khanna and Palepu, 2000). The economic transactions of these parties are also supported by the suppliers of human, physical and technological infrastructure (Teece, 1986). Essentially, these intermediaries establish links among firms with complementary resources and capabilities while providing them with necessary information involving potential exchange partners (McEvily and Zaheer, 1999). These links allow SMEs, particularly in emerging economies, to gain access to potential exchange parties, and reduce the information and search costs pertinent to locating the resources necessary for operational success (He, 2002). Therefore, when the availability of and access to these market intermediaries are not sufficient, SMEs in emerging economies are likely to find it very difficult and costly to raise the funds needed to acquire the necessary inputs and find other professionally qualified intermediary services in their home markets (Khanna and Palepu, 2000).

The literature has suggested that firms with a short history, and lack of a proven performance record, resources, legitimacy and status, generally find it very difficult to develop ties with prominent organizations, such as established firms, universities and research institutes.

Thus service intermediaries have increasingly played an important role (Zhang and Li, 2009; Hargadon and Sutton, 1997; Howells, 2006; Stinchcombe, 1965). However, this study highlights the context of transition economies and demonstrates that the prominent organizations, such as leading large manufacturing enterprises and professional specialized trading firms, may become an important facilitator in establishing ties with SMEs. In particular, based on the aforementioned theoretical perspectives, field surveys and in-depth interviews, this study highlights the roles of industry association and government departments, and specialized marketing zones, as two types of service intermediaries, and professional specialized trading enterprises and leading manufacturing enterprises as two types of prominent organizations. It then derives their associated propositions as follows.

### Industry association and government departments

Industry association and government departments create bridges between SMEs and a loose network of member firms associated with procurement, manufacturing, logistics, trading and marketing. Member firms benefit through sharing and integrating manufacturing and marketing resources, thereby increasing their overall competitiveness. The necktie manufacturing industry in Shengzhou provides a good example of strategic alliances among SMEs, facilitated by the Shengzhou Bureau of Economics and Information and the Shengzhou Necktie Industry Association. These industry associations and government departments act as leaders in bridging the gaps between SMEs in the industry cluster to form various strategic alliances. Under their guidance, Tianjia Necktie, Dayi Necktie and four other related companies established the Zhejiang Zhengtong Logistics alliance company. Also, Babei Group, Maidilang Group and eight other companies formed the Shengzhou Necktie Logistics alliance company. Besides, China Silk, Panshi Whole Industry and Jingang Silk established the Sanxin Whole Industry alliance company as well.

In addition to equity participation, the three companies participating in Sanxin Whole Industry contributed their technology, marketing, personnel and other necessary resources to the venture and shared all of the derived benefits and associated risks. The venture's success essentially stemmed from the fact that all of the collaborating companies were relatively small, with the joint venture's registered capital only coming to RMB800,000. The allocation of benefits and costs was simply based on each partner's fixed assets and manufacturing capacity. In addition, the venture was mainly associated with the logistics of finished products without the complications of product manufacturing or marketing. All of the partners put together their respective original differentiated capabilities, which clearly affected the overall quality of deliveries. Moreover, the venture provided export services, mainly to necktie-manufacturing companies within Shengzhou's clusters, and its customers knew each other very well. The pricing was almost transparent among the cluster firms and they mostly competed through the management of their production costs to earn higher profits. The collaborating partner in the venture had direct contact with the end customers rather than going through other intermediaries, thereby significantly reducing costs. Nevertheless, there were also many problems associated with the lack of international entrepreneurship experience within the venture.

Under the strong guidance of the Shengzhou Necktie Industry Association, the two necktie logistics alliances led by Tianjia Necktie and Babei Group were successful for the following reasons. The integration of preprocessing operations was achieved by unifying the procurement of sericulture and other raw material inputs, thereby strengthening the control over raw material availability and prices. A service platform was built to help the cluster of firms improve their R&D and solve various technical problems. The alliance led by Babei Group, Shengzhou Necktie Logistics, adopted a professional management system emphasizing good corporate governance. The company hired logistics professionals from outside to improve its logistics operation management and to develop a long-term business plan. In contrast, the alliance led by Tianjia Necktie, Zhejiang Zhengtong, was dominated by partners that had a kinship relationship. The operations and management of all of the partner companies were a similar family style. The chairman of the leading company had absolute authority and influence over all of the alliance's operational activities, resulting in many more management problems.

### Specialized marketing zones

Specialized marketing zones are independent entities that build their locational advantage from relatively stable collaboration networks among companies located in the zones. These companies are specialized in different areas, such as procurement, manufacturing, logistics, marketing and finance. China Textile City (CTC) is currently the largest in Asia, having the highest market turnover, operating the largest variety of textile wholesale specialized markets and supporting a number of SMEs throughout the country. CTC is also widely known and highly influential in the international textile market in that it helps domestic textile companies to explore opportunities in international markets through several initiatives. CTC attracts investments from domestic and overseas companies into this specialized zone by offering associated investment incentives. Further, CTC helps to extend international marketing channels by increasing exchanges with business or industry associations in the United States and Asia, and with other international agencies. Following these exchanges, CTC has signed long-term cooperation agreements with global SMEs, set up the first CTC overseas representative office in Dubai, and actively promoted the establishment of more overseas offices in other regions. It also enhances the connection and integration among SMEs along the supply chain, thereby increasing international competitive potential. Other initiatives include the provision of service platforms, such as Global Textiles Network and Online Textile City, to foster information exchange and online trading services, and China Textile Market Talents to promote the exchange of textile professionals.

These initiatives, however, do not help SMEs to succeed in the international markets. The SMEs are relatively passive and their willingness to collaborate with other peer companies is not very strong. Rainbow Village, for example, was involved in the entire chain of domestic supply activities, from procuring cloth and other raw materials to the finished clothes, but the company was unable to directly engage in international markets, thereby continuing to rely heavily on CTC and other foreign trading companies. Fumeilai, a manufacturer of knitting products with several plants in Fujian and Shaoxing, was unable to actively export its products due to a lack of professionals experienced in foreign trading. Shengfa believed that buyers demanded a very high-quality product that the company might not be able to profit from easily, and therefore continued to focus on domestic sales. Overall, while CTC has a strong market influence and has successfully attracted a large number of foreign buyers and trading agents to Shaoxing, the dispersed and loose connections and intense competition among relatively homogeneous peer companies in the zone have impeded the international market development of these SMEs.

### Professional specialized trading enterprises

A professional specialized trading enterprise not only provides traditional trading services but also collaborates with domestic SMEs to align their manufacturing and other activities with the demands of overseas markets. LHPI was a professional specialized trading company providing import and export services for pharmaceutical intermediate-related products. The company was not only involved in traditional international trading services but also established relatively stable collaborations with a number of SMEs that had strong pharmaceutical intermediate R&D capabilities. Through LHPI, these strategic partners mutually developed and grew overseas markets. Meibo, established in 1999 as an exporter of stationery and office supplies, daily necessities, hardware tools, and electrical and electronic products, established business relationships with more than 4,000 domestic plants. Although it helped these plants to export their products, the extent to which they collaborated with each other was not very great because they mostly relied on overseas orders available to Meibo.

Ningbo Meilian Foreign Trade Service provided member SMEs with export-related business services, such as document translation; overseas exhibition, conference and product promotion; documentation and customs clearance; inspection; verification rebates; and financing to reduce their export costs and risks. It also served as a domestic incubator for foreign trade businesses, delivering training programs for export and import companies and individual foreign trade professionals. To promote the export of domestic SMEs' products, the company specifically set up an exhibition facility of more than 6,000 square meters. Through this facility, the company was able to secure an average of three or four orders for SMEs' products and services from foreign businessmen visiting the facility. The company also organized regular trade events for new products and services while, together with other professional associations, arranging many commercial and non-commercial joint activities. With relatively large-scale trading through these SMEs' networks, the company actively collaborated and effectively negotiated with other international freight forwarders, commercial banks, insurance companies and other trade-related departments to provide member SMEs with the most cost-effective trade services once only available to large manufacturing enterprises. Through strong government support, the company became the first to domestically provide joint insurance coverage at a significantly reduced export insurance premium.

### Leading manufacturing enterprises

Leading enterprises usually have relatively strong manufacturing capabilities and are responsible for direct entry into and development in overseas markets. Other SMEs follow this leading enterprise through contract manufacturing for other peripheral products or services. Ningbo Weike Holding Group provides a good example of how a leading enterprise attracts a number of SMEs to joint its unique network. The early Weike Home Textile was first founded from the strong support of the local government by integrating and restructuring large-scale enterprises in the textile industry. The group became a leading enterprise in the home textile industry, providing a variety of support to SMEs through a number of collaborative relationships and committing significant resources to the development of international markets, such as setting up green-field overseas branches, and through mergers and acquisitions. The group had overseas subsidiaries in more than ten countries and regions worldwide, and gradually built up its own international brand.

Zhengtai Group, as another example, was founded in 1984 and mainly manufactures high- and low-voltage electrical equipment, power transmission equipment and instrumentation, communication equipment, and construction and automotive electrical products. The group had more than 50 subsidiaries with over 800 professional collaborative manufacturing plants and more than 2,000 distribution and sales companies throughout the country. Internationally, it set up five overseas subsidiaries and appointed more than 40 sales agents with products being sold in more than 90 countries and regions. The production of low-voltage electrical products was mainly delivered from the other collaborative SMEs, whereby the group was responsible for final product assembly, support, quality assurance and other core technology applications.

*Proposition 2: A transition-economy SME's ties with i) an industry association or a government department, ii) a specialized marketing zone, iii) a professional specialized trading enterprise or iv) a leading manufacturing enterprise will positively moderate each of the relationships in proposition 1.*

## Discussion and conclusion

Interest in the drivers of strategic alliance has revealed a number of benefits among the collaborative partners, but the literature has not paid enough attention to investigating the strategic alliance formation of SMEs in transition economies. In particular, entrepreneurship is a critical element in the economic development of transition economies. While moving toward a market economy, the governments in transition economies continue to exert significant influence on the development of entrepreneurship. Therefore a single-level analysis of firms in Asian emerging economies may create misleading implications for practice. Importantly, separating micro- and macro-issues in international business research on emerging economies is increasingly irrelevant. International business scholars must examine the multiple causes or consequences of firm behavior at and across different levels. Clearly, international business research on Asian emerging economies potentially uncovers a number of contributions to theoretical development and managerial practices. Scholars need to develop stronger theoretical foundations to explain why countries and associated institutions matter, as practitioners keep in mind the fact that international business skills are becoming more important than before, due to the rise in emerging economies.

Built on a resource-based view (Wernerfelt, 1984), transaction cost economics (Hennart, 1988) and institutional theory (Dacin, Oliver, and Roy, 2007), and based on extensive field surveys and in-depth interviews with SMEs in China's Zhejiang province, this study highlights the drivers for the alliance-formation processes of transition-economy SMEs in the pursuit of international entrepreneurship, which include the acquisition of critical resources, operation cost-sharing, operation risk reduction, an increase in competitive potential and governmental preferential treatment. Further, prominent organizations, such as leading large manufacturing enterprises and professional specialized trading firms and service intermediaries, such as industry associations, government departments and specialized marketing zones, are important facilitators in establishing strategic alliances among SMEs. These intermediaries play important roles in aligning firm needs and home country institutional conditions, and are crucial in many emerging economies because the level of institutional development tends to be relatively low. Institutional rules in these economies are usually insufficient, poorly enforced or even absent (Peng and Heath, 1996), and such intermediaries fill the "institutional voids" that result from a lack of reliable market information and predictable governmental actions (Khanna and Palepu, 2000). These institutional voids, if allowed to persist, make market transactions less efficient and more costly (Henisz and Zelner, 2005).

The results of this study are derived from two representative cases of SMEs based in China's Zhejiang province, where the private economy development is more advanced than in other Chinese regions. Because China exhibits a lower level of overall institutional development than its counterparts in the West, there is significant variation in the development of the private economy among different regions in the country (Chan, Isobe and Makino, 2008; Chan, Makino and Isobe, 2010). SMEs in China's various regions do not possess the same level of information about legitimate strategic choices with predictable outcomes, or the ability to reduce the uncertainty in transactions between parties in capital, product and labor markets (North, 1990). In particular, SMEs in regions that are institutionally underdeveloped may not be able to determine what constitute legitimate organizational activities (Henisz and Zelner, 2005; Scott, 1995). This elevated level of uncertainty about legitimate ways of conducting business results in SMEs engaging in a wider range of strategic actions (Chan, Makino and Isobe, 2006). Regions within a host country also vary not only because of the differences in regional endowments (Liu and Li, 2006) but also due to the geographical concentration of industrial activities (Porter, 1998). Given these regional variations, future research should extend its reach to include other regions in China.

## References

Ahlstrom, D., & Bruton, G. D. (2010) Rapid institutional shifts and the co-evolution of entrepreneurial firms in transition economies. *Entrepreneurship Theory and Practice*, 34 (3): 531–554.

Ahlstrom, D., Young, M. N., Chan, E. S., & Bruton, G. D. (2004) Facing constraints to growth? Overseas Chinese entrepreneurs and traditional business practices in East Asia. *Asia Pacific Journal of Management*, 21 (3): 263–285.

Akerlof, G. A. (1970) The market for "lemons": Quality uncertainty and the market mechanism. *Quarterly Journal of Economics*, 48: 488–500.

Baum, J. A. C., & Oliver, C. (1991) Institutional linkages and organizational mortality. *Administrative Science Quarterly*, 36: 187–218.

Baum, J. A. C., Calabrese, T., & Silverman, B. S. (2000) Don't go it alone: Alliance network composition and startups' performance in Canadian biotechnology. *Strategic Management Journal*, 21: 267–294.

Boter, H., & Holmquist, C. (1996) Industry characteristics and internationalization process in small firms. *Journal of Business Venturing*, 11: 471–487.

Chan, C. M., Isobe, T., & Makino, S. (2008) Which country matters? Institutional development and foreign affiliate performance. *Strategic Management Journal*, 29: 1179–1205.

Chan, C. M., Makino, S., & Isobe, T. (2006) Interdependent behaviour in foreign direct investment: The multi-level effects of prior entry and prior exit on foreign market entry. *Journal of International Business Studies*, 37: 642–665.

Chan, C. M., Makino, S., & Isobe, T. (2010) Does subnational region matter? Foreign affiliate performance in the United States and China. *Strategic Management Journal*, 31: 1226–1243.

Child, J., & Rodrigues, S. B. (2005) The internationalization of Chinese firms: A case for theoretical extension? *Management and Organization Review*, 1: 381–410.

Contractor, F. J., & Lorange, P. (1988) Why should firms cooperate? The strategy and economics basis for cooperative ventures. In *Cooperative Strategies in International Business*, Contractor, F. J., & Lorange, P. (Eds.) Lexington Books: Lexington, MA; pp. 3–30.

Dacin, M. T., Oliver, C., & Roy, J. P. (2007) The legitimacy of strategic alliances: An institutional perspective. *Strategic Management Journal*, 28: 169–187.

Dawar, N., & Frost, T. (1999) Competing with giants. *Harvard Business Review*, 77 (2): 119–130.

Deeds, D. L., Mang, P., & Frandsen, M. (2004) The influence of firms' and industries' legitimacy on the flow of capital into high-technology ventures. *Strategic Organization*, 2 (1): 9–34.

DiMaggio, P. J., & Powell, W. W. (1983) The iron cage revisited: Institutional isomorphism and collective rationality in organizational fields. *American Sociological Review*, 48: 147–160.

Eisenhardt, K. M., & Schoonhoven, C. B. (1996) Resource-based view of strategic alliance formation: Strategic and social effects in entrepreneurial firms. *Organization Science*, 7: 136–150.

Hargadon, A., & Sutton, R. I. (1997) Technology brokering and innovation in a product development firm. *Administrative Science Quarterly*, 42: 716–749.

Harrigan, K. R. (1988) Strategic alliance and partner asymmetries. *Management International Review*, 9: 53–72.

He, C. (2002) Information costs, agglomeration economies and the location of foreign direct investment in China. *Regional Studies*, 36 (9): 1029–1036.

Henisz, W. J., & Zelner, B. A. (2005) Legitimacy, interest group pressures, and change in emergent institutions: The case of foreign investors and host country governments. *Academy of Management Journal*, 30 (2): 361–382.

Hennart, J. (1988) A transaction costs theory of equity joint ventures. *Strategic Management Journal*, 9: 361–374.

Hennart, J. F., & Reddy, S. (1997) The choice between mergers/acquisitions and joint ventures: The case of Japanese investors in the United States. *Strategic Management Journal*, 18 (1): 1–12.

Howells, J. (2006) Intermediation and the role of intermediaries in innovation. *Research Policy*, 35: 715–728.

Katila, R., & Shane, S. (2005) When does lack of resources make new firms innovative? *Academy of Management Journal*, 48: 814–829.

Khanna, T., & Palepu, K. (2000) The future of business groups in emerging markets: Long-run evidence from Chile. *Academy of Management Journal*, 43 (3): 268–285.

Lee, C., Lee, K., & Pennings, J. M. (2001) Internal capabilities, external networks, and performance: A study on technology-based ventures. *Strategic Management Journal*, 22: 615–640.

Li, H., & Atuahene-Gima, K. (2001) Product innovation strategy and the performance of new technology ventures in China. *Academy of Management Journal*, 44: 1123–1134.

Liu, T., & Li, K. W. (2006) Disparity in factor contributions between coastal and inner provinces in post-reform China. *China Economic Review*, 17: 449–470.

Lumpkin, G. T., & Dess, G. (1996) Clarifying the entrepreneurial orientation construct and linking it to performance. *Academy of Management Review*, 21 (1): 135–172.

Luo, Y., & Tung, R. L. (2007) International expansion of emerging market enterprises: A springboard perspective. *Journal of International Business Studies*, 38 (4): 481–498.

Makino, S., Isobe, T., & Chan, C. M. (2004) Does country matter? *Strategic Management Journal*, 25: 1027–1043.

Mathews, J. A. (2006) Dragon multinationals: New players in 21st century globalization. *Asia Pacific Journal of Management*, 23: 5–27.

McEvily, B., & Zaheer, A. (1999) Bridging ties: A source of firm heterogeneity in competitive capabilities. *Strategic Management Journal*, 20 (12): 1133–1156.

Mowery, D. C., Oxley, J. E., & Silverman, B. (1996) Strategic alliances and interfirm knowledge transfer. *Strategic Management Journal*, 17: 77–91.

North, D. C. (1990) *Institutions, Institutional Change, and Economic Performance*. Cambridge and New York: Cambridge University Press.

Peng, M. W. (2003) Institutional transitions and strategic choices. *Academy of Management Review*, 28 (2): 275–296.

Peng, M. W., & Heath, P. S. (1996) The growth of the firm in planned economies in transition: Institutions, organizations, and strategic choice. *Academy of Management Review*, 21 (2): 492–528.

Peng, M. W., Wang, D., & Jiang, Y. (2008) An institution-based view of international business strategy: A focus on emerging economies. *Journal of International Business Studies*, 39: 920–936.

Porter, M. E. (1998) Clusters and the new economics of competition. *Harvard Business Review*, 76 (6): 77–90.

Reuer, J. (1999) Collaborative strategy: The logic of alliances. In *Mastering Strategy. Financial Times*, Harlow: U.K; pp. 345–350.

Ring, P. S., & Van de Ven, A. H. (1992) Structuring cooperative relationships between organizations. *Strategic Management Journal*, 13 (7): 483–498.

Scott, W. R. (1995) *Institutions and Organizations*. Thousand Oaks, CA: Sage.

Smith, K. G., Collins, C. J., & Clark, K. D. (2005) Existing knowledge, knowledge creation capability, and the rate of new product introduction in high-technology firms. *Academy of Management Journal*, 48: 346–357.

Stinchcombe, A. L. (1965) Organizations and social structure. In *Handbook of Organizations*, March, J. G. (Ed.) Rand McNally: Chicago, IL; pp. 142–193.

Teece, D. J. (1986) Transaction cost economics and the multinational enterprise. *Journal of Economic Behavior and Organization*, 7: 21–45.

Wernerfelt, B. (1984) A resource-based view of the firm. *Strategic Management Journal*, 5: 171–180.

Zhang, Y., & Li, H. 2009. Innovation search of new ventures in a technology cluster: The role of ties with service intermediaries. *Strategic Management Journal*, 31 (1): 88–109.

Zimmerman, M., & Zeitz, G. (2002) Beyond survival: Achieving new venture growth by building legitimacy. *Academy of Management Review*, 27: 414–431.

# 4
# Global Firms Competing Locally: Management Localization and Subsidiary Performance in China

*Geng Cui, T. S. Chan and Shengsheng Huang*

## Introduction

Firms face liability of foreignness and other disadvantages when operating in other countries. The pressure to engage in local isomorphism – that is, imitate the practices of domestic firms – can be great, especially in the case of large cultural distance from home (Salomon and Wu, 2012). Management localization, as a form of local isomorphism, has become an important issue in cross-national operations. In China, many foreign invested enterprises (FIEs) have embarked on the path to localize their management in the past two decades (Katrin, 1996; Keeley, 1999). As a formal and planned strategy, firms often set up a specific target and schedule for management localization. Aside from the need for cost containment, management localization is often discussed in the framework of the global integration vs. local responsiveness paradigm in an effort to balance the scale economy of global standardization with the local contingency that is necessary for success in overseas markets (Hannon et al., 1995; Prahalad and Doz, 1987). On the one hand, multinational corporations (MNCs) must efficiently transfer to the overseas subsidiaries their superior knowledge accumulated from successful operations at home and in other countries (Kogut and Zander, 1993). On the other hand, they face the risk that the knowledge may not apply to the local environment. While researchers emphasize the benefits of management localization in improving local responsiveness, its effect on subsidiary performance has been sparsely studied. A number of researchers find that the effect of management localization is not always straightforward and tends to be highly context-dependent (Lam and Yeung, 2010).

To shed light on this important issue, this study provides a succinct review of the literature and identifies the motivations and consequences of management localization on multinational subsidiaries. A theoretical framework based on the resource dependence theory and a number of testable hypotheses about several key contextual variables that moderate the effect of management localization on subsidiary performance are proposed. According to the data from foreign-invested companies in China, the results suggest that management localization (i.e., the ratio of locals in the top management team (TMT)) alone does not affect subsidiary performance per se, whereas local resource dependency, headquarters support and the participation of local managers significantly moderate the effect of management localization on subsidiary performance. Finally, the management implications for MNCs operating in emerging markets and directions for future research are explored.

## Literature review

### Motivations for management localization

There has been increasing emphasis on localizing management in the foreign subsidiaries of MNCs. First, the expansion of MNCs' cross-national operations increases the need for local managerial talent within their overseas subsidiaries. Using life-cycle theory, Cui (1998) predicts that as a new venture continues to grow and becomes mature in a foreign market, the need to localize human resources becomes apparent. As the foreign subsidiary continues to expand, the growing scale of the investment requires more qualified managers (Lasserre and Ching, 1997). Second, the cost of hiring and maintaining expatriates is extremely high compared with that of employing their local counterparts. In cost-oriented companies, reducing the number of expatriates through localization presents a viable solution (Fryxell et al., 2004). The need for more managers and large compensation packages makes it financially unaffordable to deploy more expatriates. Finally, expatriates' failure to adjust to the local living and working environments dampens their capability to exploit their skills and knowledge. The failure rate in emerging countries such as China, Russia, India and Brazil can be as high as 25–30% (Harvey, 1996). A high expatriate failure rate means unexpected costs for the companies.

From a theoretical perspective, the dependence on local resources presents another motive for localizing the top management in overseas subsidiaries (Law et al., 2009). Organizations must react to environmental uncertainty and complexity in overseas markets by adapting their strategies in non-trivial ways (e.g., Boisot and Child, 1999; Pfeffer and Salancik, 1978). In a foreign market, MNCs not only face an external environment that is different from their home country in terms of cultural, social and economic conditions but also encounter a different internal environment – that is, a workforce mostly composed of host country nationals (HCNs). In China, for example, trust and *guanxi* (personal relationships) are very important to business operations (Tsui-auch and Möllering, 2010). Unlike local managers, Western executives may not fully understand why their rivals can win business through negotiating with customers over the dinner table. Moreover, managers should know how to build trust and motivate their local employees by adopting management styles and policies that may be different from those of the parent company.

The top management of foreign subsidiaries must respond to these challenges. Given the significant differences that can exist between host countries and home environments, expatriate managers can suffer from serious biases in understanding, filtering and processing the information about the host environment due to a lack of the consistent decoding and coding needed for effective communication (Daft and Weick, 1984; Gupta and Govindarajan, 2000). Such knowledge is required to correctly decode the environmental information and to react to the environment in an appropriate way. This knowledge also constitutes firms' absorptive capabilities as it concerns the customs, religions, routines, cultures, and social and economic conditions, and it is location-specific and highly context-dependent (Cohen and Levinthal, 1990). Such knowledge is tacit and difficult to codify and transfer. In a dissimilar host environment, the "strategic failure" of expatriates is quite possible as such knowledge is not available among them. It is unlikely that they can easily obtain such knowledge and skills in a short time through "learning by doing" or training due to the tacit nature of such knowledge and the high contingency of these resources' application to daily operations.

While the expatriate managers may not adapt to the new, unfamiliar environment, involving local managers in the TMT of foreign subsidiaries may be a good substitute. Growing up in the local environment, indigenous managers represent valuable resources. Compared with outsourcing methods to gain local knowledge and skills, such as external training and consulting, bringing in or promoting local managers can be more cost-effective. In China, due to the scarcity of local talent, training and qualifying local candidates is definitely important before they can fill the important management positions. Wong and Law (1999) propose a three-stage practical model (i.e., planning-localizing-consolidating) to achieve effective localization. Fryxell et al. (2004) identify four predictors of successful localization: formal planning, local selection emphasis, retention efforts and attributions of trustworthiness. Moreover, the expatriates must be willing to localize their own positions and transfer the knowledge to the local candidates (Law et al., 2004; Selmer, 2004). The localization process is considered successful when the locals possess the same knowledge and skills as the expatriate managers.

### Consequences of management localization

Studies suggest that if management localization is effectively implemented, it can help to alleviate the problems associated with expatriates (Lasserre and Ching, 1997). A localized management can help to minimize the problems caused by cultural differences, contribute to better communication, strengthen employee relationships and create more promotion opportunities for local managers. All of these in turn will lead to employee satisfaction and loyalty, improve management effectiveness, and relieve the heavy financial burden on the new ventures. Unlike others who have supported the localization effort, however, a number of authors have shared their concern about the effect of management localization on subsidiary performance. Kobrin (1988) argues that a reduction in expatriates would weaken global integration and consistent MNC identification. Moreover, based on case studies in China, Gamble (2000) points out that the development of culturally literate expatriates could become a more valuable resource for subsidiaries than substituting expatriates with local managers, and thus the costs of expatriates should be considered by MNCs as a long-term investment. From the perspective of the subsidiary–parent relationship, Gong (2003b) emphasizes the importance of expatriates in the MNCs' control mechanisms, especially in culturally distant countries.

Meanwhile, Festing (1997), and Erdener and Torbiörn (1999) analyze the differences in terms of the transaction costs incurred by the locals and the expatriates. Their study suggests that the benefits of the locals or the expatriates depend on the total transaction costs, and that a certain mixture of the HCNs and parent country nationals would achieve minimum transaction costs. In a study of organizational learning within a team of heterogeneous staff, Gong (2003a) proposes that the heterogeneous staffing composition would have a negative effect on short-term performance and a positive effect on long-term performance, implying a bell-shaped curve in the relationship between management localization and subsidiary performance.

Based on empirical findings, a number of studies examine the effect of management localization on subsidiary performance. An A.T. Kearney (1997) survey of global companies in China found that companies that had achieved large market shares in China had less than 10 expatriates, far fewer than other firms. Konopaske et al. (2002) found that while expatriate management contributes to subsidiary financial performance for wholly owned subsidiaries, more localized management is better for joint ventures. Lam and Yeung (2010) observed an inverted U-curve between the degree of management localization and subsidiary performance, while Law et al. (2009) revealed a positive effect of management localization, dependent on a number of factors, such as resource dependence and commitment. These findings suggest that the effect of management localization on performance may be conditional on other factors. Thus while it is possible that the local managers equipped with local knowledge and skills are valuable to the subsidiaries, the role of local managers and the effect of management localization requires more theoretical discussion and rigorous investigation.

## Theoretical framework and hypotheses

A fundamental assumption of foreign direct investment (FDI) is that the MNC's motivation for cross-national operation is to use the existent resources, knowledge and skills to maximize its return on such resources (Penrose, 1959). Moreover, firms tend to invest in other countries when their knowledge is so tacit that it cannot be transferred through market transactions (Kogut and Zander, 1993). An MNC is a centralized bureaucratic organization, and its subsidiaries share the basic common organizational culture and core resources. The hierarchical arrangement rather than arm's-length market transaction ensures the efficient transfer of knowledge and resource exploitation. To ensure the success of new ventures in foreign countries, a parent company should exert strict control over its subsidiaries, regardless of their ownership structure (Child and Yan, 1999). Therefore the initial status of an overseas subsidiary can be regarded as a replication of the parent company, or part of it. In other words, all of the operations are replicated from the parent country before localization occurs. Prior to localization, the TMT is composed of the expatriates from the parent company and/or other subsidiaries in third countries.

According to the resource-based view (RBV), if a firm owns resources that are valuable, rare and imperfectly imitable and substitutable, it can obtain sustained competitive advantages, which in turn lead to superior performance (Barney, 1991). Such resources include proprietary assets, organizational processes, firm attributes, information and knowledge, and so on. The managerial skills and knowledge of the TMT represent valuable rent-generating resources for a firm (Castanias and Helfat, 2001; Wright et al., 1994). As an intangible resource that is socially complex and causally ambiguous, human resources (HR) are more likely to produce competitive advantages (Hitt et al., 2001). Meanwhile, how firms use these resources is equally, if not more, important for generating competitive advantages and superior performance. Penrose (1959) argued that a firm's inputs are the combination of various resources in different ways, rather than the resources themselves. Some scholars have emphasized firms' "capabilities," which come from resource integration and thus are more intangible and inimitable sources of competitive advantages than the simple input of resources (Barney, 1991; Peteraf, 1993).

Recent studies propose that the link between resource and performance is contingent on important contextual variables. Brush and Artz (1999) suggest that the "value" of resources might vary according to context. Grant (1996) believes that knowledge resources must be integrated into the value-adding process before the knowledge can be a source of competitive advantage. Based on an empirical investigation of the service sector, Hitt et al. (2001) found that the return on resources also depended on firms' strategies. Thus, according to the contingent RBV perspective, the resource's effect on firm performance is conditional. For instance, the strong bargaining power of suppliers and market imperfection could weaken the tie between competitive advantage and measurable performance (Coff, 1999; Hitt et al., 2001).

Following the contingent perspective of RBV, this study proposes a conceptual model regarding the relationship between management localization and subsidiary performance (Figure 4.1), which posits that the effect of management localization on subsidiary performance is conditional on several key contextual variables and firm characteristics. The contextual factors include cultural distance and local resource dependence (e.g., Law et al., 2009), and the firm factors include headquarters support and the participation of local managers in the subsidiaries' important decisions (Fryxell et al., 2004; Wong and Law, 1999). The following sections elaborate on how the contextual factors and

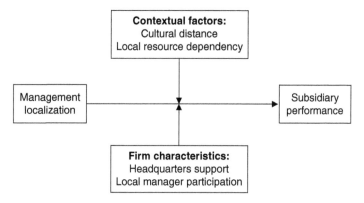

*Figure 4.1*   The effect of management location based on the contingent RBV

firm characteristics moderate the effect of management localization on subsidiary performance, and propose the research hypotheses.

First, although management localization can help a subsidiary adjust to the local environment, it is difficult to justify the idea that management localization alone can improve the performance of foreign subsidiaries. The literature suggests that expatriates have more functions than as vehicles of managerial resources in the subsidiary–parent relationship. Expatriate managers are important to the subsidiaries in several areas, such as cultural control, the absorptive capability of the inflow of knowledge, and the channels of knowledge transfer. Ouchi (1979) posited that expatriates can help the parent companies to exert cultural control over the subsidiaries by duplicating the same organizational climate as the parent company. In addition, the common shared knowledge between the expatriates and their parent company will improve the absorptive capability and ensure that the inflow of knowledge from the parent company and other subsidiaries can be correctly decoded and efficiently absorbed by the TMT at the new subsidiary (Cohen and Levinthal, 1990). Finally, richer social ties between and closer relationships with the parent company and other subsidiaries also provide broad channels through which to transfer knowledge to the new subsidiary (Gupta and Govindarajan, 2000). In this sense, expatriate managers might not be perfectly substitutable as a managerial resource. A reduction in expatriate managers may result in the loss of valuable resources not available among local managers, even if a successful localization process is conducted. While local managerial resources have the potential to bring competitive advantages, the valuable managerial resources embedded in the expatriate managers, who made the company a success to begin with, might be lost after localization. Therefore management localization alone may not lead to superior performance at the new subsidiary. Thus

*Hypothesis 1: Management localization has no significant direct effect on subsidiary performance.*

The contingent RBV suggests that the value of resources may differ across environments and contexts (Hitt et al., 2001; Brush and Artz, 1999). First, it is posited that the cultural distance between the home and host countries may affect the value of the local managerial resources generated by management localization (Law et al., 2009; Li and Guisinger, 1991). As previously discussed, the managerial resources of the expatriate managers may not match the local environment, which can be very different from that of the parent company. Then the local knowledge and skills embedded among the local managers can help a subsidiary to achieve effective exchange between the firm and the local environment, especially in the case of great cultural distance (Salomon and Wu, 2012). In contrast, if the subsidiary is in an environment similar to that of the home country, the expatriate managers will encounter a better match. Consequently, management localization might not be a necessary choice and its effect would be limited. Thus

*Hypothesis 2: Management localization leads to better performance for firms from culturally distant countries than for those from culturally similar countries.*

In a multinational environment, a subsidiary's external parties might be dispersed and not constrained to the local environment. The subsidiary also depends on the parent company, foreign suppliers and customers, and so on. Depending on the nature and the subsidiary's strategic purpose, its dependence on local managerial resources may differ. The greater its dependence on local resources, the more it must identify with and react to the local environment (Law et al., 2009). If a firm is a resource-seeker in the host country, such as in export-oriented operations, its local managerial resource needs are more limited. For firms that are market-seekers in the host country, however, local managerial resources are critical to its success as the firm needs the knowledge and skills to gain access to critical resources that are important in a number of areas, such as access to local market opportunities, an enhanced understanding of local customer needs, and the necessary knowledge and skills to navigate the local market. Therefore the local knowledge and skills could be more useful and valuable to those subsidiaries that are dependent on local managerial resources. In other words, management localization can bring more benefits if local resource dependence is high.

*Hypothesis 3: Management localization leads to better performance for firms with high resource dependence on the local environment than for those with low resource dependence.*

Furthermore, it is believed that whether a localized management can help to shore up subsidiary performance is also contingent on important firm variables. Wong and Law (1999) and Fryxell et al. (2004) define "effective localization" as successful knowledge transfer from expatriate managers to the locals. The literature on management localization suggests a strong positive correlation between headquarters support and the effectiveness of management localization (Fryxell et al., 2004; Wong and Law, 1999). Because parent-company-related managerial resources may not be perfectly transferred to the local successors, headquarters support and commitment are absolutely necessary for an effective localization program. Thus, the headquarters support of management localization has two important effects on the subsidiary. First, it ensures the effective transfer of critical knowledge and skills from expatriates to the local managers, and can help the latter acquire the necessary knowledge and skills from the parent company and apply them within the subsidiary after the departure of expatriate managers. Second, through socialization during the localization process, local managers might have assimilated into the culture and norms of the parent company. Their shared common "language" could reduce the conflicts and frictions within the mixed TMT and, therefore, improve internal efficiency. Both of these effects can magnify the benefits of management localization by reducing the disruption caused by the departure of expatriate managers.

*Hypothesis 4: Management localization leads to better performance for firms with strong headquarters support than for those with poor headquarters support.*

Grant (1996) suggests that the resources that firms possess will not generate maximum rents until they are effectively integrated into the rent-generating system. Unlike in a domestic company, expatriate managers and local managers in multinational subsidiaries may exercise varying levels of decision power. If the participation of the local managers in the decision-making processes is limited to symbolic values or figurehead posts, exploitation of the local managerial resources will not materialize. In contrast, if the local managers actively participate in the subsidiary's decision-making processes and their opinions are well respected and considered, the subsidiary's response to the environment can be more effective. Thus

*Hypothesis 5: Management localization leads to better performance for firms with good decision participation by local managers than for those with limited participation.*

## Research method

### Measures and instrument

The localization of the TMT is operationalized as the ratio of locally hired managers among the top management positions in 11 functional areas (e.g., CEO, operations, finance, marketing, sales and HR). The ratio approach is more objective because it satisfies the face validity of the management localization construct. It is also consistent with the theoretical framework based on the RBV. As the knowledge and skills embedded in top managers are unique and hard to imitate (Castanias and Helfat, 2001), it is likely that when the ratio of local managers increases, the local knowledge pool will be enlarged accordingly. This measure is consistent with those used in previous studies (Gupta and Govindarajan, 2000; Gong, 2003b).

The origins of top managers were classified into the following categories: local managers from China, overseas Chinese expatriates and non-Chinese expatriates from other countries. Most of the Chinese returnees, if assigned by the parent company, are not considered locals because they have notable knowledge about the parent company and know little about their home-country business environment because they left the country years ago. For joint ventures, some local top-level managers are representatives of the parent companies of local partners. They are hired by local parent companies to safeguard local partners' rights and interests. Therefore the respondents were asked to exclude top-level managers who are representatives of local partners when calculating the number of top managers.

Multidimensional scales were used to measure the other major variables. Because financial performance is complex and may reflect non-operating factors, this study adopts subjective measures of subsidiary performance in terms of the subsidiary company compared with the top three competitors in the local market in i) total sales, ii) market shares and iii) sales growth. Using Hofstede's culture indices (Hofstede, 2001) and the method developed in Kogut and Singh (1988), cultural distance is calculated based on the deviation along each of the four dimensions (i.e., power distance, uncertainty avoidance, masculinity/femininity and individualism) for each home country from China's scores. The local resource dependence refers to the relative importance of the local resources to the subsidiaries (Law et al., 2009), and its measures are adapted from Prahalad and Doz (1981) and Ghoshal and Bartlett (1990). Following Fryxell et al. (2004) and Wong and Law (1999), headquarters support or commitment is measured by a group of items judging the headquarters' i) attitude toward localization, ii) localization planning and iii) training of local managers. The decision participation of local managers refers to their involvement in the firms' routine operations and decision processes. Even though local managers may hold senior positions, their participation in decision-making may be limited. Thus the respondents were asked whether formal routines and regulations were in place to motivate the local managers to exert their authority. Except for the ratio of management localization, all of the above variables were measured on a seven-point Likert scale. The firm-level control variables are length of operation, total assets, number of employees and entry mode (wholly owned subsidiary vs. joint venture, coded as 0 and 1, respectively).

### Sample and survey

The data were collected through a questionnaire survey conducted in mainland China. The sampling areas included Beijing, Shanghai, Jiangsu and Guangdong, which in total attracted nearly half of the FDI in China. The sampling framework is composed of the manufacturing firms in 11 Economic and Technology Development Zones (ETDZs) in the major cities of these areas. The population is defined as the legally independent foreign invested enterprises (FIEs) in manufacturing industries that have been in operation for more than two years. For those FIEs with two or more foreign investors, the "parent company" is defined as the foreign firm with the largest equity ratio in the subsidiary. The total number of eligible FIEs from these ETDZs was around 500.

A questionnaire-based survey was conducted to collect data from these firms. Research assistants at these locations delivered the questionnaires to the general managers or human resources managers of the companies. Two weeks later, after reminder phone calls, a second round of questionnaires were delivered to the companies that had not replied. Finally, 86 valid questionnaires were returned, resulting in a response rate of 16%. Among them, 68% of the respondents were top-level managers and 32% were mid-level managers (primarily HR managers because in some FIEs they are treated as mid-level executives). As for the ethnic origin of the respondents, 53.5% were local Chinese and others were expatriates, among which 23.7% were overseas Chinese and 23.7% were non-Chinese expatriates.

## Results

The descriptive statistics suggest that among the valid responses, 61.8% were from wholly owned subsidiaries and others were from joint ventures. As for the country of origin of parent companies, 16 firms were from Europe, 20 from North America, 25 from Hong Kong and Taiwan, and 25 from other Asian countries. The invested capital ranged from USD200,000 to USD460 million; the number of employees ranged from 40 to 12,000; and the length of operation ranged from 2 to 26 years. Thus the sample represents different types of FDI operation in China. After data processing, the reliability of the measures for the key variables was calculated. The alpha values ranged from 0.69 to 0.88, which shows adequate reliability. Table 4.1 shows the means and standard deviations of the variables and the correlations among them.

A hierarchical regression analysis was performed on subsidiary performance, using the mean-centered method to minimize the multicollinearity problem. All of the variables have a variance inflation factor score of less than 10. Due to the small sample size, the results are reported with a significance level of less than 0.1 (Luo, 1998). Table 4.2 shows the results of the hierarchical regression analysis using subsidiary performance as the dependent variable. Model 1 includes the control variables and management localization. Model 2 adds the moderating variables. Model 3 adds the interactions of management localization with the moderating variables. The adjusted R-square of Model 3 (0.293) shows that the fit of the regression model is very good. In Model 3, management localization has no significant main effect on market performance. Thus Hypothesis 1 is supported.

However, the interaction between cultural distance and management localization is not significant, thus Hypothesis 2 is not supported. Meanwhile, the positive coefficient of the interaction between management localization and local resource dependence ($\beta = 0.336$, $p \leq 0.05$) shows that the higher the local resource dependence, the greater the

Table 4.1 Means, standard deviations and correlation matrix

| Variables | Mean | SD | | | | | | | | |
|---|---|---|---|---|---|---|---|---|---|---|
| Length of operation | 9.76 | 5.64 | | | | | | | | |
| Total assets | 59.3 | 147 | -.11 | | | | | | | |
| No. of employees | 1075.28 | 1853.62 | 0.34** | 0.00 | | | | | | |
| Localization | 0.53 | 0.25 | -0.03 | -0.07 | -0.38** | | | | | |
| Cultural distance | 2.00 | 1.25 | -0.21 | 0.18 | -0.13 | 0.14 | | | | |
| Resource dependence | 4.40 | 1.22 | 0.11 | 0.01 | -0.01 | 0.27** | -0.15 | | | |
| Headquarters support | 4.93 | 0.98 | 0.16 | -0.03 | -0.01 | 0.25* | -0.14 | 0.07 | | |
| Local participation | 5.05 | 0.86 | 0.31** | 0.02 | -0.08 | 0.14* | -0.03 | 0.32** | 0.04 | |
| Market performance | 4.79 | 0.95 | 0.15 | 0.23* | 0.06 | 0.25* | 0.25* | 0.27* | -0.06 | 0.11 |

Notes: (1) *: sig. $\leq$ 0.1, **: sig. $\leq$ 0.05. (2) Total assets in millions of US dollars.

*Table 4.2*  Results of hierarchical regression analysis for subsidiary performance

| Variables/models | Model 1 | Model 2 | Model 3 |
|---|---|---|---|
| R-square | 0.166 | 0.272 | 0.417 |
| Adjusted R-square | 0.106 | 0.172 | 0.293 |
| F value | 2.754 | 2.703 | 3.363 |
| Sig. level | 0.025 | 0.010 | 0.001 |
| Length of operation | 0.106 | 0.118 | 0.236† |
| No. of employees | 0.152 | 0.151 | −0.081 |
| Total assets | 0.270* | 0.232* | 0.234* |
| Entry mode | −0.053 | 0.008 | 0.002 |
| Management localization (ML) | 0.339 | 0.266 | 0.047 |
| Cultural distance (CD) | | 0.248 | 0.267 |
| Local resource dependence (RD) | | −0.098 | −0.023 |
| Headquarters support (HS) | | 0.240* | 0.238* |
| Local participation (LP) | | −0.036 | −0.137 |
| ML*CD | | | −0.046 |
| ML*RD | | | 0.279* |
| ML*HS | | | 0.157† |
| ML*LP | | | 0.204† |

*Notes*: (1) †: sig. ≤ 0.1, *: sig. ≤ 0.05. (2) Entry mode: joint venture = 1, wholly owned subsidiary = 0.

effect that management localization has on subsidiary performance. Thus Hypothesis 3 is supported. The interaction term between management localization and headquarters support ($\beta = 0.129$, $p \leq 0.1$) is also significant and the coefficient is positive, supporting Hypothesis 4 – that is, that localization with headquarters support can bring superior performance to the subsidiary. Similarly, the significant positive coefficient of the interaction term between localization and local manager participation supports Hypothesis 5 ($\beta = 0.204$, $p \leq 0.1$).

## Discussion

### Conclusions and implications

This study attempts to furnish a coherent framework to assess the effect of management localization on subsidiary performance. It posits that the value of local managers depends on several key contextual and firm variables. The results of the study suggest that the benefit of management localization is not determined by the ratio of local managers in the TMT. Despite the cultural difference, management localization may not bring any benefits for FIEs in China because the success of subsidiaries goes far beyond overcoming cultural differences. Focusing on the parent–subsidiary relationship, previous studies have argued that expatriate managers are necessary for MNCs to exert control over overseas subsidiaries (Kobrin, 1988). Thus it is not advisable to replace expatriates with locals just for cultural reasons. However, for firms with a high level of dependence on local resources, management localization helps to improve subsidiary performance. This is also true for firms that have ensured support from the headquarters in their localization effort. Meanwhile, FIEs should also consider how to delegate more power to local managers and involve local managers in the decision-making processes for management localization to be truly beneficial.

This research has both significant theoretical and practical implications for management localization. Previous studies largely focus on cost reduction, training qualified locals and their effect on internal efficiency. Practically speaking, management localization should be considered not only based on concerns of operational efficiency, such as cultural differences, cost reduction and expatriate failure but also from a more strategic perspective. In fact, having local managers on board may help to close the gap in cultural differences but it does not necessarily shore up subsidiary performance. Management localization should be planned and carried out to acquire and exploit the valuable resources that the subsidiaries depend on. Moreover, having commitment and support from the headquarters and actually involving local managers in the decision-making process are critical for the success of localization programs. Multinationals can maximize the benefits of management localization strategies through coordinated efforts – for example, carefully planned and implemented localization processes and decision-making mechanisms that exploit the resources embedded in the local managers.

*Limitations and suggestions*

The most serious limitation of the present study is the small sample size. First, more data should be collected to arrive at accurate estimates of the parameters regarding the relationships between variables. Second, the sample of firms comes from a single host country, and other countries may have very different environments in terms of economic development, cultural distance and managerial resource availability. This may produce varied effects of management localization. Finally, other correlates of management localization, such as market orientation, may lead to a potential confounding effect and should be controlled in future studies. Meanwhile there are several directions for future research. First, management localization might not only influence subsidiary performance but also affect employee morale and satisfaction. Therefore it would be interesting for future research to include the other consequences of management localization. Second, the indirect effect of management localization is also worth studying. This study only explores the direct effect of management localization on subsidiary performance. Many MNCs prevent knowledge spillover and leakage by using more expatriates, because the locals are more likely to spread the knowledge to competitors through turnover. An integrative model including both the direct and the indirect effects would capture a more comprehensive picture of the effect of management localization. Finally, future studies may examine the benefits of inpatriation – that is, transferring local managers to the home-country headquarters to monitor the subsidiaries in various country locations and improve the responsiveness of global companies to the local markets around the world.

## References

Barney, J. (1991) Firm resources and sustained competitive advantage. *Journal of Management*, 17(1): 99–120.

Boisot, M., and Child, J. (1999) Organizations as adaptive systems in complex environments: The case of China. *Organization Science*, 10(3): 237–252.

Brush, T. H., and Artz, K. W. (1999) Toward a contingent resource-based theory: The impact of information asymmetry on the value of capabilities veterinary medicine. *Strategic Management Journal*, 20(3): 223–250.

Castanias, R. P., and Helfat, C. E. (2001) The managerial rents model: Theory and empirical analysis. *Journal of Management*, 27(6): 661–678.

Child, J., and Yan, Y. (1999) Investment and control in international joint ventures: The case of China. *Journal of World Business*, 34(1): 3–15.

Coff, R. W. (1999) Why competitive advantage does not lead to performance: The resource-based view and stakeholder bargaining power. *Organization Science*, 10(2): 119–133.

Cohen, W. M., and Levinthal, D. A. (1990) Absorptive capacity: A new perspective on learning and innovation. *Administrative Science Quarterly*, 35(1): 128–152.

Cui, G. (1998) The evolutionary process of global market expansion: Experiences of MNCs in China. *Journal of World Business*, 33(1): 87–110.

Daft, R. L., and Weick, K. E. (1984) Toward a model of organizations as interpretation systems. *Academy of Management Review*, 9(2): 284–295.

Erdener, C., and Torbiorn, I. (1999) A transaction costs perspective on international staffing patterns: Implications for firm performance. *Management International Review*, 39(3): 89–106.

Festing, M. (1997) International human resource management strategies in multinational corporations: Theoretical assumptions and empirical evidence from German firms. *Management International Review*, 37(1): 43–64.

Fryxell, G. E., Butler J., and Choi, A. (2004) Successful localization programs in China: An important element in strategy implementation. *Journal of World Business*, 39(3): 268–282.

Gamble, J. (2000) Localizing management in foreign-invested enterprises in China: Practical, cultural, and strategic perspectives. *International Journal of Human Resource Management*, 11(5): 883–903.

Ghoshal, S., and Bartlett, C. A. (1990) The multinational corporation as an inter-organizational network. *Academy of Management Review*, 15(4): 603–625.

Gong, Y. (2003a) Toward a dynamic process model of staffing composition and subsidiary outcomes in multinational enterprises. *Journal of Management*, 29(2): 259–280.

Gong, Y. (2003b) Subsidiary staffing in multinational enterprises: Agency, resources, and performance. *Academy of Management Journal*, 46(6): 728–739.

Grant, R. M. (1996) Prospering in dynamically-competitive environments: Organizational capability as knowledge integration. *Organization Science*, 7(4): 375–387.

Gupta, A. K., and Govindarajan, V. (2000) Knowledge flows within multinational corporations. *Strategic Management Journal*, 21(4): 473–496.

Hannon, J. M., Huang, I. C., and Jaw, B. S. (1995) International human resource strategy and its determinants: The case of subsidiaries in Taiwan. *Journal of International Business Studies*, 26(3): 531–554.

Harvey, M. (1996) The selection of managers for foreign assignments: A planning perspective. *Columbia Journal of World Business*, 31(4): 103–118.

Hitt, M. A., Bierman L., Shimizu, K., and Kochhar, R. (2001) Direct and moderating effects of human capital on strategy and performance in professional service firms: A resource-based perspective. *Academy of Management Journal*, 44(1): 13–28.

Hofstede, G. (2001) *Cultures Consequences: International Differences in Work-Related Values*, Second Edition. Sage: Beverly Hills.

Katrin, N. (1996) Localization of expatriates. *Benefits and Compensation International*, 26(3): 2–6.

Kearney, A. T. (1997) Global companies in China – A white paper on the changing landscape. Chicago: A. T. Kearney.

Keeley, S. (1999) The theory and practice of localization. In B. Rogers (ed.), *Localization in China: Best Practice*, Asia Law and Practice: Hong Kong, pp: 1–23.

Kobrin, S. J. (1988) Expatriate reduction and strategic control in American multinational corporations. *Human Resource Management*, 27(1): 62–74.

Kogut, B., and Singh, H. (1988) The effect of national culture on the choice of entry mode. *Journal of International Business Studies*, 19(3): 411–432.

Kogut, B., and Zander, U. (1993) Knowledge of the firm and the evolutionary theory of the multinational corporation. *Journal of International Business Studies*, 24(4): 625–645.

Konopaske, R., Werner, S., and Neupert, K. E. (2002) Entry mode strategy and performance: The role of FDI staffing. *Journal of Business Research*, 55(9): 759–770.

Lam, S. S. K., and Yeung, J. C. K. (2010) Staff localization and environmental uncertainty on firm performance in China. *Asia Pacific Journal of Management*, 27(4): 677–695.

Lasserre, P., and Ching, P. S. (1997) Human resources management in China and the localization challenge. *Journal of Asian Business*, 13(4): 85–99.

Law, K. S., Song, L. J., Wong, C., and Chen, D. (2009) The antecedents and consequences of successful localization. *Journal of International Business Studies*, 40(8): 1359–1373.

Law, K. S., Wong, C.-S., and Wang, K. D. (2004) An empirical test of the model on managing the localization of human resources in the People's Republic of China. *International Journal of Human Resource Management*, 15(4–5): 635–648.

Li, J. T., and Guisinger, S. (1991) Comparative business failures of foreign-controlled firms in the United States. *Journal of International Business Studies*, 22(2): 209–224.

Luo, Y. (1998) Timing of investment and international expansion performance in China. *Journal of International Business Studies*, 29(2): 391–407.

Ouchi, W. G. (1979) A conceptual framework for the design of organizational control mechanisms. *Management Science*, 25(9): 833–848.

Penrose, E. (1959) *The Theory of the Growth of the Firm*, Oxford University Press: Oxford.

Peteraf, M. A. (1993) The cornerstones of competitive advantage: A resource based view. *Strategic Management Journal*, 14(3): 179–191.

Pfeffer, J., and Salancik, G. R. (1978) *The External Control of Organizations: A Resource Dependence Perspective*. Stanford University Press: Stanford.

Prahalad, C. K. and Doz, Y. L. (1987) The Multinational Mission: Balancing Local Demands and Global Vision. New York: The Free Press.

Prahalad, C. K., and Doz, Y. (1981) An approach to strategic control in MNCs. *Sloan Management Review*, 22(4): 5–13.

Salomon, R., and Wu, Z. (2012) Institutional distance and local isomorphism strategy. *Journal of International Business Studies*, 43(4): 343–367.

Selmer, J. (2004) Expatriates hesitation and the localization of Western business operations in China. *International Journal of Human Resource Management*, 15(6): 1094–1107.

Tsui-auch, L. S., and Möllering, G. (2010) Wary managers: Unfavorable environments, perceived vulnerability, and the development of trust in foreign enterprises in China. *Journal of International Business Studies*, 41(6): 1016–1035

Wong, C., and Law, K. S. (1999) Managing localization of human resources in the PRC: A practical model. *Journal of World Business*, 34(1): 26–40.

Wright, P. M., McMahan, G. C., and McWilliams, A. (1994) Human resources and sustained competitive advantage: A resource-based perspective. *International Journal of Human Resource Management*, 5(2): 301–316.

# 5

# The Influence of Culture on Budgetary Characteristics and Managerial Effectiveness: An Empirical Investigation of National and Multinational Companies in Thailand

*Somboon Saraphat and Joseph Aiyeku*

## Introduction

Budgeting is the cornerstone of nearly all organizations' management control systems (MCSs) but, despite its widespread use, it is far from perfect (Hansen, Otley and Van der Stdede, 2003). Phadoongsitthi (2003: 59) provided empirical evidence of the importance of budgeting as one of the keys to effective MCSs in organizations located in Thailand.

The study featured in this chapter shows that Thai-listed manufacturing and non-manufacturing companies implement budgeting as the highest ranked practice for operational planning and control. Budgeting has been one of the most extensively researched topics in management accounting and has been studied from the theoretical perspectives of economics, psychology and sociology (Covaleski, Evans and Luft, 2003).

The importance of budgeting styles in enhancing MCS effectiveness has received increasing attention in recent years, with the management accounting literature suggesting that budgetary characteristics (here defined as the seven aspects of budgeting: budgetary participation, budget goal difficulty, budget goal clarity, budgetary evaluation (general), budgetary evaluation (punitive), budgetary feedback and budgetary slack) are significant and negatively or even positively related to either individual job or firm performance. This indicates that empirical evidence has been inconclusive and some of the evidence from various countries has provided conflicting results (Brownell, 1981). In this regard, Hofstede (1967) suggests that one explanation for these results is the different cultural setting, which is an important conditioning factor.

Hofstede (2001) proposes that many management concepts, practices and techniques are affected by cultural values, such as planning, control, accounting, corporate governance, motivation and compensation, leadership and subordinates' empowerment, managerial and organizational development, and performance evaluation. Thus it would seem reasonable to assume that cultural differences are able to provide competitive advantages in addition to disadvantages in increasingly competitive global business environments (Hofsted, 2001: 442).

The effectiveness of budget controls in multinational companies (MNCs) and organizational management as an issue has generated significant attention in recent years. Notably, normative discussions suggest that distinctions should be made between the budget processes of foreign and domestic subunits due to environmental, strategic emphasis, geographic distance, language, and cultural differences (Bartlett and Goshal, 1989: 100; Egelhoff, 1988: 163).

In the only empirical studies on the subject, Hassel and Cunningham (1996) note that the effectiveness of budget controls varies between the domestic and foreign business units of MNCs in some contexts. These studies have been limited because they have only considered a few budget-related variables. However, the present study explores additional budget-related variable dimensions by incorporating goal-setting theory and psychology-based budgeting.

The influence that culture has had on management styles in various countries has generated interest for many years because very limited or no studies have been conducted on culture's influence on the preference for and the design of MCSs (i.e., budgetary characteristics) as comprehensive models incorporating all of the classical budget-related variables in a single study. Hence this study attempts to rectify this missing link.

Effective budgeting systems should motivate employees while simultaneously providing the perceptions of procedural fairness resulting from budgetary practices. It is pervasively believed that budgetary characteristics may give rise to these attitudes. The ways in which the budget systems interact with participants might be considered fair, unfair or motivational. It is apparent that more research on cultural differences in perceptions of fairness and other key organizational constructs is needed to test the generalizability of key justice concepts across cultures (Pillai, Wiliams and Tan, 2001). It may be useful to investigate the effects of MCSs on perceptions of procedural fairness and individual motivation because these positive attitudes are likely to affect firm performance.

Despite the recognition of motivational effect and perceptions of procedural fairness by which aspects of budgeting bring about the benefits of enhancements in subordinates' managerial performance, to date no studies have investigated these issues in the context of cultural differences.

Thus the purpose of this study is to develop a conceptual framework model of budgetary characteristics in determining firm managerial effectiveness that examines whether culture is a significant moderating variable in considering the effects of the former on the latter. In addition to the influence of different cultures, there will be other mediating variables intervening; specifically, the budgetary fairness and motivation perceived by various functional managers who are, to some extent, held accountable for preparing budgets and controlling operations.

### Chapter organization

This chapter is organized as follows. The first section is the introduction. The next section describes the theoretical background of contingency and psychology theory, particularly as they relate to budgetary control systems. The literature review and development of hypotheses appear in the third section. The fourth section discusses the research methodology used in this study. The results and discussion follow in the next section. The last section contains a summary, presents theoretical and managerial implications, and notes the limitations of the findings.

## Theoretical background

### Contingency theory

Contingency theory proposes that firm performance can be enhanced by the fit between organizational structure and contextual variables. In reality, organizational structure varies significantly across organizations. MCSs, including management accounting techniques (e.g., budgeting systems), are considered to be components of organizational structure. Contextual variables, such as external environment, technology, organizational size, organizational strategy and culture, are collectively known as contingency theory. This study attempts to consider the influence of culture as the moderating variable on the fit between particular budgeting practices and managerial effectiveness in firm performance.

## Psychological theory

Motivation plays a vital role in functioning, improving and maintaining organizational capability and sustainable competitive advantage. To understand how MCSs influence individual behavior, the three facets of psychological theory – cognitive, motivational and social psychological – are applied in MCS research to study the influence of the various aspects of MCSs (i.e., budgeting practices) on individual motivation (Birnberg et al., 2007), which, in turn, can affect managerial performance. The psychology-related variables in this study are concerned with the perceived fairness and motivation of budgeting practices.

## Literature review and hypothesis development

The research model for this study is illustrated in Figure 5.1, which shows that budgetary characteristics (budgetary participation, budget goal difficulty, budget goal clarity, budgetary evaluation (general and punitive), budgetary feedback and budgetary slack) are independent variables while managerial effectiveness is the dependent variable.

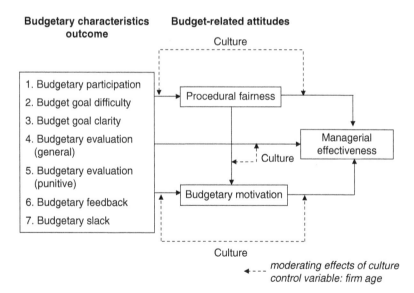

*Figure 5.1* Conceptual model of effects of budgetary characteristics on managerial effectiveness via procedural fairness and budgetary motivation with moderating effects of cultural influences

In addition, there are two mediators of budgetary characteristics, procedural fairness and budgetary motivation, and culture is identified as the moderating variable.

*Budgetary participation*

The first characteristic of budgeting in this study is budgetary participation, defined as a process whereby subordinates are given opportunities to get involved in and have an influence on the budget-setting process (Brownell, 1982c). Budgetary participation is expected to affect perceptions of procedural fairness, budgetary motivation and managerial effectiveness.

Procedural fairness is defined here as managers' perceptions of the fairness of budget procedures and implementation. Such perceptions of fairness are likely to result in favorable managerial reactions, both positive and negative, including motivation, which in turn affects managerial effectiveness. The perceptions of fairness depend on a number of factors, such as annual budget outcomes and resource-allocation practices (Dittmore, Mahony, Andrew and Hums, 2009: 430). Lindholm (2000: 48) suggests that an effective MCS is dependent on to what extent it is considered fair. Little, Magner and Welker (2002) provide support for the interaction between the fairness perceptions of formal budgetary procedures and their enactment by supervisors. Specifically, the fairness of formal budgetary procedures is significantly and positively related to job performance, which helps behavior. The results suggest that managers exhibit particular positive organizational behavior when they view both the formal budgetary procedures and the supervisory enactment of these procedures as fair. Lau and Lim (2002) find that procedural fairness is positively related to managerial performance and they suggest that budgetary participation may be more effective in enhancing managerial performance when procedural fairness is lower, compared with when it is high. Later, they note the positive relationship between budgetary participation and procedural fairness (Lau and Tan, 2005, 2006). Similarly, Kyj and Parker (2008: 424) state that perceived procedural fairness may be improved by budgetary participation because organizational decision may affect them (i.e., goal-setting). In addition to perceptions of procedural fairness, budgetary participation may lead to improved motivation.

Budgetary motivation in this study refers to the desire to attain a select budgetary goal (the goal congruence aspect), combined with the resulting pursuit of that goal (the effort aspect) (Horngren et al., 2009: 796). Motivation may be improved by the level of participation because participation provides a sense of accomplishment (Brownell, 1983a: 457; Chenhall and Brownell, 1988: 229; Iriyadi and Gurd, 1998; Kenis, 1979; Schnake, Bushardt and Spottswood, 1986). Thus this study proposes that budgetary participation will lead to greater budgetary motivation.

Regarding the relation between budgetary participation and managerial effectiveness, extant studies have provided conflicting findings (Agbejule and Saarikoski, 2006; Guilding, Lamminmaki and Drury, 1998: 575). Budgetary participation is a negotiation process based on the best-known information (Brown et al., 2009; Dunk, 1995; Shields and Shields, 1998; Tsui, 2001). Participation not only provides top management with more insight into business practices and possible obstacles but also helps parent companies to coordinate all of their responsibility centers (De and Dijkman, 2008). Some studies have found a positive relationship between budgetary participation and managerial performance (Brownell and McInnes, 1986; Kenis, 1979; Lau, Low and Eggleton, 1995; Schnake, Bushardt and Spottswood, 1986; Shields and Shields, 1998) while others have failed to provide support (Milani, 1975). Overall the effect that budgetary participation has on managerial effectiveness has been inconclusive. This study expects that budgetary participation may improve perceptions of procedural fairness, budgetary motivation and organizational managerial effectiveness. This reasoning suggests the following hypothesis:

*Hypothesis 1. Budgetary participation will be positively related to (a) procedural fairness, (b) budgetary motivation, and (c) managerial effectiveness.*

Unlike budgetary participation, the studies that have examined the effects of budget goal difficulty, budget goal clarity, budgetary evaluation (general), budgetary evaluation (punitive), budgetary feedback and budgetary slack on perceptions of procedural fairness have been very scarce. Unsurprisingly, it is apparent that the remaining hypotheses are contingency-based propositions in MCSs.

*Budget goal difficulty*
Budget goal difficulty refers to how challenging the budget goals and standards are (Schnake et al., 1986). Budget goals can range from very loose and easily attainable to very tight and unattainable. Easily attainable goals fail to present a challenge to participants and therefore have little motivational effect. Very tight and unattainable goals lead to feelings of failure, frustration, lower aspiration levels and the rejection of participants' goals (Kenis, 1979). Managers are much more likely to

reject a high level of budget goal difficulty, meaning that the resistance exists mentally (Su, 2010: 3). Hence budget goal difficulty may be negatively related to the perceptions of procedural fairness.

For motivational purposes, both the budget goal and its target should be challenging (Merchant and Van der Stede, 2007). A difficult goal is likely to affect performance by prompting the exertion of more effort (Jeffery et al., 2010; Locke and Latham, 2002) toward better achievement, implying that budgetary motivation may be improved by difficult goals. Thus budget goal difficulty may be positively related to budgetary motivation.

With regard to budget goal difficulty and managerial effectiveness, Carroll and Tosi (1970) find a positive relationship between managers' perceived task-goal difficulty and their self-rated performance. Gerard (1997) notes that high and very high goals led to better performance compared with low goals. Budget goals are frequently claimed to increase the level of task performance. Chow (1983: 683) also suggests that job standard tightness had a significant effect on performance, especially for those who were assigned an average performance standard and a compensation scheme. Accordingly, budget goal difficulty is likely to have a positive effect on managerial effectiveness. Thus the following hypothesis is presented:

*Hypothesis 2. The budget goal difficulty will be negatively related to (a) procedural fairness and will be positively related to (b) budgetary motivation and (c) managerial effectiveness.*

### Budget goal clarity

Budget goal clarity refers to the extent to which budget goals are stated specifically and clearly, and are understood by those who are responsible for meeting them (Kenis, 1979).

Perceptions of procedural fairness may be improved by budget goal clarity. A specific goal is better than an ambiguous or no goal because responsible managers are more likely to understand how to achieve a specific goal, whereas an ambiguous goal can lead to confusion, tension and dissatisfaction (Kenis, 1979). Thus budget goal clarity may be positively related to perceptions of procedural fairness.

For motivational purposes, the budget goal and its target should be specific (Merchant, 1984). As previously discussed, a specific goal is more likely to affect motivation (Jeffreyet et al., 2010: Locke and Latham, 2002). Thus budget goal clarity is likely to have a positive effect on budgetary motivation.

For improved managerial effectiveness via budget goal clarity, Locke (1968) suggests that setting specific goals is more productive than not setting goals and urging employees to do their best. Previous studies have provided support for the positive relationship between budget goal clarity and managerial performance. For example, Kenis (1979) indicates a positive relationship between budget goal clarity and budgetary performance and cost efficiency. Schnake et al. (1986), hypothesizing that employees perform better when specific challenging goals are established than when general, easy to attain goals are set, indicate a significant relation between goal clarity, effort and performance. Gerard, Ree and Gerjo (1997) learned that a specific goal led to higher performance than an absence of goals. For this study it is proposed that managerial effectiveness may also be improved by budget goal clarity. Accordingly, it would seem reasonable to propose the following hypothesis:

*Hypothesis 3. Budget goal clarity will be positively related to (a) procedural fairness, (b) budgetary motivation and (c) managerial effectiveness.*

### Budgetary evaluation

Budgetary evaluation refers to the extent to which budget variances are traced back to individual department heads and used in evaluating their performance (Kenis, 1979). Budgetary evaluation in this study is categorized into two approaches: budgetary evaluation (general) and budgetary evaluation (punitive).

### Budgetary evaluation (general)

Budgetary evaluation (general) is defined here as the extent to which budget variances are traced back to responsible managers and used in evaluating them in supportive ways. For example, if a supervisor has held a subordinate personally accountable for budget variances in the respective department, then budget variances have been mentioned by supervisors as factors in being considered for a raise. This study expects budgetary evaluation (general) to have a positive effect on procedural fairness perceptions.

Budgetary evaluation can also motivate managers to use the information to improve performance (Shield and Shield, 1998: 270). A reward structure based primarily on budget achievement is likely to motivate subordinates only if they are heavily involved in the budget-setting process (Lau et al., 1995), and the fashion in which budgets are used in evaluating tends to influence individual motivation to achieve goals is noted (Kenis, 1979: 710). Thus it is anticipated that the higher the degree of budget used to evaluate individuals in supportive ways (general), the more likely it is that firms will create more budgetary motivation and also tend to achieve greater managerial effectiveness. Hence the following hypothesis is proposed:

> *Hypothesis 4. Budgetary evaluation (general) will be positively related to (a) procedural fairness, (b) budgetary motivation and (c) managerial effectiveness.*

### Budgetary evaluation (punitive)

Budgetary evaluation (punitive) in this study refers to the extent to which budget variances are traced back to responsible managers and used to evaluate them in punitive ways. For example, supervisors tend to show their dissatisfaction with budget variances, apportioning blame when the budget has not been met and thus becoming angry about variances. Welsch et al. (1988) state that lower motivation and negative attitudes may be caused by the punitive approach to budgetary evaluation. Hofstede (1984) suggests that a cost-conscious boss interprets negative results as being punitive rather than corrective, which can lead to higher pressure and lower performance. Kenis (1979) finds a negative relationship between budgetary evaluation (punitive) and budgetary and job performance. Unlike budgetary evaluation (general), if the firm's budgetary evaluation systems are characterized by a punitive approach, it tends to emphasize placing blame on others. In contrast with budgetary evaluation (general), it is anticipated that this approach to evaluation will have negative effects on perceptions of procedural fairness, budgetary motivation and organizational managerial effectiveness. The following hypothesis is thus formulated:

> *Hypothesis 5. Budgetary evaluation (punitive) will be negatively related to (a) procedural fairness, (b) budgetary motivation and (c) managerial effectiveness.*

### Budgetary feedback

In this study, budgetary feedback refers to the activity of providing information to responsible individuals about their achievements, and guidance about budget goals and variances. As the plan is implemented, continuous feedback is needed to evaluate actual results. If these are compared with planned activities on a timely basis, corrective action may be taken as needed to achieve ultimate goals (Cherrington et al.,

1974). Budgetary feedback may be related to procedural fairness, budgetary motivation and organizational managerial effectiveness.

Feedback provides additional knowledge that can be used to establish the most efficient way to perform tasks (Hirst and Yetton, 1999: 207). Feedback from superiors is much more crucial for significant job improvement (Brown and Porter, 2006). Budgetary feedback plays an important role in establishing a work environment in which subordinates are motivated to perform at their maximum potential. Subordinates in such an environment know exactly how well they are performing in terms of achieving budget goals and receive guidance on how to improve performance through useful feedback (Hillman et al., 2007). Yet there has been limited evidence to support this assumption. In this regard, Erez (1997) argues that knowledge alone is not sufficient for effective performance, providing support for the positive relationship between feedback and performance and also the interactive effects of goal-setting and feedback on performance (Erez, 1977). Other studies have shown that feedback (as it interacts with budget goal difficulty) has a positive effect on budgetary performance (Hirst and Lowy, 1990). Likewise, feedback has been found likely to affect performance through consideration effort (Cianci and Bierstaker, 2008; Schnake et al., 1986). Thus it is anticipated that budgetary feedback is likely to have a positive effect on perceptions of procedural fairness, budgetary motivation and organizational managerial effectiveness. The following hypothesis is therefore proposed:

*Hypothesis 6. Budgetary feedback will be positively related to (a) procedural fairness, (b) budgetary motivation and (c) managerial effectiveness.*

### Budgetary slack

Budgetary slack refers to an amount designated in the budget, during the budget-setting process, that may be generally believed to be unnecessary but is nonetheless included for the sole purpose of creating a buffer to insure that the budget is easily achieved (Wu, 2005: 30). The lower level of budgetary slack, as budget-related behavior, represents management's ability to plan and control. Onsi (1973) suggests that budget goal difficulty may play a major role in creating anxieties about the possibility of goal attainment. Thus creating budgetary slack seems to be a general management trait. The motivation to do so is to ensure the availability of extra resources, thereby increasing the likelihood that subordinates will achieve better individual job performance (Lukka, 1988).

While empirical evidence of budgetary slack's effect on procedural fairness and budgetary motivation is limited, such slack is used by members of the coalition to satisfy personal motives that may not otherwise be explicitly approved, and slack can be created by managers who influence the budgeting process through successful bargaining (Onsi, 1973: 535). Thus it would seem reasonable to conclude that slack is a function of successful bargaining on behalf of the managers who influence the budgeting process. Although slack in the budget can be considered unethical behavior, it has the potential to improve procedural fairness and budgetary motivation.

In addition, studies examining the effect of budgetary slack on managerial effectiveness are also lacking, hence the hypothesis is contingent. However, Armesh et al. (2010) propose that budgetary slack remains a major concern in budget practices because it may have a negative effect on long-term performance. Based on the abovementioned assumptions, this study proposes that the greater the degree of propensity to create budgetary slack, the less likely it is that firms will achieve managerial effectiveness due to their inefficient resource allocation, and the following hypothesis is investigated:

*Hypothesis 7. Budgetary slack will be positively related to (a) procedural fairness and (b) budgetary motivation, and negatively related to (c) managerial effectiveness.*

### The consequences of budget-related attitudes

Budgetary motivation may be improved via perceived procedural fairness, as Kyj and Parker (2008: 424) suggest. Superiors have a number of reasons for treating their subordinates fairly, and superiors with a reputation for fairness may be more effective managers because their goals will be easily accepted by subordinates. Acceptable plans indicate a sense of accomplishment or motivation. Hence it is anticipated that the higher the degree of procedural fairness, the more likely it is that individuals will be motivated. With regard to procedural fairness and managerial effectiveness, Wang (2010) suggests that fair management can influence managerial effectiveness. Lua and Tan (2005, 2006) suggest that procedural fairness can improve organizational commitment and trust in supervisors, which, in turn, affects firm performance. The following hypothesis is thus proposed:

*Hypothesis 8. Procedural fairness will be positively related to (a) budgetary motivation and (b) managerial effectiveness.*

This study employs psychology-theory-based investigations of budgeting, the success of which in motivating employees and planning depends on how it influences employees' mental states and behavior (Covaleski et al., 2003: 24). Some aspects of budgetary control (i.e., budgetary participation, budgetary evaluation and budget goal difficulty) may improve manager motivation, which, in turn, affects managerial effectiveness (Brownell, 1983a; De and Dijkman, 2008; Wong-On-Wing, Guo and Lui, 2010; Wu, 2005). Thus managerial effectiveness should be assessed based on the motivation and morale of employees (Analoui, Ahmed and Kakabadse, 2009: 59). De and Dijkman (2008) argue that managerial motivation depends on the ways in which the company develops targets. The motivation to attain the targets will be greater for managers who have worked on the development of their budget, thus it is reasonable to assume that budgetary motivation is likely to have a positive effect on managerial effectiveness. The following hypothesis is therefore stated:

*Hypothesis 9. Budgetary motivation will be positively related to managerial effectiveness.*

### The moderating effects of culture

Culture is the collective programming of the mind, distinguishing the members of one group or society from those of another (Hofstede, 1984: 82). Cultural dimensions comprise i) individualism vs. collectivism, ii) large vs. small power distance, iii) strong vs. uncertainty avoidance, iv) masculinity vs. femininity and v) long-term orientation (Confucian dynamism). Because the interpretation of culturally different contexts is very complex, previous researchers (Iriyadi and Gurd, 1998; O'Connor, 1995; Tsui, 2001; Wu, 2005) have not focused on all of the cultural dimensions, attempting instead to directly measure the significant differences in cultural values because there is solid evidence that cultural dimensions are universal (Hofstede, 1984: 84). The first two cultural values are the focal cultural dimensions through which to derive expectations about the perceived appropriateness of budget practices at the organizational context level. At an organizational level, Hofstede (1993: 11) suggests that individualism and power distance are the most relevant cultural dimensions for the type of leadership style and its attributes, such as degree of participation in planning and decision-making. National culture can moderate the effects of MCS practices in organizations as it influences the ways in which managers and other employees respond to MCS practices (Gong and Tse, 2009). Thus a firm's cultural background is considered to be a moderating variable because the availability of MCSs in improving managerial effectiveness is likely to be influenced by cultural differences. Hence while positive and negative relationships between budgetary characteristics, procedural fairness, budgetary motivation and managerial effectiveness are expected, they are more likely to be moderated by cultural differences, which suggests that the two way-interaction hypothesis should be examined. We expect the interaction effects of budgetary characteristics and the cultural background of the firm on procedural fairness, budgetary motivation and managerial effectiveness to be different, depending on the organization's cultural background. The following contingent hypotheses are therefore proposed:

> *Hypothesis 10. Depending on the organizations' cultural backgrounds, managers working for US manufacturing firms in Thailand will exhibit a different correlation between budgetary characteristics and budgetary fairness compared with those working for local Thai manufacturing firms.*

> *Hypothesis 11. Depending on the organizations' cultural backgrounds, managers working for US manufacturing firms in Thailand will exhibit a different correlation between budgetary characteristics, procedural fairness and budgetary motivation compared with those working for local Thai manufacturing firms.*

> *Hypothesis 12. Depending on the organizations' cultural backgrounds, managers working for US manufacturing firms in Thailand will exhibit a different correlation between budgetary characteristics, procedural fairness, budgetary motivation and managerial effectiveness compared with those working for local Thai manufacturing firms.*

## Research methodology

### Data collection

Data were collected with a field survey involving functional managers (purchasing, production and sales) working for Thai-listed manufacturing firms (representatives of collectivism and high-power distance societies), and those working for US manufacturing MNCs in Thailand (representatives of high individualism and low-power distance societies). A cross-sectional population of 600 managers was selected from each group, of which 231 and 252 usable questionnaires were returned, resulting in response rates of 43% and 47%, respectively. Non-response bias analysis was conducted to verify the representativeness of the responses by comparing early responses with late responses (Armstrong and Overton, 1977; Lau and Lim, 2002). The first 50% of responses were defined as early responses and the second 50% as late. In this regard, a two-sample t-test was performed to test the response differences. The result provided support for the absence of a non-response bias between early and late responses for budgetary characteristics, procedural fairness, budgetary motivation and organizational managerial effectiveness.

### Variability measurements

All of the variables in this study were measured by the five sections of the questionnaire. The first section covered the demographics of the respondents and their firms. The remaining sections measured budgetary characteristics, procedural fairness, budgetary motivation and managerial effectiveness, respectively. The respondents were asked to respond to a set of relevant statements by circling or crossing out a number from 1 (strongly disagree) to 7 (strongly agree), except for managerial effectiveness, which will be discussed later. The second part of the questionnaire measured the seven aspects of budgetary characteristics: i) the budgetary participation measure, adapted from Milani's (1975) six-item measure and used to assess the extent to which the budget systems involved functional managers; ii) the budget goal difficulty measure, comprising five items used to assess the difficulty of the budget goal; iii) the budget goal clarity measure, with five items used to assess the clarity of the budget goal; iv) the budgetary evaluation (general) measure, with four items used to determine the extent to which the functional managers were held accountable for budget variances and evaluated based on budgeting; v) the budgetary evaluation (punitive) measure, which used five items to indicate whether the budget systems were used to punish functional managers; vi) the budgetary feedback measure, which used five items to provide a set of feedback on how well subordinates were doing compared with budgetary goals; and vii) the budgetary slack measure, which used six items adapted from Onsi (1973) to reflect the extent of the propensity to create slack in the budget preparation. The measures of budget goal difficulty, budget goal clarity, budgetary evaluation (general and punitive) and budgetary feedback were adapted from Kenis (1979). Next, six items adapted from Folger and Cropanzano (1998) and Hamman-Fisher (2008), related to the procedural fairness for which budget systems are implemented, were used to measure the extent to which functional managers are treated fairly, especially in a budgeting context. Then budgetary motivation measures developed by Wong-On-Wing et al. (2010) were used to measure managers' motivation in the budgeting practices. Nine items pertaining to budgetary motivation were used to measure the effect of budget systems on managerial motivation. Finally, managerial effectiveness dimensions were measured with an eight-dimensional scale introduced by Mahoney et al. (1963), which has been used extensively in budgeting research (e.g., Agbejule and Saarikoski, 2006; Brownell, 1982b, 1983a; Brownell and Hirst, 1986; Brownell and McInnes, 1986; Lua et al., 2002; Leach-Lopez et al., 2007; Su, 2010; Yahya, 2008). This scale measures eight performance dimensions: planning, investigating, coordinating, evaluating, supervising, staffing, negotiating and representing. The respondents were asked to rate their own recent performance as 1, 2 or 3 for below average performance; 4, 5 or 6 for average performance; and 7, 8 or 9 for above average performance. Managerial effectiveness was taken as the sum of these eight individual measures.

## Method

Confirmatory factor analysis (CFA) was used to investigate the validity of the constructs. Furthermore, the factor scores were used to estimate the regression analysis. Table 5.1 depicts the factor loadings and Cronbach's alpha coefficients. With respect to the CFA, this analysis has a high potential to inflate the component loadings based on a higher rule-of-thumb at a cut-off value of 0.40 (Hair, Black, Babin, Anderson and Tatham, 2010: 117). All of the factor loadings were greater than 0.6 and statistically significant. The reliability of the measurements, or internal consistency, was evaluated by Crobach's alpha coefficients, which are based on a value of greater than 0.70 (Hair et al., 2010: 125). Overall, the results in Table 5.1 indicate the reliability of these constructs.

*Table 5.1*  Validation of measures

| Variables | Cronbach's alpha | Factor loadings |
| --- | --- | --- |
| Budgetary participation | 0.916 | 0.807–0.894 |
| Budget goal difficulty | 0.796 | 0.716–0.849 |
| Budget goal clarity | 0.898 | 0.861–0.905 |
| Budgetary evaluation (general) | 0.879 | 0.812–0.889 |
| Budgetary evaluation (punitive) | 0.920 | 0.872–0.922 |
| Budgetary feedback | 0.838 | 0.625–0.848 |
| Budgetary slack | 0.743 | 0.720–0.840 |
| Procedural fairness | 0.900 | 0.770–0.932 |
| Budgetary motivation | 0.940 | 0.675–0.855 |
| Managerial performance | 0.919 | 0.748–0.843 |

The ordinary least squares regression analysis was used to estimate parameters in hypothesis testing. To test the proposed hypotheses, the following models were applied:

Model 1: $PF = \beta_{01} + \beta_1 BP + \beta_2 BGD + \beta_3 BGC + \beta_4 BEG + \beta_5 BEP + \beta_6 BF$
$+ \beta_7 BS + \beta_8 Age + \varepsilon$

Model 2: $BM = \beta_{02} + \beta_9 BP + \beta_{10} BGD + \beta_{11} BGC + \beta_{12} BEG + \beta_{13} BEP$
$+ \beta_{14} BF + \beta_{15} BS + \beta_{16} PF + \beta_{17} Age + \varepsilon$

Model 3: $ME = \beta_{03} + \beta_{18} BP + \beta_{19} BGD + \beta_{20} BGC + \beta_{21} BEG + \beta_{22} BEP$
$+ \beta_{23} BF + \beta_{24} BS + \beta_{25} PF + \beta_{26} BM + \beta_{27} Age + \varepsilon$

Model 4: $PF = \beta_{04} + \beta_{28} BP + \beta_{29} BGD + \beta_{30} BGC + \beta_{31} BEG + \beta_{32} BEP$
$+ \beta_{33} BF + \beta_{34} BS + \beta_{35} CUL + \beta_{36} (BP^*CUL)$
$+ \beta_{37} (BGD^*CUL) + \beta_{38} (BGC^*CUL) + \beta_{39} (BEG^*CUL)$
$+ \beta_{40} (BEP^*CUL) + \beta_{41} (BF^*CUL) + \beta_{42} (BS^*CUL)$
$+ \beta_{43} Age + \varepsilon$

Model 5: $BM = \beta_{05} + \beta_{44} BP + \beta_{45} BGD + \beta_{46} BGC + \beta_{47} BEG + \beta_{48} BEP$
$+ \beta_{49} BF + \beta_{50} BS + \beta_{51} PF + \beta_{52} CUL + \beta_{53} (BP^*CUL)$
$+ \beta_{54} (BGD^*CUL) + \beta_{55} (BGC^*CUL) + \beta_{56} (BEG^*CUL)$
$+ \beta_{57} (BEP^*CUL) + \beta_{58} (BF^*CUL) + \beta_{59} (BS^*CUL)$
$+ \beta_{60} (PF^*CUL) \beta_{61} Age + \varepsilon$

Model 6: $ME = \beta_{06} + \beta_{62} BP + \beta_{63} BGD + \beta_{64} BGC + \beta_{65} BEG + \beta_{66} BEP$
$+ \beta_{67} BF + \beta_{68} BS + \beta_{69} PF + \beta_{70} BM + \beta_{71} CUL + \beta_{72} (BP^*CUL)$
$+ \beta_{73} (BGD^*CUL) + \beta_{74} (BGC^*CUL) + \beta_{75} (BEG^*CUL)$
$+ \beta_{76} (BEP^*CUL) + \beta_{77} (BF^*CUL) + \beta_{78} (BS^*CUL)$
$+ \beta_{79} (PF^*CUL) + \beta_{80} (BM^*CUL) + \beta_{81} Age + \varepsilon$

Here, PF = procedural fairness; BP = budgetary participation; BGD = budget goal difficulty; BGC = budget goal clarity; BEG = budgetary evaluation (general); BEP = budgetary evaluation (punitive); BF = budgetary feedback; BS = budgetary slack; ME = managerial effectiveness; BM = budgetary motivation; CUL = a dummy variable for cultural background, with 1 representing managers working for US MNCs in Thailand and 0 representing managers working for Thai firms; Age = firm age; and $\varepsilon$ = error term.

Firm age, as a control variable, is included and measured as the number of years that a firm has been in operation. Procedural fairness, budgetary motivation and managerial effectiveness may be influenced by firm age because it may be able to achieve superior performance (Banker, Bardhan and Chen, 2008).

## Results and discussion

### Descriptive statistics

In both the national and multinational companies, over 50% of the respondents reported being in their 40s to 50s. On average the respondents had over 10 years of working experience for all of the companies, over 8 years for their present employer and about 6 years in their present position with the average number of subordinates being 24 people. Of the respondents 65 had bachelor's, master's or professional qualifications. They were all Thais and they all had budget responsibilities. These data indicate that the respondents were highly experienced, held highly responsible positions, and were generally highly educated and qualified. Table 5.2 presents the descriptive statistics, by culture, for each of the study's variables. While it is not the main hypothesis, we also empirically test the significant differences in budgetary characteristics,

*Table 5.2* Descriptive statistics and results of t-tests by cultural background

| Variables | Mean | | t-value | p-value |
| --- | --- | --- | --- | --- |
| | Multinational | National | | |
| **Budgetary characteristics** | | | | |
| Budgetary participation | 4.11 | 3.83 | 3.23 | 0.00*** |
| Budget goal difficulty | 4.15 | 3.89 | 3.67 | 0.00*** |
| Budget goal clarity | 5.07 | 4.99 | 0.79 | 0.21 |
| Budget evaluation (general) | 4.21 | 3.65 | 4.46 | 0.00*** |
| Budget evaluation (punitive) | 3.86 | 3.51 | 2.43 | 0.00*** |
| Budgetary feedback | 4.80 | 4.56 | 3.63 | 0.00*** |
| Budgetary slack | 3.97 | 3.90 | 4.28 | 0.00*** |
| **Budget-related attitudes** | | | | |
| Procedural fairness | 4.56 | 4.31 | 1.96 | 0.04** |
| Budgetary motivation | 4.65 | 4.50 | 1.88 | 0.06* |
| **Outcome** | | | | |
| Managerial effectiveness | 5.89 | 5.90 | 0.11 | 0.45 |

*, ** and *** indicate significance at $p < 0.10$, $p < 0.05$ and $p < 0.01$, respectively, based on two-tailed tests.

budget-related attitudes and managerial effectiveness before testing the main hypotheses. Based on Hofstede's cultural dimensions, the cultures of local Thai countries are different from those of the US-controlled subsidiaries. If these expectations are proved to be the case, it would seem more reasonable to assume that further analysis of the relations between budgetary characteristics and managerial effectiveness should be appropriate as the cultural differences may influence them. As expected, the preference for and design of budget systems in MNCs (high individualism and low-power distance societies) in Thailand do not fall far from the tree (the parent company) because almost all of the budgetary characteristics are consistent with those used in Western countries. In this regard, US MNCs in Thailand tend to participate more in the setting and implementation of budgets – specifically, setting more difficult budget goals, using budgeting systems to evaluate their subordinates to a larger extent, giving more budgetary feedback to responsible managers and creating more slack in budget preparation than local Thai firms. With regard to budget-related attitudes, this study finds that procedural fairness and budgetary motivation in individualism and low-power distance societies is statistically significantly larger than those in their low individualistic culture, high-power distance counterparts. In addition, there is no difference in the mean of the budget goal clarity and managerial effectiveness when grouped by cultural background.

### Direct effects of procedural fairness, budgetary motivation and managing effectiveness

Table 5.3 shows the descriptive statistics and correlation matrix between variables analyzed by Pearson correlation coefficients. Although it indicates a strong correlation between independent variables, the multicollinearity problem is not severe. The results show that variance inflation factors range from 1.06 to 2.54. They are all well below the cut-off value of 10 recommended by Hair et al. (2010: 204), indicating that there are no substantial multicollinearity problems encountered in this study. Table 5.4 illustrates the multiple regression results based on the first three proposed models. Regardless of the cultural differences, the results indicate that budgetary participation is largely and positively related only to budgetary motivation ($p < 0.01$) and minimally related to managerial effectiveness ($p < 0.10$). Thus hypotheses 1b and 1c are supported. With regard to the second aspect of budgetary characteristics, the results reveal that budget goal difficulty is only negatively related to budgetary motivation ($p < 0.01$). Hence Hypothesis 2b is supported. As expected, budget goal clarity has significant positive effects on all

*Table 5.3* Descriptive statistics and correlation matrix

| Variables | 1 | 2 | 3 | 4 | 5 | 6 | 7 | 8 | 9 | 10 |
|---|---|---|---|---|---|---|---|---|---|---|
| Mean | 3.98 | 4.03 | 5.04 | 3.95 | 3.70 | 4.69 | 3.94 | 4.45 | 4.58 | 5.90 |
| Standard deviation | 1.21 | 0.97 | 1.11 | 1.41 | 1.42 | 1.03 | 0.67 | 1.39 | 0.89 | 1.44 |
| 1. Budgetary participation | 1.00 | 0.19*** | 0.29*** | 0.58*** | 0.12*** | 0.42*** | 0.27*** | 0.44*** | 0.43*** | 0.22*** |
| 2. Budget goal difficulty | | 1.00 | 0.15*** | 0.33*** | 0.46*** | 0.12* | 0.24*** | 0.10*** | 0.16*** | -0.11** |
| 3. Budget goal clarity | | | 1.00 | 0.28*** | 0.03 | 0.52*** | 0.13*** | 0.41*** | 0.60*** | 0.43*** |
| 4. Budgetary evaluation (general) | | | | 1.00 | 0.28*** | 0.40*** | 0.34*** | 0.53*** | 0.43*** | 0.16*** |
| 5. Budgetary evaluation (punitive) | | | | | 1.00 | 0.19*** | 0.16*** | -0.11** | 0.10* | -0.20*** |
| 6. Budgetary feedback | | | | | | 1.00 | 0.20*** | 0.44*** | 0.57*** | 0.38** |
| 7. Budgetary slack | | | | | | | 1.00 | 0.25*** | 0.21*** | -0.03 |
| 8. Procedural fairness | | | | | | | | 1.00 | 0.59*** | 0.32*** |
| 9. Budgetary motivation | | | | | | | | | 1.00 | 0.56*** |
| 10. Managerial effectiveness | | | | | | | | | | 1.00 |

*, **, and *** indicate significant correlations at $p < 0.10$, $p < 0.05$ and $p < 0.01$, respectively, based on two-tailed tests.

*Table 5.4* Results of effects of budgetary characteristics on procedural fairness, budgetary motivation and managerial effectiveness[a]

| Independent variables | Dependent variables | | |
|---|---|---|---|
| | Procedural fairness (Model 1) | Budgetary motivation (Model 2) | Managerial effectiveness (Model 3) |
| Budgetary participation | 0.05 | 0.09 | 0.09 |
| | (0.05) | (0.04)*** | (0.07)* |
| Budget goal difficulty | −0.03 | −0.09 | −0.00 |
| | (0.05) | (0.04)*** | (0.06) |
| Budget goal clarity | 0.18 | 0.40 | 0.09 |
| | (0.04)*** | (0.04)*** | (0.06)* |
| Budgetary evolution (general) | 0.36 | −0.01 | −0.04 |
| | (0.06)*** | (0.05) | (0.08) |
| Budgetary evaluation (punitive) | −0.32 | 0.30 | −0.27 |
| | (0.04)*** | (0.04) | (0.06)*** |
| Budgetary feedback | 0.19 | 0.17 | 0.12 |
| | (0.05)*** | (0.04)*** | 0.07)*** |
| Budgetary slack | 0.07 | 0.00 | −0.09 |
| | (0.04)* | (0.04) | (0.06)*** |
| Procedural fairness | | 0.36 | 0.10 |
| | | (0.04)*** | (0.07)* |
| Budgetary motivation | | | 0.59 |
| | | | (0.05)*** |
| Firm age | 0.00 | 0.00 | 0.00 |
| | (0.00)*** | (0.00)*** | (0.00)** |
| Adjusted R² | 0.43 | 0.60 | 0.50 |
| F-value | 39.96*** | 70.42*** | 41.59*** |

*, ** and *** indicate significance at $p < 0.10$, $p < 0.05$, and $p < 0.01$, respectively, based on two-tailed tests.
[a]Beta coefficients with standard errors in parentheses.

of its consequences, which are procedural fairness ($p < 0.01$), budgetary motivation ($p < 0.01$) and managerial effectiveness ($p < 0.10$). Accordingly, all subsets of Hypothesis 3 are fully supported. Next, budgetary evaluation (general) only has a significant positive effect on procedural fairness ($p < 0.01$). Thus, only Hypothesis 4a is supported. However, when the budget is used for punitive purposes, it has negative effects on procedural fairness ($p < 0.01$) and managerial effectiveness ($p < 0.01$). Thus hypotheses 5a and 5c are supported. With regard to budgetary feedback, the findings provide support for the notion that budgetary feedback is more likely to have positive effects on all of its consequences ($p < 0.01$). Thus hypotheses 6a to 6c are fully supported. For the last dimension of budgetary characteristics, we provide partial support for the hypotheses – that is, the higher the degree of creating budgetary slack, the more likely it is that individuals will consider the budget to be fair ($p < 0.10$). Likewise, budgetary slack leads to less managerial effectiveness ($p < 0.01$). Based on these results, hypotheses 7a and 7c are supported. In addition, procedural fairness is significantly and positively related to budgetary motivation ($p < 0.01$) and procedural fairness ($p < 0.10$). Hence all of the subsets of Hypothesis 8 are fully supported. The findings show that budgetary motivation appears to have a positive effect on managerial effectiveness ($p < 0.01$), such that Hypothesis 9 is supported. Regarding the control variables, a positive relationship was found between firm age, procedural fairness, budgetary motivation and managerial effectiveness at varying degrees of significance.

## Cultural moderating effects on the relationships between budgetary characteristics, procedural fairness, budgetary motivation and managerial effectiveness

Table 5.5 presents the results of the moderating effects of culture on the relationships between budgetary characteristics, procedural fairness, budgetary motivation and managerial effectiveness. With regard

*Table 5.5* Results of main and cultural moderating effects

| Independent variables | Dependent variables | | |
| --- | --- | --- | --- |
| | Procedural fairness (Model 4) | Budgetary motivation (Model 5) | Managerial effectiveness (Model 6) |
| Budgetary participation | −0.01 | 0.21 | 0.03 |
| | (0.06) | (0.05)*** | (0.09)* |
| Budget goal difficulty | −0.02 | −0.14 | −0.07 |
| | (0.06) | (0.04)*** | (0.08) |
| Budget goal clarity | 0.14 | 0.50 | 0.42 |
| | (0.06)** | (0.04)*** | (0.09)*** |
| Budgetary evaluation (general) | 0.28 | 0.04 | −0.06 |
| | (0.07)*** | (0.05) | (0.11) |
| Budgetary evaluation (punitive) | −0.28 | −0.02 | −0.44 |
| | (0.06)*** | (0.04) | (0.09)*** |
| Budgetary feedback | 0.20 | 0.14 | 0.24 |
| | (0.06)*** | (0.05)*** | (0.09)** |
| Budgetary slack | 0.05 | −0.09 | −0.24 |
| | (0.06)*** | (0.04) | (0.09)*** |
| Procedural fairness | | 0.25 | 0.00 |
| | | (0.04)*** | (0.10)* |

| | | | |
|---|---|---|---|
| Budgetary motivation | | | 0.51 |
| | | | (0.09)*** |
| Culture | 0.05 | 0.15 | −0.02 |
| | (0.07) | (0.06) | (0.11) |
| Budgetary participation * | 0.07 | −0.27 | 0.42 |
| culture | (0.10) | (0.08)*** | (0.15)*** |
| Budget goal difficulty * culture | 0.03 | 0.15 | 0.00 |
| | (0.09) | (0.07)** | (0.14) |
| Budget goal clarity * culture | 0.02 | −0.51 | −0.46 |
| | (0.09) | (0.07)*** | (0.14)*** |
| Budgetary evaluation (general) | 0.19 | −0.09 | −0.14 |
| * culture | (0.10)* | (0.08) | (0.17) |
| Budgetary evaluation | −0.10 | −0.10 | 0.13 |
| (punitive) * culture | (0.08) | (0.08) | (0.17) |
| Budgetary feedback * culture | 0.05 | 0.07 | −0.19 |
| | (0.10) | (0.07) | (0.16) |
| Budgetary slack * culture | −0.14 | 0.11 | 0.15 |
| | (0.08)* | (0.06)* | (0.12) |
| Procedural fairness * culture | | 0.83 | 0.69 |
| | | (0.86)*** | (0.18)*** |
| Budgetary motivation * culture | | | −0.41 |
| | | | (0.16)*** |
| Firm age | 0.00 | 0.00 | 0.00 |
| | (0.00)** | (0.00)*** | (0.00)** |
| Adjusted $R^2$ | 0.46 | 0.72 | 0.49 |
| F-value | 27.00*** | 60.72*** | 20.45*** |

*, ** and *** indicate significance at $p < 0.10$, $p < 0.05$, and $p < 0.01$, respectively, based on two-tailed tests.

to procedural fairness as the independent variable, it is noted that the firms' cultural backgrounds do not moderate the effects of budgetary characteristics on procedural fairness to a greater extent. Only the effects of budgetary evaluation (general) ($p < 0.10$) and budgetary slack on procedural fairness ($p < 0.10$) are, to a lesser extent, moderated by the cultural background. Thus Hypothesis 10 is partially supported. Regarding budgetary motivation, the interaction between culture and the following elements – i) budgetary participation ($p < 0.01$); ii) budget goal difficulty ($p < 0.05$); iii) budget goal clarity ($p < 0.01$); (iv) budgetary slack ($p < 0.10$); and v) procedural fairness ($p < 0.01$) – affects budgetary motivation, and these effects are significantly different depending on cultural variables. Hence Hypothesis 11 is partially supported. Additionally, the effects of i) budgetary participation ($p < 0.01$), ii) budget goal clarity ($p < 0.01$), iii) procedural fairness ($p < 0.01$) and iv) budgetary motivation ($p < 0.01$) on managerial effectiveness are also statistically different, depending on the cultural influence. Accordingly, Hypothesis 12 is partially supported.

### Additional analyses of the mediating effects of procedural fairness and budgetary motivation on the relationships between budgetary characteristics and managerial effectiveness

To examine the mediating effects of procedural fairness and budgetary motivation, we follow the three-step regression analysis of Baron and Kenny (1986), and conduct three steps of mediation testing to find that procedural fairness mediates the effects of i) budgetary participation, ii) budget goal clarity and iii) budgetary feedback on managerial effectiveness (Table 5.6). Furthermore, only an indirect effect of budget goal clarity on managerial effectiveness through its effect on budgetary motivation is revealed (Table 5.7). In summary, only budget goal clarity's effect on managerial effectiveness is mediated by both procedural fairness and budgetary motivation.

First, the mediator (e.g., procedural fairness) should be regressed on the independent variable (e.g., budgetary participation). Second, the dependent variable (i.e., managerial effectiveness) should be regressed on the independent variable (e.g., budgetary participation). Finally, the dependent variable (i.e., managerial effectiveness) should be regressed on both the independent variable (e.g., budgetary participation) and the

*Table 5.6*  Results of mediating effects of procedural fairness

| Variables | Step1 | Step2 | Step3 | Result |
|---|---|---|---|---|
| 1. Budgetary participation | 0.43*** | 0.25*** | 0.13*** | supported |
| Procedural fairness | | | 0.29*** | |
| 2. Budget goal difficulty | 0.08* | −0.12*** | −0.15*** | not supported |
| Procedural fairness | | | 0.36*** | |
| 3. Budget goal clarity | 0.41*** | 0.45*** | 0.38*** | supported |
| Procedural fairness | | | 0.18*** | |
| 4. Budgetary evaluation (general) | 0.53*** | 0.17*** | −0.13 | not supported |
| Procedural fairness | | | 0.35*** | |
| 5. Budgetary evaluation (punitive) | −0.18*** | −0.24*** | −0.18*** | not supported |
| Procedural fairness | | | 0.34*** | |
| 6. Budgetary feedback | 0.44*** | 0.35*** | 0.25*** | supported |
| Procedural fairness | | | | |
| 7. Budgetary slack | 0.31*** | 0.02 | −0.10** | not supported |
| Procedural fairness | | | 0.37*** | |

*, ** and *** indicate significance at $p < 0.01$, $p < 0.05$ and $p < 0.10$, respectively, based on two-tailed tests.

*Table 5.7* Results of mediating effects of budgetary motivation

| Variables | Step1 | Step2 | Step3 | Result |
|---|---|---|---|---|
| 1. Budgetary participation | 0.42*** | 0.25*** | −0.02 | not supported |
| Budgetary motivation | | | 0.61*** | |
| 2. Budget goal difficulty | 0.09** | −0.12*** | −0.18*** | not supported |
| Budgetary motivation | | | 0.63*** | |
| 3. Budget goal clarity | 0.65*** | 0.45*** | 0.10** | supported |
| Budgetary motivation | | | 0.54*** | |
| 4. Budgetary evaluation (general) | 0.44*** | 0.17*** | −0.12*** | not supported |
| Budgetary motivation | | | 0.66*** | |
| 5. Budgetary evaluation (punitive) | 0.02 | −0.24*** | −0.25*** | not supported |
| Budgetary motivation | | | 0.61*** | |
| 6. Budgetary feedback | 0.59*** | 0.35*** | −0.00 | not supported |
| Budgetary motivation | | | 0.61*** | |
| 7. Budgetary slack | 0.26*** | 0.02 | −0.15*** | not supported |
| Budgetary motivation | | | 0.65*** | |

*, ** and *** indicate significance at $p < 0.01$, $p < 0.05$ and $p < 0.10$, respectively, based on two-tailed tests.

mediator (i.e., procedural fairness). For mediation to hold, the independent variable (e.g., budgetary participation) must have an effect in all three steps and the effect of the independent variable in step 3 must be less than in step 2 (Baron and Kenny, 1986).

## Discussion

### Procedural fairness
Regardless of cultural perspective, budget goal clarity, budgetary evaluation (general), budgetary feedback and budgetary slack appear to have positive effects on procedural fairness, whereas budgetary evaluation (punitive) has a negative effect on the perceptions of procedural fairness. From a cultural difference perspective, the two-way interaction term by itself does not provide any information about the nature and direction of the difference. Thus the interaction term in the regression can be explained mathematically as a partial derivative equation (Tsui, 2001). Given this application (figures not provided), the findings suggest that for managers working for the US MNCs in Thailand, the effect of budgetary evaluation (general) on perceptions of procedural fairness is stronger than it is for those working for Thai counterparts. This suggests that those who work for US MNCs in Thailand prefer to be evaluated and rewarded by comparing budgets and actual performance. The more the firms make use of this evaluative style, the more the managers perceive

the budget implementation as fair. However, the results also suggest that for managers working for local Thai firms, there is a strong relationship between budgetary slack and perceptions of procedural fairness. It is notable that budgetary slack is positively related to budgetary fairness. As previously discussed, slack in the budget is the result of the successful bargaining of managers who influence the budgeting process. Hence the ability to create budgetary slack appears to improve the perceptions of procedural fairness because it may ameliorate discontent among organization members, especially in Thai societies. Given the absence of theoretical and empirical literature on the relationships among aspects of budgeting and perceptions of procedural fairness, especially in the context of cultural differences, the ability to compare these findings with the literature is limited.

*Budgetary motivation*
Without taking cultural issues into account, we find that budgetary participation, budget goal difficulty, budget goal clarity, budgetary feedback and procedural fairness are positively related to budgetary motivation, with only a negative relationship between budget goal difficulty and budgetary motivation. The effects of budgetary participation on budgetary motivation are evidenced by prior studies (Chenhall and Brownell, 1988; Iriyadi and Gurd, 1998; Schnake, Bushardt and Spottswood, 1986). It is also consistent with Kenis (1979), who identifies the positive relationship between budget goal clarity and budget goal difficulty, and budgetary feedback on motivation. Lau et al. (2005) provide evidence to support the proposition that procedural fairness is positively associated with motivation as the results of the various procedures used for budget preparation and implementation.

   When compared by cultural background, the results indicate that the effect of budget goal difficulty and budgetary slack on budgetary motivation is stronger in US MNCs, suggesting that managers in this culture prefer more challenging budget goals than those working in Thai firms. In addition, if they are able to create more slack in the budget, they will be increasingly motivated. Conversely, the relationship between budgetary participation, budget goal clarity and budgetary motivation is more strongly observed in local Thai companies. Consequently, to improve the high level of motivation in this cultural context, firms should provide participatory budgeting systems for the managers and establish specific budget goals that are clearly identified.

*Managerial effectiveness*
Contingency-based research examines the effectiveness of MCSs through some of the aspects of a particular MCS (i.e., budgeting).

Overall, this study indicates that managerial effectiveness may be improved through budgetary participation, budget goal clarity, budgetary feedback and budgetary motivation. In contrast, an increased use of budget in punitively evaluating managers leads to decreased managerial effectiveness. Furthermore, the interactive effect of cultural background and the antecedents of managerial effectiveness provides evidence that managers working for US-owned subsidiaries in Thailand achieve greater managerial effectiveness through enhanced participation in budget preparation and procedural fairness perceptions.

In individualism and low-power distance cultures, if managers are actually able to establish objectives and goals, they are more likely to better understand how to enhance goal attainment. Thus managerial effectiveness may be greater through this participatory process. This study is consistent with previous studies on the direct positive relationship between budgetary participation and managerial effectiveness (Brownell and McInnes, 1986; Kenis, 1979; Lau, Low and Eggleton, 1995; Lau and Lim, 2002; Leach-Lopez, 2002; Schnake et al., 1986). For Thai cultures, budgetary participation has a weak association with managerial performance, as seen in the work of Milani (1975) and Tsui (2001), suggesting that managerial performance decreases as budgetary participation increases for Asian managers. Similarly, Iriyadi and Gurd (1998) find that performance in Asian countries (Indonesia) is not affected by budgetary participation. However, among those who work for local Thai companies, people tend to be collectivist and have more power distance, thus to enhance their managerial effectiveness, budget goals should be more specific and clear, and firms should provide a high level of motivation for their managers. In this regard, Locke (1968) posits that setting specific goals is more productive than not setting goals and urging employees to do the best they can. The evidence also supports Kenis (1979), who notes a positive relationship between budget goal clarity, budgetary performance and cost-efficiency. This study also provides support for the notion that procedural fairness and budgetary motivation can mediate the relationships between budgetary characteristics (only budget goal clarity) and managerial effectiveness.

## Summary, implications and limitations

The objective of this study was to provide a clear understanding of the roles of budgetary characteristics in the organizational managerial effectiveness as understood through the perceptions of procedural fairness and budgetary motivation in the context of cultural differences. In general it is obvious that US-owned subsidiaries in Thailand, as in many

Southeast Asian countries, can transfer the assumptions of budgetary control systems through cultural differences. Because the findings of this study are consistent with those of previous studies and the literature review of the characteristics of budgeting in Western countries, it is argued that the low power distance culture found in the Western parent companies would dominate the high power distance found in the Southeast Asian countries, such as Thai subsidiaries, thereby enhancing the uniqueness and effectiveness of MCSs. Thus it would seem reasonable to conclude that culture influences the preference for and design of budgetary characteristics, and these different dimensions may influence the relationships between budgetary characteristics and managerial effectiveness. This study provides important theoretical contributions expanding on previous knowledge and the MCS literature, specifically in relation to budgetary characteristics, procedural fairness, budgetary motivation and managerial effectiveness in the context of cross-cultural differences.

Regarding theoretical contributions, this study is one of the first to examine the influence of national culture on the preference for and design of MCSs (budgetary control systems) in Thailand. It is the first study to investigate the effects of the seven aspects of budgeting (in a single study) on organizational managerial effectiveness through procedural fairness and budgetary motivation in the context of cultural differences. An important theoretical implication is that national cultures can be changed as the result of globalization, and how to design an effective MCS that fits both organizational cultures – Western and Southeast Asian – can be considered as valuable knowledge.

Regarding the managerial implications, we find that national companies operating in Southeast Asian countries should improve their managerial effectiveness by increased budget goal clarity and increased motivation for functional managers. MNCs from the West should improve their managerial effectiveness by focusing on greater participation in budget-setting and the perceptions of procedural fairness.

Regardless of cultural dimensions, we note that the organizational managerial effectiveness decreases as budgetary slack increases. Thus controlling slack in the budget via a strong budget committee is also recommended. An effective, clear-cut budget process and optimal pressure, for example, have played major roles in identifying unnecessary or excessive resources in some departmental budgets and would reduce slack in the budget. Moreover, for both national and multinational companies, the findings indicate that increased budgetary evaluation (punitive) appears to have negative effects on managerial effectiveness.

Great care should therefore be taken when considering using budget evaluation as a punitive approach. Perhaps the use of budgeting to punish managers should be sparsely used or completely abandoned because, based on the results of this study, budgetary evaluation (punitive) appears to have a negative effect on organizational management effectiveness.

As with all research, this study is subject to limitations. Hence the results of this study should be interpreted accordingly. This is a cross-sectional study taken at one point in time and concentrating solely on the manufacturing sector, so generalizing the results to other industries should be done with caution. Finally, this study employed self-reported measures for all constructs. A multimethod approach would improve the validated findings.

## References

Agbejule, A., & Saarikoski, L. (2006) The effect of cost management knowledge on the relationship between budgetary participation and managerial performance. *The British Accounting Review*, 38, 427–440.

Analoui, F., Ahmed, A. A., & Kakabadse, N. (2009) Parameters of managerial effectiveness: The case of senior managers in the Muscat Municipality, Oman. *Journal of Management Development*, 29 (1), 56–78.

Armesh, H., Slarzehi, H., & Kord, B. (2010) Management control system. *Interdisciplinary Journal of Comtemporary Reserch in Business* 2 (6), 193–206.

Armstrong, J. S., & Overton, T. (1977) Estimating non-response bias in mail surveys. *Journal of Marketing Research*, 14 (3), 396–402.

Baron, R. M., & Kenny, D. A. (1986) The moderator-mediator variable distinction in social psychological research: Conceptual, strategic, and statistical considerations. *Journal of Personality and Psychology*, 51 (6), 1173–1182.

Bartlett, C. A., & Goshal, S. (1989) *Managing across Borders: The Transnational Solution*. Boston, Mass: Harvard Business School Press.

Birnberg, J. G., Luft, J., & Shields, M. D. (2007) *Psychology Theory in Management Accounting Research*. Handbook of Management Accounting Research. Elsevier.

Brown, D. S., & Porter, T. (2006) Enhance individual, team and firm performance by creating a feedback culture, *CPA Practice Management Forum*, 2, 14–15.

Brown, J. L., III, J. E., & Moser, D. V. (2009) Agency theory and participative budgeting experiments. *Journal of Management Accounting Research*, 21, 317–345.

Brownell, P. (1981) Participation in budgeting, locust of control, and organizational effectiveness. *The Accounting* Review, LVI (4), 844–860.

Brownell, P. (1982a) A field study examination of budgeting participation and locus of control. *The Accounting Review*, LVII (4), 766–777.

Brownell, P. (1982b) The role of accounting data in performance evaluation, budgetary participation, and organizational effectiveness. *Journal of Accounting Research*, 20(1), 12–27.

Brownell, P. (1982c) Participation in the budgeting process: When it works and when it doesn't. *Journal of Accounting Literauture*, 1(2), 124–153.

Brownell, P. (1983a) Leadership style, budgeting participation and managerial behavior. *Accounting, Organizations and Society,* 8(4), 307–321.

Brownell, P. (1983b) The motivational impact of management-by-exeption in a budgeting context. *Journal of Accounting Research,* 21(2), 456–472.

Brownell, P., & Hirst, M. (1986) Reliance on accounting information, budgeting participation, and task uncertainty: Tests of a three-way interaction. *Journal of Accounting Research,* 24 (2), 241–249.

Brownell, P., & McInnes, M. (1986) Budgeting participation, motivation, and managerial performance. *The Accounting Review,* LXI (4), 587–600.

Carroll, S. J. & Tosi, H. L. (1970) Goal characteristics and personality factors in a management by objectives program. *Administrative Science Quarterly,* (September), 295–305.

Chenhall, R. H. & Brownell, P. (1988) The effect of participative budgeting on job satisfaction and performance: Role of ambiguity as an intervening variable. *Accounting, Organizations and Society,* 13 (3), 225–233.

Cherrington, D. J., & Cherrington, J. O. (1974) Participation, performance, and appraisal. *Business Horizons,* 17 (6) 35–43.

Cianci, A. M., & Bierstaker, J. L. (2008) The effect of performance feedback and client importance on auditors' self-and public-focused ethical judgments. *Managerial Auditing Journal,* 24 (5), 455–474.

Chow, C. W. (1983) The effects of job standard tightness and compensation scheme on performance: An exploration of linkages. *The Accounting Review,*VIII (4), 667–685.

Chow, C. W., Shields, M. D., & Wu, A. (1999) The importance of national culture in design of and preference for management controls for multi-national operations. *Accounting, Organizations and Society,* 24, 441–461.

Covaleski, M. A., Evans III, J. H., & Luft, J. L. (2003) Budgeting research: Three theoretical perspectives and criterial for selective integration. *Journal of Management Accounting Research,* 15, 3–49.

De With, E., & Dijkman, A. (2008) Budgeting practices of listed companies in the Netherlands. *Management Accounting Quarterly,* 10 (1), 26–36.

Dittmore, S. Mahony, D., Andrew, D. P. S. & Hums. (2009) Examining fairness perceptions of financial resources allocation in U.S. Olympic Sport. *Journal of Sport Management,* 23, 429–456.

Douglas, P. C. & Wier, B. (2005) Cultural and ethical effects in budgeting systems: A comparison of U.S. and Chinese Managers. *Journal of Business Ethics,* 60, 159–174.

Dunk, A. S. (1995) The joint effect of participative budgeting and managerial interest in innovation on departmental performance. *Scandinavian Journal of Management,*11 (1), 75–85.

Egelhoff, W. G. (1988) Strategy and structure in multinational corporations: A revision of the Stopford and Wells model. *Strategic Management Journal,* 9, 1–14.

Erez, M. (1977) Feedback: A necessary condition for the goal setting-performance Relationship. *Journal of Applied Psychology,* 62 (5), 624–627.

Fogler, R., & Cropanzano, R. (1998) *Organizational Justice and Human Resource Management.* California: Sage.

Gerard, S., Ree, M., & Gerjo, K. (1997) The effects of task importance and publicness on the relationship between goal difficulty and performance. *Canadian Journal of Behavioral Science,* 29 (1), 54–62.

Gong, M. Z., & Tse, M. S. C. (2009) Pick, mix or match? A discussion of theories for management accounting research. *Journal of Accounting, Business and Management*, 16 (2), 54–66.

Goodwin, D., & Sethapokin (1996) The impact of cultural influence on the relationship between budgetary participation, role stress, and job satisfaction. *Asian Review of Accounting*, 4 (2), 1996.

Guilding, C., Lamminmaki, D., & Drury, C. (1998) Budgeting and standard costing practices in New Zealand and the United Kingdom. *The International Journal of Accounting*, 33 (5), 569–588.

Hair, J. F., Black, W. C., Babin, B. J., Anderson, R. E., & Tatham, R. L. (2010) *Multivariate Data Analysis* (7th ed.), Pearson Prentice Hall.

Hamman-Fisher, D. A. (2008) *The Relationship between Job Satisfaction and Organizational Justice Amongst a Academic Employees in Agricultural Colleges in South Africa*. Unpublished Dissertation's Thesis, University of the Western Cape, South Africa.

Hansen, S. C., Otley, D. T., & Van der Stdede, W. A. (2003) Practice developments in budgeting: An overview and research perspective. *Journal of Management Accounting Research*, 15, 95–116.

Harrision, G. L., McKinnon, J. L, Panchapakesan, S., & Leung, M. (1994) The influence of culture on organizational design and planning control in Australia and the United States compared with Singapore and Hong Kong. *Journal of International Financial Management Accounting*, 5 (3), 242–261.

Hassel, L. G., & Cunningham, G. M. (1996) Budget effectiveness in multinational corporations: An empirical test of the use of budget controls moderated by two dimensions of budgetary participation under high and low environmental dynamism. *Management International Review*, 36 (Third Quarter): 245–266.

Hillman, L. W., Schwandt, D. R., & Bartz, D. E. (2007) Enhancing staff members' performance through feedback and coaching. *JMD* 9 (3), 20–27.

Hirst, M. K., & Lowy, S. M. (1990) The linear additive and interactive effects of budgetary goal difficulty and feedback on performance. *Accounting, Organizations and Society*, 15 (5), 425–436.

Hirst, M. K., & Yetton, P. W. (1999) The effect of budget goals and task interdependence on the level of and variance in performance: A research note. *Accounting, Organizations and Society*, 24, 205–216.

Hofstede. G. (1967) *The Game of Budget Control*. Assen, The Netherlands: Van Gorcum.

Hofstede, G. (1984) Cultural dimensions in management and planning. *Asia Pacific Journal of Management*, 1(2), 81–99.

Hofstede, G., & Bond, (1993) The Confucius connection: From cultural roots to economic growth, In: Ed. Blunt, P., & Richards, D. (Eds.), *Management, Organization and Culture in East and South-East Asia*, Darwin: Northern Territory University Press, 105–121.

Hofstede, G. (2001) *Culture's Consequences: Comparing Values, Behaviors, Institutions, and Organizations Across Nations*, 2nd ed. Thousand Oaks, CA: Sage Publication.

Horngren, C. T., Datar, S. M., Foster, G., Rajan, M., & Ittner, C. (2009) *Cost Accounting: A Managerial Emphasis* (13th ed.). New Jersey: Pearson Prentice Hall.

Iriyadi & Gurd, B. (1998) Cultural effects of budgetary participation: Indonesian evidence. *Asian Review of Accounting*, 6 (7): 71–99.

Jeffrey, W. A., Scott, A., & Axel, S. (2010) Factors affecting goal difficulty and performance when employees select their own performance goals: Evidence from the field. *Journal of Management Accounting Research, 22*, 209–232.

Kennis, I. (1979) Effects of budgeting goal characteristics on managerial attitudes and performance. *The Accounting Review, LIV* (4),707–721.

Kyj, L., & Parker, R. J. (2008) Antecedents of budget participation: Leadership style, information asymmetry, and evaluative use of budget. *A Journal of Accounting, Finance and Business Studies, 44* (4), 423–423.

Lau, C. M., & Lim, E. W. (2002) The effects of procedural justice and evaluation styles on the relationship between budgeting participation and performance. *Advances in Accounting, 19*, 139–160.

Lau, C. M., Low, L. C., & Eggleton, Ian, R. C. (1995) The impact of reliance on accounting performance measures on job-related tension and managerial performance: Additional evidence. *Accounting, Organizations and Society, 20* (5), 359–381.

Lau, C. M., & Tan, S. L. C. (2005) The importance of procedural fairness in budgeting. *Advances in Accounting, 21*, 333–356.

Lau, C. M., & Tan, S. L. C. (2006) The effects of procedural fairness and interpersonal trust on job tension in budgeting. *Management Accounting Research, 17*, 171–186.

Leach-Lopez, M. A. (2002) Participative budgeting, performance and job satisfaction: A cultural study of managers working for multinational firms in southeasterm United States and the US-Mexican border. *Dissertation Abstracts International.* (UMI No. 3043142).

Leach-Lopez, M. A., Stammerjohan, W. W., & McNair, F. M. (2007) Differences in the role of job-relevant information in the budget participation-performance relationship among U.S. and Mexican Managers: A question of culture or communication. *Journal of Management Accounting Research, 19*, 105–135.

Lindholm, N. (2000) National culture and performance management MNC subsidiaries. *International Studies of Management & Organization, 29* (4), 45–66.

Little, H., Magner, N., & Welker, R. B. (2002) The fairness of formal budgetary procedures and their enactment relationships with managers' behavior. *Group & Organization Management, 27* (2), 209–225.

Locke, E. A. (1968) Toward a theory of task motivation and incentives. *Organizational Behavior and Human Performance* (May), 157–189.

Locke, E. A., & Latham, G. P. (2002) Building a practically useful theory of goal setting and task motivation. *American Psychologist, 57* (9), 705–717.

Lukka, K. (1988) Budgeting biasing in organizations: Theoretical framework and empirical evidence. *Accounting, Organization and Society, 13*, 281–301.

Mahoney, T. A., Jerdee, T. H., & Carroll, S. J. (1963) The design of management. *Industrial Relations, 4*, 97–110.

Merchant, K. A. (1984) The design of the corporate budgeting system: Influences on managerial behavior and performance. *The Accounting Review, LVI* (4), 813–829.

Merchant, K. A. & Van der Stede, W. A. (2007) *Management Control Systems, Performance Measurement, Evaluation and Incentives* (2nd ed.). Prencitce-Hall: Upper Saddle Rive, N.J.

Milani, K. (1975) The relationship of participation in budget-setting to industrial supervisor performance and attitude: A field study. *The Accounting Review*, 50 (2), 274–287.

O'Connor, N. G. (1995) The influence of organizational culture on the usefulness of budget participation by Singaporean-Chinese managers. *Accounting, Organizations and Society*, 20 (5), 383–403.

Onsi, M. (1973) Factor analysis of behavioral variables affecting budgetary slack. *The Accounting Review*,48 (3), 535–548.

Phadoongsitthi, M. (2003) The role of managerial accounting in emerging economies: An empirical study of Thailand. *Dissertation Abstracts International*. (UMI No. 3112505).

Pillai, R. Wiliams, S., & Tan, J. J. (2001) Are the scales tipped in favor of procedural or distributive justice? An investigation of the U.S., India, Germany, and Hong Kong (China). *International Journal of Conflict Management*, 12, 312–332.

Schnake, M. E., Bushardt, S. C., & Spottswood. (1986) Internal work motivation and intrinsic job satisfaction: The effects of goal clarity, goal difficulty, participation in goal setting and task complexity. *Group and Organization Studies*, 9 (2): 201–220.

Shield, J. F., & Shield, M. D. (1998) Antecedents of participative budgeting. *Accounting, Organizations and Society*, 23 (1), 49–76.

Su, C. C. (2010) The role of trust in supervisor in participative budgeting systems. *Journal of Modern Accounting and Auditing*, 6 (10), 1–11.

Tsui, J. L. (2001) The impact of culture on the relationship between budgetary participation, management accounting systems, and managerial performance: An analysis of Chinese and Western managers. *The International Journal of Accounting*, 36, 125–146.

Ueno, S., & Sekaran, U. (1992) The influence of culture on budget control practices in the USA and Japan: An empirical study. *Journal of International Business Studies*, 23 (4), 659–674.

Wang, J. (2010) Understanding managerial effectiveness: A Chinese perspective. *Journal of European Industrial Training*, 35 (1), 6–23.

Welsch, G. A., Hilton, R. W., & Gordon, P. N. (1988) *Budgeting Profit Planning and Control* (5th ed.). New Jersey: Prentice-Hall Inc.

Wong-On-Wing, B., Guo, L., & Lui, G. (2010) Intrinsic and extrinsic motivation and participation in budgeting: Antecedents and consequences. *Behavioral Research in Accounting*, 22 (2), 133–153.

Wu, Eng C. (2005) Convergence of attitudes in different cultures towards the budgeting process. *Journal of Business and Management*, 11 (2): 29–47.

Yahya, M. N., Ahmad, N. N., & Fatima, A. H. (2008) Budgetary participation and performance: Some Malaysian evidence. *International Journal of Public Sector Management*, 21 (6), 658–673.

# Part II
# International Business and FDI

# 6
# Understanding the Entrepreneurial Process of Learning through Network Dynamics: Insights from China's Young International Firms

*Lianxi Zhou, Bradley R. Barnes and T. S. Chan*

## Introduction

Research in the field of international entrepreneurship (IE) has advanced the traditional process theory of internationalization by focusing on young firms that are international at their inception, or shortly thereafter (Knight and Cavusgil, 1996; Oviatt and McDougall, 1994). Empirical evidence has shown that despite lacking resources and experience, young entrepreneurial firms have the capability to internationalize proactively and rapidly (Rialp et al., 2005). Building on this line of research, Autio, Sapienza and Almeida (2000) introduce the concept of "learning advantages of newness" (LAN) as a theoretical foundation to explain the success of new venture internationalization.

The main premise underlying the LAN concept is that young firms suffer less from the organizational inertia that develops in their home market, thus they enjoy internal flexibilities that facilitate their ability to learn from international endeavors. However, given that early internationalizing firms are typically associated with deficits in terms of their adsorptive capacity for organizational learning (Zahra and George, 2002), and liabilities of newness and foreignness (Henderson, 1999; Zaheer, 1995), much remains relatively unexplored, particularly with regard to the question of how it is possible for young entrepreneurial firms to venture into foreign markets almost immediately from their inception and achieve learning advantages and subsequent success from early internationalization (Zahra, 2005).

Researchers have begun to explicate the idea of LAN and deepen their theorizing regarding its origin and nature (e.g., Carr et al., 2010; Sapienza et al., 2006; Zahra et al., 2006; Zhou et al., 2010). Such research has significantly advanced knowledge of the role that learning plays in young international firms by focusing on the firms' ability to exploit existing resources and capabilities to absorb new knowledge from foreign markets. From an organizational learning perspective, gains made through the exploitation of existing capabilities for new knowledge much depend on the proximity between a firm's existing knowledge base and its external knowledge domain (Zahra and George, 2002). Further, learning through exploitation has often resulted in a tendency for firms to get locked out of certain types of knowledge, to the extent that they never manage to acquire it early on (Hannan, 1998).

Without an adequate knowledge base or some degree of familiarization with new foreign markets, young international ventures may find it necessary to acquire learning advantages by engaging in exploration activities (Zahra, 2005). Exploring new knowledge bases and upgrading capabilities are thus instrumental to a firm's ability to learn about the challenges and opportunities that reside in international markets (Autio et al., 2000; Sapienza et al., 2006; Zhou et al., 2010). In turn, it is particularly important for young international firms not only to proactively access and deploy external resources but also to turn these into new skills and capabilities.

This study seeks to advance the theoretical argument pertaining to LAN by focusing on network dynamics and the upgrading of learning advantages in early and rapid internationalization. Drawing on network dynamics, Coviello (2006) explains the importance and significance of networks, particularly in the very early stages of new venture internationalization, and how they may evolve over time. Her conceptualization emphasizes the process nature of network relationships (i.e., dynamic rather than static) to accommodate the network theory of internationalization developed in the past.

Other scholars also recognize the importance of network dynamics specifically pertaining to international new ventures (INVs) in overcoming the liabilities of newness and foreignness generated by early internationalization (e.g., Arenius, 2002; Andersson and Wictor, 2003; Sharma and Blomstermo, 2003; Autio, 2005; Coviello and Cox, 2006; Elango and Pattnaik, 2007). In addition to the literature on the network approach in internationalization (e.g., Coviello and Munro, 1997; Ellis and Pecotich, 2001; Zain and Ng, 2006), research on network dynamics in the context of new venture internationalization places a greater emphasis on the network characteristics and patterns of resource changes over time (Coviello and Cox, 2006).

In turn, this study builds on the network dynamics perspective to examine the changing nature of network type with respect to young entrepreneurial firms' strategic mobilization of resources and the upgrading of new knowledge in absorbing the capacity to achieve learning advantages from early internationalization. The aim is to reveal how young entrepreneurial firms mobilize and upgrade their network resources for LAN. The mechanisms underlying LAN are not entirely obvious through causal reflection but rather are more associated with exploratory learning through network dynamics. The premise of LAN is that when a firm internationalizes earlier, it is less constrained by any established routines and operations and thus can learn more effectively from international activities (Autio et al., 2000; Carr et al., 2010). That causal reasoning is extended in this study by focusing on entrepreneurial action and network dynamics as a "positional advantage" pertaining to the LAN argument.

This notion is investigated using 11 case studies – an approach that not only reflects on the need to acquire greater insights into the entrepreneurial process of resource mobilization (Coviello and Cox, 2006) but also responds to the call for more qualitative research in the field of new venture internationalization (Rialp et al., 2005). Further, this study is built by drawing on a sample of young international firms in China. The focus on young and entrepreneurial Chinese firms is partially due to the accessibility of such links through well-established research connections in the market, but more importantly it is due to the pivotal role played by the internationalization of emerging market firms (EMFs), which provides a more complete framework for new venture internationalization (Mathews, 2006; Yamakawa et al., 2008). In a review of studies on the internationalization of EMFs, Gaur and Kumar (2010) highlight several unique aspects of EMFs, including their networking skills and connections, which they found were particularly useful in helping such firms to expand into foreign markets.

As the world's largest emerging economy, China clearly presents a marketplace of significant interest and has attracted a considerable amount of academic and practitioner discourse in recent years. In particular, a number of international business scholars have examined the internationalization process in the context of China. Their findings suggest that network linkages, both business connections and social ties, are instrumental and play a very significant role with respect to initiating foreign market entry or international entry decisions, such as foreign direct investment (FDI) location choice (e.g., Chen and Chen, 1998; Child, Ng and Wong, 2002; Qiu, 2005; Wong and Ellis, 2002). While the pertinent literature provides i) an empirical understanding of initial firm internationalization, particularly in high-tech industries, and ii) greater knowledge relating to the significance of networks in successful foreign market entry decisions by Chinese firms, relatively less has been concluded regarding young firms' network dynamics and upgrading within the general domain of IE research. The LAN, in particular, also have yet to be addressed. This study offers an empirical examination of the network dynamics and upgrading of young internationalizing firms in escalating learning advantages and provides readers with a greater understanding of new venture internationalization from the context of China, while offering additional insights into the theoretical development of IE research from an emerging market perspective.

## Theoretical background

### Learning Advantages of Newness

LAN have been described as a unique feature of new venture internationalization (Autio et al., 2000; Sapienza et al., 2006). This notion suggests that the earlier firms internationalize, the more effective they are in developing new knowledge from their foreign activities. Autio et al. (2000) explained that young firms typically have not established rigid organizational structures and routines, thus they tend to have certain structural, cognitive and relational organizational characteristics that allow them to benefit from LAN.

Sapienza et al. (2006) further substantiates the LAN argument by providing additional commentary on these three characteristics. In terms of the structural advantage, compared with older firms, newly established ventures tend to have fewer established routines and fewer internal constraints, and can often more easily detect new international market opportunities. With respect to the cognitive advantage, new ventures face fewer competency traps than more established businesses and are not generally isolated from certain types of knowledge. Due to such cognitive advantages, new ventures are apt to learn quickly and view international territories in an open-minded manner.

As for relational advantages, new ventures generally have relatively fewer bonded ties with domestic partners. As a result, they often face less resistance in developing relationships overseas as they are not overdependent on having to serve the domestic market. The relational aspect thus provides a unique "positional advantage" that enables young internationalizing firms to be more flexible than established firms – allowing them to undertake new initiatives without any impeding obstacles arising from domestic business partners by way of formal contracts, moral obligation or informal agreements (Sapienza et al., 2006). Given that the LAN concept points to the reduced effect of organizational routines and historic dependence on young firms acquiring new knowledge in international markets, it implies that early internationalizing firms will systematically enjoy learning advantages (Zahra, 2005). As LAN is somewhat contrary to other established concepts, such as experiential learning (Levitt and March, 1988) and absorptive capacity (Cohen and Levinthal, 1990; Zahra and George, 2002), one might expect young firms to require time-based learning experience to acquire the capacity necessary to absorb and integrate diverse knowledge bases for developing new internationalization capabilities (Johanson and Vahlne, 1990). Likewise, the international initiation process typically exposes firms to unfamiliar market environments with potentially more risk. This may pose serious threats, particularly in relation to liabilities of newness or foreignness, and can impede the internationalization process when initiated at an early stage in a firm's life cycle (Hymer, 1976; Zaheer, 1995).

In response, some scholars stress the significance of entrepreneurial activities directed at learning from international markets. De Clercq et al. (2005), for example, suggest that an entrepreneurial orientation drives the international learning effort in young firms. Knight and Cavusgil (2004) show that young internationalizing firms can improve their learning ability in foreign markets through successfully leveraging their product-market strategies and by having a strategic orientation (international entrepreneurial and market orientations).

Jones and Coviello (2005) develop an entrepreneurial process behavior framework for describing how young firms are better positioned to recognize opportunities and acquire knowledge by acting proactively in international territories. Finally, building on the entrepreneurial process of new venture internationalization, Zhou (2007) demonstrates the crucial role of international entrepreneurial proclivity, defined as an organization's predisposition to accept entrepreneurial processes, practices and decision-making ( Matsuno et al., 2002) in facilitating learning advantages at a rapid pace among young internationalizing firms.

Sapienza et al. (2006), however, maintain that the learning advantages of early internationalization may be contingent on the founders' or entrepreneurs' managerial experience, and the fungibility of firm resources. In their view, LAN can offset newness and foreignness when a venture has the organizational capability to absorb new knowledge from its international activities. In turn, Zhou et al. (2010) highlight the significance of an entrepreneurship-driven capability-upgrading mechanism pertaining to the learning benefits of early internationalization. The theoretical framework presented by Mathews and Zander (2007) clearly emphasizes the dynamic nature of entrepreneurial actions for driving new ventures, discovering growth opportunities and rapidly learning from international operations.

In short, within the context of new venture internationalization, the nature and outcome of LAN has emerged as a subject of heightened scholarly IE enquiry. This line of research emphasizes the notion of entrepreneurial process learning (Oviatt and McDougall, 2005; Zahra, 2005) and the dynamics of entrepreneurial behavior (Shane and Venkataraman, 2000; Zahra et al., 2006) in facilitating and enhancing LAN through early internationalization. The theoretical arguments surrounding the network dynamics related to new venture internationalization are reviewed next, and a perspective is given on those network dynamics as a source of entrepreneurial process learning driven by the "positional advantages" that young firms have in going international (Autio et al., 2000; Sapienza et al., 2006).

### Network dynamics as a source of learning advantage

Relationship networks are generally regarded as firm-specific resources that can help to leverage new and small firms into internationalizing (Coviello and Munro, 1995; Zain and Ng, 2006). A growing body of literature is examining the influence of relationship networks or social ties on firm internationalization (see Harris and Wheeler, 2005; Qiu, 2005). For example, a variety of network resources including information, knowledge and connections have been found to play significant roles in a firm's internationalization process. Specifically, the literature suggests that relationship networks can be useful in assisting with export initiation (Ellis and Pecotich, 2001), identifying international opportunities (Ellis, 2000), assessing location choice (Chen and Chen, 1998) and providing learning mechanisms in international markets (Johanson and Vahlne, 2003).

The need for a greater understanding of the network approach, specific to new venture internationalization, has been acknowledged in the IE literature (e.g., Andersson and Wictor, 2003; Sharma and Blomstermo, 2003; Coviello, 2006; Coviello and Cox, 2006; Yiu et al., 2007; Zhou et al., 2007). A key consideration in this line of research is understanding how networks enable new ventures to acquire and mobilize resources and develop capabilities for early and rapid internationalization. Insights from the literature suggest that networks are dynamic resources that can be leveraged to access social capital through resource acquisition.

Given firms' resource-based view (RBV) and research on entrepreneurship and strategic management, Coviello and her colleague (Coviello, 2006; Coviello and Cox, 2006) suggest a network dynamics perspective for understanding new venture internationalization that considers networks of INVs to be process-based, shifting their structural and interactional patterns as the new venture evolves through the various stages of internationalization. They maintain that the network constitutes a dynamic resource base, through which the young venture acquires stock and an ongoing flow of social capital for achieving a competitive position in early international expansion.

Coviello (2006) shows that during the course of a new venture's international development in technology-oriented firms, several changing characteristics, such as size (the number of ties), density (the proportion of ties that are interconnected) and the dominant nature of economic or business ties involved in network interactions, are associated with network structures. This suggests that network dynamics reflect an increase in social capital pertaining to new venture internationalization. Related to these findings and building on this case evidence, Coviello and Cox (2006) investigate network dynamics in terms of the type of resources (human and financial capital) that are transferred to international ventures, and the nature of the resource flow, including resource acquisition and mobilization. Their findings particularly highlighted the significance of organizational capital, such as technology know-how and the flow of resource mobilization, in the early stages of new venture development. Specifically, this research suggests that without owning network resources, young internationalizing firms can embrace the strategic value of network dynamics for international expansion.

While the network dynamics perspective and the empirical evidence presented have provided a fundamental understanding of how the evolution of networks per se might be related to the various developmental stages of new venture internationalization, this perspective is extended here through an investigation into the entrepreneurial process of learning via network dynamics. Taking the view of new venture internationalization as an entrepreneurial dynamic of learning (Mathews and Zander, 2007), this study posits that by mobilizing and upgrading different types of network resources at the very early stages of internationalization, an entrepreneurial firm is not only able to acquire social capital but more importantly can develop the capacity to embrace the LAN.

Young international ventures' learning advantages through network dynamics do not seem to have been fully addressed in the literature. As previously explained, due to their structural, cognitive and positional advantages (Sapienza et al., 2006), young international ventures should have greater flexibility compared with established firms. Thus they are able to take bold steps to acquire, mobilize and configure their business and social networks to achieve learning advantages from early internationalization.

## Research context and approach

### Internationalization of EMFs

This study focuses on the internationalization of EMFs. Such internationalization is receiving increased research attention due to its pivotal role in the development of a new framework specific to these firms (Child and Rodrigues, 2005; Elango and Pattnaik, 2007; Luo and Tung, 2007). In their review of major studies on the internationalization of EMFs, Gaur and Kumar (2010) draw a conclusion that mirrors the theoretical arguments advanced by Mathews and Zander (2007), confirming that the internationalization process of EMFs is not only different from that of firms from developed economies but also varies within different emerging economies. Of particular relevance to the phenomenon of INVs, Yamakawa et al. (2008) point out the need to expand theoretical approaches that consider the unique aspects of the "accelerated internationalization" of EMFs.

According to Gaur and Kumar (2010), some of the distinctive aspects associated with EMF internationalization include their motivation, the international pathways followed, business processes and performance. EMFs' ability to go abroad, despite their often weak resource constraints and lack of foreign knowledge and experience, is considered an interesting departure from the major internationalization theories in the literature (Dunning, 1980, 2006; Johanson and Vahlne, 1977, 1993). In what they describe as a "springboard perspective" of internationalization, Luo and Tung (2007) argue that large EMFs can overcome latecomer disadvantages in internationalization by aggressively acquiring assets from multinationals in developed economies.

Mathews (2006) maintains that the rapid internationalization that some EMFs have achieved can be attributable to entrepreneurial actions through network-based learning – described as a "linkage-leverage-learning" perspective. Thus taking advantage of their networking skills and connections and combining them with production know-how, technological assets and transferable capabilities obtained through operating in emerging domestic markets, EMFs seem to be able to develop the unique capabilities needed to successfully enter other similar emerging economies (Elango and Pattnaik, 2007; Sol and Kogan, 2007; Yiu et al., 2007; Young et al., 1996; Zhou et al., 2007).

Although the literature has identified the role of networks as a unique and distinguishing aspect of EMF internationalization, the dynamic features of networking and network linkages have yet to be fully developed in relation to the accelerated or rapid internationalization of EMFs, particularly among smaller and younger international ventures. This research expands the literature by aiming to bridge this gap.

### Description of research approach

This research focused on the entrepreneurial processes of young international firms learning through network dynamics. A case study approach was considered most appropriate for investigating how the various network types evolve over time. The selected approach reflects the call for more qualitative research on new venture internationalization (Rialp et al., 2005), and for the development of new IE theory using network dynamics and learning as a theoretical foundation (Coviello, 2006; Keupp and Gassmann, 2009). Given the complexity of international markets and the changing dynamics associated with young firms' international expansion plans, research of a qualitative nature may prove useful (Jones and Coviello, 2005; Mathews and Zander, 2007). In particular, it is believed that an in-depth analysis through case-study investigations will probe deeper and gain additional insights into "how" and "why" such early and rapid internationalization issues emerge (Yin, 1989; Keupp and Gassmann, 2009).

Specifically, this study provide insights into the process of how young entrepreneurial firms from China mobilize and leverage a range of different networks (i.e., domestic agents, overseas Chinese merchants, international distributors, etc.) in driving their learning advantages to enable early and rapid internationalization. While INVs may experience a lack of resources in their domestic markets, their network dynamics can act as a substitute for such resources and provide learning opportunities in international territories.

The work reported here was undertaken in two major cities within Zhejiang province in southeastern China – Wenzhou and

Hangzhou – where private entrepreneurial small and medium-sized enterprises (SMEs) have prospered in recent years. Zhejiang is located to the south of the Yangtze Delta region along the southeastern coastline, and is one of the most economically developed regions in the country. In recent years its foreign trade has developed rapidly and the value of the region's international trade ranks among the top four in China, despite a shortage of land and natural resources (Zhejiang Statistics Bureau, 2007).

Traditionally, due to limited land space in the province, family members in Zhejiang were not solely engaged in agricultural farming and many were occupied with household crafts. Even under China's former planned economy, craftsmen from Zhejiang could be found all over the country. After China's economic reform, family-based entrepreneurial firms in Zhejiang began to grow rapidly. Wenzhou has been widely considered the root of private businesses in Zhejiang, whereas Hangzhou is the capital city of the province. As such, these two cities provide an ideal focus for the study as they are home to an abundance of thriving internationally oriented SMEs.

The fieldwork was undertaken during late 2007 and early 2008, and was restricted to the study of private, predominantly small and medium-sized INVs from the Zhejiang region of China. Given the primary focus on small and young internationalizing firms, the first task was to conduct a baseline information search of local sources, such as newspapers, periodicals and government agencies featuring entrepreneurs and their businesses. From there, potential cases involving internationalization activities, such as exporting, were identified and well-established local contacts (in local government and two of the region's universities) further helped in collating additional first-hand information to verify both the feasibility and the suitability of the cases chosen from secondary information sources.

This led to the withdrawal of several cases that were either not feasible or not suitable to participate in the study due to a lack of INV status. This study adopts a broader definition when considering a firm as an INV (i.e., up to six years from inception to generate international sales orders (Fan and Phan, 2007; Zahra et al., 2000)). There tends to be no clear consensus in the literature on defining INVs using the timespan between foundation and the beginning of their international activities. It can range from two (Moen and Servais, 2002) to eight (McDougall et al., 1994) years.

The selection criteria thus fall within the range of previous studies. In addition, only firms that were established post-1990 were sampled. This represented an economic period in China when young entrepreneurial firms flourished and export-driven businesses were encouraged via governmental policies. Other criteria, such as the percentage of international sales to firms' total sales at first internationalization or the geographic scope of international operations are not included because the intention was to focus on young international firms with various scales of international operations. Among the qualified cases, 11 founding entrepreneurs or senior managers were successfully interviewed and, on average, two hours was spent with each of them. All of the firms in the sample were privately run and located in either Wenzhou or Hangzhou.

The vast majority of the sampled firms were founded during the 1990s and employed between 60 and 300 staff members. They operated in a range of industrial sectors, including the production of textiles and clothing, leather goods, footwear, pearls, packaging and hardware. Exporting represented their primary mode of international activity, and international sales growth ranged between 15% and 70% in the three years preceding the research. The Appendix provides an overview of the demographic profile for the firms sampled in this study. To protect their identity, pseudonyms have been used for the illustrative purposes of this research.

As previously highlighted and in light of the exploratory nature of the investigation, in-company personal interviews with key respondents served as the principal research method adopted in this study. As with similar research in the area (Coviello and Munho, 1997; Ellis and Pecotich, 2001), multiple case studies were identified to provide a more optimum approach than a survey for collecting data relating to the rapid internationalization process among young entrepreneurial firms. The idea was that case studies can generate sensitive, confidential or sequential data, which might not otherwise be obtained (Coviello, 2006).

Before meeting the firms, a trail of evidence relating to each company was sought from various sources (i.e., local newspapers, periodicals, governmental agencies, etc.). The local government and university contacts in the region further helped in collating additional first-hand information. Moreover, during company visits and in line with Yin's (1989) suggestions for obtaining construct validity and convergence, further evidence was also requested and obtained during each interview. In some instances, repeat contacts with the entrepreneurial founders and managers were initiated in various social contexts to verify the evidence obtained during each interview, and to gain further insight into sensitive and context-specific issues. This provided rich data supporting the in-depth interviews exploring the evolution of networks during early and rapid internationalization.

To strengthen the associated reliability of the research, a file on each company case was created to store the chain of evidence. The files contained the entire literature collated from each company, the transcripts of the interviews and any other artifacts. The chain of evidence provided a useful practical solution as an audit trail to enable other researchers or auditors access, should it be needed in the future (Yin, 1994). Rather than focusing on network characteristics, or resource dynamics by stage of firm evolution (Coviello, 2006; Coviello and Cox, 2006), the data file contained evidence relating to the changing pattern of network type during the early stages of firm internationalization.

Next, the case studies are presented, with a focus on how young entrepreneurial firms develop their learning capacity by mobilizing and upgrading various network and linkage types in the early stages of internationalization.

## Case analyses and results

As evidence was sought from INVs using a multicase approach, the analysis of the dynamic nature of network type is presented on an across-case basis (Yin, 1989). The entrepreneurial process of learning through the evolution of network type from the home environment to international markets was explored, paving the way for new theories explaining early and rapid internationalization.

### Experiential learning acquisition

According to this study, the most common way for small and young INVs to engage in exporting business was to work with domestic agents, especially state-owned professional trade companies. At the initial stage of internationalization, the destinations for their export orders were primarily in other developing or geographically close countries, including Thailand, Korea, Taiwan and Russia. Mr Huang, the general manager of H.T. Leather Goods, described the initial export business:

> Because of our limited knowledge and experience with international markets, the main way for our company to acquire international market information is through a state-operated foreign trade company.

By taking advantage of the experience of state-operated foreign trade companies, this firm quickly expanded its products into international markets. In particular, regarding its initial overseas order, it was noted that the first consignment of export goods was achieved largely through the help of a provincial state-operated foreign trade organization that exhibited the company's products at the China Export Commodities Fair. There it began to establish contacts with overseas buyers from Thailand and other developing countries.

The case of Shu Fu Hardware Co. was similar. The founding entrepreneur, Mr Chang, explained that the first overseas sale was initiated shortly after inception. Prior to establishing his company, the entrepreneur foresaw potential opportunities in overseas markets, particularly in other emerging countries, and purposely prepared to target markets outside China. However, due to a lack of international exposure and experience, he was introduced to a large trading merchant in northeastern China through his local contacts. The merchant used his contacts in Russia to test-market the supplier's hardware tools. He quickly discovered that the Russians wanted to countertrade and he told us that "the result of the test marketing was delightful, from which we developed more confidence and desire to deepen our international expansion."

Obviously, the key to such enterprises with initial foreign market entry was to obtain help from agencies and obtain foreign market information. For example, the knowledge associated with the trade merchants at the frontier of northeastern China regarding the Russian market (general acquaintance with transportation, familiarity with the foreign language and negotiation), or acquiring information from people in resourceful positions (i.e., from state-operated foreign trade companies attending international trade fairs), initially proved to be critical.

During this investigation, evidence was also found that suggested that some overseas Chinese merchants undertook similar roles. For example, the general manager of a company operating in the textile industry recalled the conditions of the company's first export order in 2004:

> Before this period, our company sold textile fabrics in the domestic market through China Light Textile City in Shaoxing [a local city]. During this period, only a fraction of our products was exported to overseas markets via a local trading company. But after 2004, surplus domestic production capacity led to weak market conditions in China, so our company became more proactively involved with foreign markets. At the China Export Commodities Fair of 2004, our company's first overseas transaction was with an overseas Chinese

merchant based in Thailand. Since then we have found that overseas Chinese merchants act as a "window" or a "gateway" for our learning of foreign customers and competition.

Other senior manager respondents in various SMEs also expressed the facilitating and learning functions that overseas merchants have played in their early international activities. One manager emphasized:

> A big advantage of undertaking foreign trade by partnering with overseas Chinese is that there tends not to be any cultural barriers as such. Both parties can communicate easily and get to know each other quickly – therefore the transaction costs are much lower.

Taken together, the case evidence suggests that the engagement of early internationalization provided the founding entrepreneurs or senior managers with unique opportunities to proactively gain "experiential learning" from either domestic or overseas Chinese trading agencies. This seems to contrast with the incremental learning approach observed in the traditional stage models of internationalization. By securing initial international orders from countries in close geographical proximity through either home-based business networks or overseas ethnic merchants, early internationalizing firms developed confidence and a higher tolerance for risk, and were able to seek out opportunities to gain experiential learning. This initial pattern of network linkages may reflect on the idea that a lack of experience in international operations and the liability of foreignness from a developing country led Chinese entrepreneurs to initiate their international activity indirectly through professional trade agencies at home and abroad.

### Industrial clusters as a knowledge base

Industrial clusters are specialized manufacturing groups that are concentrated in specific geographical areas throughout China. Zhejiang is the home of more than 500 such clusters, ranging from the production of garments in Ningbo to leather shoes in Wenzhou, other leather goods in Haining, pearls in Zhuji and hardware in Yongkang. Research suggests that enterprises can benefit from industrial clusters not only in terms of their production efficiency but also due to being better positioned to respond more rapidly to changes in the external business environment (Zhang et al., 2004). The "clustering effect" enables firms to collaborate with one another on joint market-screening activities, to better regulate and attain desired product quality standards, to share the innovation costs associated with developing new products and to significantly raise brand profile and credibility (Cai, 2002).

While industrial clusters may vary in terms of such benefits, little evidence has been concluded from the literature concerning their effect on internationalization activities among enterprises. In this study, industrial clusters were found to strengthen both cooperation and competition among enterprises. They represent a knowledge resource that firms can use to obtain access to numerous network relationships, which can potentially contribute to the development of new technologies and markets to enhance international performance.

Mr Tong from T. P. Optical Co. explained why he felt that such industrial clusters can be particularly useful for relatively smaller firms in facilitating overseas sales:

> Our enterprise is one of many small firms in the region and we benefit from the larger companies that operate in our regional cluster. Through observing their rapid growth in overseas markets, they have motivated us to quickly establish an international identity and we were able to learn from their actions.

Through various connections between the larger, more established companies and their foreign clients, smaller firms like T. P. Optical can recognize and capitalize on benefits through the international exposure that such large companies bring to the region. Having an international identity and recognition associated with an industrial cluster therefore enables entrepreneurial firms to become more proactive and confident in their approach to international trade.

The research findings also reveal that industrial clusters help to promote young and small firm internationalization activity through original equipment manufacturing (OEM). While OEM remains popular among SMEs in China, most manufacturers tend to operate in a passive fashion by serving as production units for larger domestic companies that receive export orders. In contrast, the research suggests that owing to a favorable reputation and their economies of scale, industry clusters seem to be able to attract visits from foreign companies, which enables local firms to establish direct business relationships via such OEM operations.

Through their interactions with foreign companies, some entrepreneurial OEM firms are able to build "absorptive capacity" (Cohen and Levinthal, 1990) that can be leveraged to enhance their international learning effort (Sapienza et al., 2005). Therefore, even in the absence of entering foreign markets, Chinese OEM suppliers can still build their knowledge base and upgrade their capabilities to increase learning advantages for internationalization. The following statement from Mr Yang of Yulong Garment Inc. reflects this observation:

> I started our business as an OEM supplier for a large garment company based in Zhejiang. After just one year in operation, I had the opportunity to make branded clothing [also OEM] for a Hong Kong based apparel company. Soon after I realized that we would be better off if we could establish our own brands in foreign markets. Gladly we later successfully entered Russia and several South American markets with our own branded products.

During the period of this investigation, Mr Yang's company operated at two distinct business levels. The first involved supplying OEM at the high end of the market, and the second involved exporting mid-range-level branded garments directly. In general, although respondents had different views and opinions about the potential benefits of industrial clusters, most agreed that such specialized industrial groups can provide useful insights into the opportunities arising from the transmission of information and knowledge through both formal business ties and social interactions. The evidence suggests that some entrepreneurial firms can build on home-based learning advantages – particularly through OEM operations for early and rapid internationalization.

### Influence of international experience

The extent to which entrepreneurs' international experience influences learning advantages in early internationalization has been discussed in the IE literature (Sapienza et al., 2006; Zahra et al., 2006). Some researchers have argued that entrepreneurs may have international experience prior to establishing their business, and this serves as a knowledge base to facilitate learning in early internationalization (e.g., Zucchella et al., 2007). In contrast with the literature, we found that most entrepreneurs or senior managers in the sample had a lack of foreign market knowledge and international experience initially. However, they quickly acquired such knowledge through their early contact with trading agencies.

An interesting pattern emerged as the function of the domestic agent changed gradually after such enterprises realized their full international potential. While domestic agents proved useful in the initial stage of internationalization, none of the firms in the sample maintained working relationships with such parties. Instead, most firms had established their own export department that took responsibility for international sales. One reason for this phenomenon was the change in governmental regulations allowing SMEs new legal rights to develop and manage their own international business affairs. Likewise, such firms had gained vital experience from operating in foreign markets and developed an appetite for absorbing foreign market knowledge and upgrading their foreign language abilities, negotiation skills and understanding of cultural trade styles and international marketing.

For example, the chairman of Hangzhou Jiewei Handicrafts had a vision of recruiting employees with the experience, skills and ability to successfully manage the firm's international markets. Many entrepreneurs work relentlessly to learn at least one foreign language (usually English), and receive export training by attending many courses in their spare time, hosted by the local government and specific industrial trade associations. Several of the entrepreneurs studied registered in executive MBA programs, rendering the classroom an important platform for learning more and broadening one's knowledge base in addition to establishing further social contacts with like-minded individuals.

As more international knowledge was acquired and absorbed within the firms, the domestic agents tended to play a less prevalent role in most exporting channels. Only the China South East Textile Company and the Zhejiang Pearl Co. retained some domestic agents. The former claimed:

> Many foreign wholesalers are accustomed to contacting China's foreign trade companies to save costs in searching for suppliers directly. Such foreign wholesalers realize that foreign trading companies operating in China have access to many companies and products, thus they save much time and effort.

It may also relate to credibility, as the latter added: "Because foreign trade companies have a long professional history, I think they are perceived as being more trustworthy among foreign clients." The two firms shared similar views and felt that it was feasible to establish successful relationships with foreign wholesalers by acquiring information and working alongside foreign trading companies in China.

In addition to the role of domestic trading agents, the function of overseas Chinese merchants has also weakened somewhat, despite the fact that they remain key players in some of the enterprises studied. Mr Yu, the senior manager of Yulong Garment Inc., commented:

> Whilst in the very early days of our company's export business we depended heavily on overseas Chinese merchants and current export orders from overseas Chinese merchants occupy only about 10%, whereas the other 90% comes from local agents and distributors.

The general manager of Liangwen Footwear Co. remarked:

> For us, overseas Chinese merchants provide a solid platform as they continue to knock on doors and provide a gateway for generating new business. When a firm wishes to consider a new foreign market, it always asks whether it has friends in the local market, or potentially friends of friends. From our experience, if such people are found, they often prove useful for introducing our firm to other friends and assisting us in finding trade partners. Whilst such friends do not become business partners, a long-term friendship can be easily established, and when such friends visit our city, we always try our best to accompany them and provide business assistance where possible.

The export manager of Y. Tee Package Co. further commented:

> Overseas Wenzhou people mostly act as a gateway during the early stage when exploring new markets. The function of many people from north east China living in Russia is the same. Cooperation usually begins by establishing a foreign distributor relationship with the aim of expanding into the international market and fulfilling mutual rewards.

However, the facilitating function of overseas Chinese merchants appears to weaken as the extent of firm internationalization deepens. The general manager of China South East Textile Company explained:

> The rapid growth of our company and demand for our products from overseas places a burden on the Chinese merchants who do not have sufficient capacity to manage our entire foreign market sales... Many overseas Chinese merchants are not particularly trustworthy, as they cannot always be relied upon when supplying goods on credit.

Mr. Tong, the general manager of T. P. Optical Co., experienced similar problems:

> Compared with major foreign buyers, some overseas Chinese merchants have a poor credit history. Therefore, once our company has established a good working relationship with a foreign buyer, the function of overseas Chinese merchants becomes less prevalent and is weakened step by step.

These findings provide interesting insights of both a corroboratory and a contrasting nature. On the one hand, there is evidence to suggest that merchants of Chinese ethnic origin are to some extent responsible for the initiation of international activities among the Chinese INVs – advocating the significance of familiarity and trust in initiating affairs in the Chinese culture (Child and Möllering, 2003; Yen et al., 2007). On the other hand, and as a result of INV experience, it appears that merchants may not always be trustworthy (i.e., there is evidence that they cannot be relied on when they have goods supplied on credit). This contradicts most of the research relating to the evolution of buyer–seller relations (Ford, 1980; Dwyer et al., 1987) and suggests a dark side to relationships in which the business fails to progress in an incremental linear trajectory (Grayson and Ambler, 1999; Barnes, 2005).

It is also apparent that because merchants play a third-party role in promoting business on behalf of their principals, they are likely to be evaluated at different intervals by INVs. While they serve a purpose in facilitating early international activities and provide a stepping stone to the international marketplace, it appears that they are not able to meet the requirements and aspirations of the Chinese INVs attempting to penetrate international markets at a rapid pace. At this stage there is evidence of a "shake-up" taking place, whereby the Chinese INVs mobilize their resources and networks to focus more on motivating their international channel intermediaries to seize opportunities in international markets. In sharp contrast, Wenzhou H. R. Electronic Security Products Co. did not share this experience. Instead, the firm preferred a more direct approach to managing distribution operations. As a result, it decided to open a sales subsidiary in Europe to manage established relations with its network of distributors in the EU, which has subsequently weakened the function of overseas Chinese merchants.

In brief, the findings suggest that as firms' international experience increases, there is a movement away from engaging both domestic and overseas Chinese parties and toward developing business relationships with foreign intermediaries. This pattern of network change seems to reflect the fact that Chinese entrepreneurs strategically mobilize external sources of expertise and knowledge at a rapid pace during the course of early internationalization. While firms with international aspirations would traditionally look to first export and then engage in more committed modes of internationalization, here we demonstrate that young international Chinese entrepreneurs appear to be engaging in network interactions to develop "absorptive capacity" very early in the internationalization process.

## Discussion, implications and conclusion

Based on a review of the pertinent literature and in providing suggestions for developing the field of IE research, Keupp and Gassmann (2009) identified several knowledge gaps, one of which relates to a lack in understanding of how the process of entrepreneurially driven internationalization evolves. These scholars specifically highlighted the fact that there appears to be no clear theoretical understanding of the initial stages of early and rapid internationalization to explain why new venture internationalization is possible. In an effort to address the knowledge gap, scholars have attempted to analyze a firm's entrepreneurial dynamics of resource-acquisition behavior (Mathews and Zander, 2007), and the evolution of network structure and resource flows (Coviello, 2006; Coviello and Cox, 2006).

This study contributes further to this line of enquiry by highlighting the entrepreneurial process of learning through network dynamics. In this approach, network dynamics are considered to be interactive sources of knowledge and a resource base for enabling young entrepreneurial firms to develop capabilities in the early stages of internationalization. In contrast with the RBV of network evolution (Coviello and Cox, 2006), the investigation captures the linkage-leverage-learning process (Mathews, 2006), particularly as it pertains to the rapid development of the absorptive capability of achieving learning advantages from early and rapid internationalization.

The aim of this study was to explain how INVs mobilize and upgrade their network resources to achieve the LAN at a fast pace. We found significant evidence that resource scarcity can be a driver of, rather than an obstacle to, early and rapid internationalization (Mathews and Zander, 2007). Although the use of network resources may not be a feature that distinguishes INVs from those that follow more traditional internationalization pathways (Antonio Dib et al., 2010), their networking skills and network dynamics appear to more closely characterize the process of new venture internationalization. An important insight obtained from this research is that young entrepreneurial Chinese ventures build on the dynamics of networks by engaging a combination of domestic agents, overseas Chinese merchants and international distributors to develop the absorptive capacity needed for early and rapid internationalization.

In contrast with the important role of social relationships in facilitating international exposure or entry into foreign markets among small Chinese exporters (Ellis, 2000; Ellis and Pecotich, 2001), a tendency among the sample of INVs was found to leverage economic or business linkages with external parties. Domestic foreign-trade agencies or overseas ethnic merchants seemed to be a preferred choice early on in the internationalization process. Such network sources are considered to serve as an appropriate base for mitigating the liabilities of newness and foreignness associated with INVs, and at the same time increasing their risk tolerance for early and rapid internationalization.

The case analysis helps to demonstrate the connection between inward and outward internationalization (Welch and Luostarinen, 1993). In the early stages of China's catch-up economy, most Chinese firms sought to gain strategic assets from multinationals based in industrialized countries through different forms of FDI, including OEM or technology licensing. The phrase "borrow ships to navigate abroad" suitably characterizes the leveraging of resources and capabilities from foreign firms. For example, the structure of OEM is regarded as a stepping stone to expand domestic products into international markets, as it enables Chinese enterprises to acquire international competence, learn international rules and build a reputation among foreign manufacturers by expanding their marketing channels to indirectly serve international markets (Child and Rodrigues, 2005; Lu, 2006).

Similarly and also indirectly, this study found that Chinese firms can relatively easily participate in industrial clusters within their domestic market to achieve learning advantages for internationalization. Industrial clusters can improve production efficiency, resource capabilities and innovation in international markets (Zhang et al., 2004). The clustering approach enables differentiation to occur through large-scale economies, sharing a cluster's advanced technologies, reputation and brand identity (Cai, 2002). Research has shown that activities associated with certain enterprises of a network cluster (involved in international activities) can positively enhance other firms. In brief, advantages emerged from home-based networks, through either OEM connections or industrial clusters, and these were all readily available for young entrepreneurial firms to connect with to speed up their internationalization process.

It is quite clear that the sample of INVs had the aspiration to develop organizational and strategic positions, which more than compensated for their lack of international experience. To a large extent, the early internationalization of the sample was focused and directed toward other emerging markets that were geographically close and represented locations where they could take the advantages accrued from operating in similar, harsh institutional market environments (Wright et al., 2005; Del Sol and Kogan, 2007). This is reflective of the changing nature of the INVs' network dynamics, as they embrace the legitimacy of their international presence to local idiosyncrasies – that is, from home-based relationships to overseas Chinese-based network connections and beyond.

Specifically, this study discovered a pattern of change in the types of network among INVs as they became more internationally experienced – a shift from using domestic and overseas Chinese agents to appointing foreign distributors. In the Chinese context, trusting outside parties tends to occur less frequently and at a slower pace (Child and Möllering, 2003; Huff and Kelley, 2005). Previous research suggests that interfirm relationship trust is more difficult to build when partners originate from diverse cultures and it takes a significant amount of time to accumulate, as the Chinese prefer to work with commercial counterparts with whom they are familiar (Zhang, Cavusgil and Roath, 2003; Yen et al., 2007). Establishing personalized trust is particularly important in Chinese relationships, and this is usually cultivated through networking (Davies et al., 1995). Hence the experience factor appears to explain the rationale behind why the INVs moved from their initial networks with parties of the same ethnic origin to explore other relationships outside when seeking international advantage.

In light of the theoretical background and the case insights offered in this study, it concludes by providing a conceptual model (Figure 6.1) as a guideline for future research. This suggests that learning from those networks of their own ethnic origin can often drive rapid international exposure, which in turn leads to the evolution of networks characterized by resource upgrading and international network leverage. As a result, INVs are able to improve their absorptive capacity for achieving LAN-related international performance. While the efficacy of networks in the internationalization process has been widely documented in the literature (e.g., Johanson and Vahlne, 1977, 1993), the model further captures

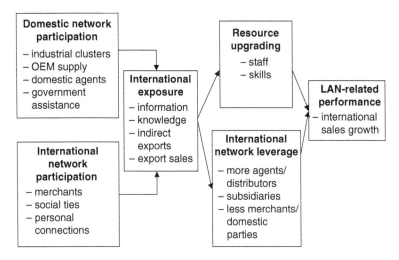

*Figure 6.1* The evolution of network connections as a source of learning advantages in early internationalization

the entrepreneurial process of learning through network dynamics in early and rapid internationalization. The network dynamics approach advocates that although young entrepreneurial firms may experience a lack of resources in early internationalization, it is the linkage, leverage and learning – in contrast with the knowledge and resource intensity – that attracts entrepreneurs and their new ventures into cross-border activities (Mathews, 2006; Luo, 2000). In doing so, such firms are able to upgrade their absorptive capacity and cultivate their learning advantages from early and rapid internationalization (Zahra, 2005).

This study fills a gap in the under-researched area of the literature surrounding the internationalization of EMFs (Yamakawa et al., 2008). Consistent with the position of Gaur and Kumar (2010), the research indicates that entrepreneurial action and networking skills that allow EMFs to operate in harsh domestic markets form their capacity when venturing into new international territories. Some EMFs have also taken advantage of their linkages with international players through OEM and the resource base of industrial clusters within their home markets to indirectly expand overseas at a rapid pace.

There are a number of limitations associated with this study. First, as INVs were selected based on foreign market success stories that were found in the local press and through some reliance on local contacts, there was the possibility of a self-selection bias in favor of high-performing firms. Arguably there could be further examples of internationalization among other young entrepreneurial firms in China. Despite this, the strategic use of network dynamics to upgrade learning advantages remains a distinguishing feature associated with EMF internationalization.

Second, as with any qualitative research, the findings cannot be generalized. In this respect they should therefore be open to further validation and serve as a foundation on which to build (Eisenhardt, 1989; Yin, 1989). The scope of the case analyses is preliminary in nature. However, this investigation provides a solid theoretical background by highlighting the theoretical perspectives relevant to the study. With regard to further advancing knowledge, the theoretical framework outlined provides a useful avenue for future research.

Third, the approach used in this study does not fully capture the complexity and key constructs regarding the nature of network dynamics, nor the nature of resource flows. While depending on a number of relational ties and measuring the flow of resources are arguably important for understanding network dynamics as an INV evolves, this approach may not be fully predictable in developing novel theories to guide empirical research on new venture internationalization (Coviello and Cox, 2006). By considering different types of network and their strategic positions for developing learning advantages in early internationalization, the findings provide fresh insights detailing a process perspective of entrepreneurial behavior (Mathews and Zander, 2007).

Finally, the INVs in the sample mostly took the form of exporting as their dominant mode of internationalization and, historically, EMFs have tended to focus on export-based strategies (Child and Rodriguez, 2005). Export-led growth from emerging markets such as China has also been reinforced via other forms of international market entry, including strategic alliances and FDI (Luo and Tung, 2007), particularly for larger multinationals. For most young entrepreneurial firms, exporting remains the optimum internationalization approach, and this is perhaps the reason why most studies in the IE research domain have focused on exporting as a proxy for internationalization (e.g., Autio et al., 2000; Knight and Cavusgil, 2004). Future research should therefore further investigate the network dynamics associated with other forms of internationalization and market-entry strategies in the context of new venture internationalization.

Although there are obvious geographical constraints that are also associated with the company cases used in this research, this study has attempted to provide a more comprehensive review of the relevant literature to set up a solid theoretical foundation for the knowledge base, seeking a better understanding of the network dynamics of learning within the context of accelerated EMF internationalization. Three aspects of the case analyses – industrial clusters serving as a knowledge base, experiential learning from trading agents and the influence of international experience – reflect on something that is rather distinct from other young international venturing firms based in more advanced economies. In this regard, this investigation adds to the theoretical development of new venture internationalization, with a particular focus on the internationalization of EMFs.

## Appendix

Demographic profile of the cases in the study

| Cases | Founding year | Location | No. of employees | Industry type/ business | Year at first internation-alization | International sales growth |
|---|---|---|---|---|---|---|
| 1. H.T. Leather Goods | 1994 | Wenzhou | 137 | leather goods | 1998 | 30% |
| 2. Shu Fu Hardware Co. | 1992 | Wenzhou | 86 | hardware tools | 1993 | 40% |
| 3. Taihao Texitle and Garment | 1995 | Hangzhou | 165 | textile | 2000 | 35% |
| 4. Hangzhou Jiewei Handicrafts | 1992 | Hangzhou | 110 | bamboo weaving handicrafts | 1993 | 70% |
| 5. China South East Textile Company | 2002 | Hangzhou | 105 | textiles | 2003 | 50% |
| 6. Zhejiang Pearl Co. | 1996 | Hangzhou | 120 | pearls | 1999 | 40% |
| 7. Yulong Garment Inc. | 1995 | Wenzhou | 90 | clothing | 1998 | 20% |
| 8. Liangwen Footwear Co. | 1998 | Wenzhou | 200 | footwear | 1999 | 25% |
| 9. Y.Tee Package Co. | 2000 | Wenzhou | 150 | plastic bags | 2002 | 60% |
| 10. Wenzhou H.R. Electronic Security Products Co. | 1993 | Wenzhou | 300 | door locks | 1998 | 15% |
| 11. T.P. Optical Co. | 1999 | Wenzhou | 60 | optical frames | 2002 | 40% |

## References

Andersson, S., and Wictor, I. (2003) Innovative internationalization in new firms: Born globals – the Swedish case. *Journal of International Entrepreneurship*, 1 (3): 249–276.

Antonio Dib, L., Da Rocha, A., and Da Silva, J. F. (2010) The internationalization process of Brazilian software firms and the born global phenomenon: Examining firm, network, and entrepreneur variables. *Journal of International Entrepreneurship*, 8: 233–253.

Arenius, P. M. (2002) *Creation of Firm-level Social Capital, Its Exploitation and the Process of Early Internationalization*. Helsinki University of Technology, Helsinki Finland.

Autio, E. (2005) Creative tension: The significance of Ben Oviatt's and Patricia McDougall's article "Toward a theory of international new ventures". *Journal of International Business Studies*, 36 (1): 9–19.

Autio, E., Sapienza, H. J., and Almeida, J. G. (2000) Effects of age at entry, knowledge intensity, and imitability on international growth. *Academy of Management Journal*, 43 (5): 909–924.

Barnes, B. R. (2005) Is the seven-year hitch premature in industrial markets? *European Journal of Marketing*, 39 (5/6): 560–581.

Cai, N. (2002) On enterprise clustering and the development of small and medium-sized enterprises' internationalization. *China Soft Science*, 5 (1), 54–56.

Carr, J. C., Haggard, K. S., Hmieleski, K. M., and Zahra, S. A. (2010) A study of the moderating effects of firm age at internationalization on firm survival and short-term growth. *Strategic Entrepreneurship Journal*, 4 (2): 183–192.

Chen, H., and Chen, T. J. (1998) Network linkages and location choice in foreign direct investment. *Journal of International Business Studies*, 29 (3): 445–468.

Child, J., Ng, S. H., and Wong, C. (2002) Psychic distance and internationalisation. *International Studies of Management and Organizations*, 32 (1): 36–56.

Child, J., and Möllering, G. (2003) Contextual confidence and active trust in the Chinese business environment. *Organization Science*, 14 (1): 69–80.

Child, J., and Rodrigues, S. B. (2005) The internationalization of Chinese firms: A case for theoretical extension? *Management and Organization Review*, 1(3): 381–410.

Cohen, M. D., and Levinthal, D. A. (1990) Absorptive capacity: A new perspective on learning and innovation. *Administrative Science Quarterly*, 15: 128–152.

Coviello, N. E. (2006) The network dynamics of international new ventures. *Journal of International Business Studies*, 37 (5): 713–728.

Coviello, N. E., and Cox, M. (2006) The resource dynamics of international new venture networks. *Journal of International Entrepreneurship*, 4: 113–132.

Coviello, N., and Munro, H. (1995) Growing the entrepreneurial firm: Networking for international market development. *European Journal of Marketing*, 29 (7): 49–61.

Coviello, N., and Munro, H. (1997) Network relationships and the internationalisation process of small software firms. *International Business Review*, 6 (4): 361–386.

Davies, H., Leung, K. P., Luck, T. K., and Wong, Y-H. (1995) The benefits of "guanxi". *Industrial Marketing Management*, 24 (3): 207–215.

De Clercq, D., Sapienza, H. J., and Crijns, H. (2005) The internationalization of small and medium-sized firms: The role of organizational learning effort and entrepreneurial orientation. *Small Business Economics*, 24 (4): 409–419.

Dunning, J. H. (1980) Toward an eclectic theory of international production: Some empirical tests. *Journal of International Business Studies*, 11 (1): 9–31.

Dunning, J. H. (2006) Comment on dragon multinationals: New players in 21st century globalization. *Asia Pacific Journal of Management*, 23 (2): 139–141.

Dwyer, R. F, Schurr P. H. and Oh, S. (1987) Developing buyer-seller relationships. *Journal of Marketing*, 51 (2): 11–27.

Eisenhardt K. M. (1989) Building theories from case study research. *Academy of Management Review*, 14 (4): 532–550.

Elango, B. and Pattnaik, C. (2007) Building capabilities for international operations through networks: A study of Indian firms. *Journal of International Business Studies*, 38 (4): 541–555.

Ellis, P. (2000) Social ties and foreign market entry. *Journal of International Business Studies*, 31 (3): 443–469.

Ellis, P. D. and Pecotich, A. (2001) Social factors influencing export initiation in small and medium-sized enterprises. *Journal of Marketing Research*, 38 (February), 119–130.

Fan, T. and Phan, P. (2007) International new ventures: Revisiting the influences behind the "born-global" firm. *Journal of International Business Studies*, 38: 1113–1131.

Ford, D. (1980) The development of buyer-seller relationships in industrial markets. *European Journal of Marketing*, 14 (5/6): 339–354.

Gaur, A. S. and Kumar, V. (2010) Internationalization of emerging market firms: A case for theoretical extension. In the *Proceedings of 2010 Global Marketing Conference*, Tokyo, Japan, September 9–11.

Grayson, K. and Ambler, T. (1999) The dark side of long-term relationships in marketing services. *Journal of Marketing Research*, 36 (2): 132–141.

Hannan, M. (1998) Rethinking age dependence in organizational mortality: Logical formalizations. *American Journal of Sociology*, 104: 126–164.

Harris, S., and Wheeler, C. (2005) Entrepreneurs' relationships for internationalization: Functions, origins and strategies. *International Business Review*, 14 (2): 187–207.

Henderson, A. D. (1999) Firm strategy and age dependence: A contingent view of the liabilities of newness. *Administrative Science Quarterly*, 44 (2): 281–314.

Huff, L., and Kelley, L. (2005) Is collectivism a liability? The impact of culture on organizational trust and customer orientation: A seven-nation study. *Journal of Business Research*, 58 (1): 96–118.

Hymer, S. H. (1976) *The International Operations of National Firms: A Study of Foreign Direct Investment*, MIT Press, Cambridge, MA

Johanson, J. and Vahlne, J. E. (1977) The internationalization process of the firm: A model of knowledge development and increasing foreign market commitments. *Journal of International Business Studies*, 8 (1): 23–32.

Johanson, J. and Vahlne, J. E. (1990) The mechanism of internationalization. *International Marketing Review*, 7 (4): 11–24.

Johanson, J. and Vahlne, J. E. (2003) Business relationship learning and commitment in the internationalization process. *Journal of International Entrepreneurship*, 1 (1): 83–101.

Jones, M. V. and Coviello, N. E. (2005) Internationalization: Conceptualizing an entrepreneurial process of behavior in time. *Journal of International Business Studies*, 36: 284–303.

Keupp, M. and Gassmann, O. (2009) The past and the future of international entrepreneurship: A review and suggestions for developing the field. *Journal of Management*, 35(3): 600–633.

Knight, G. A. and Cavusgil, S. T. (1996) The born global firm: A challenge to traditional internationalization theory. *Advances in International Marketing*, 8: 11–26.

Knight, G. A. and Cavusgil, S. T. (2004) Innovation, organization capabilities, and the born-global firm. *Journal of International Business Studies*, 35: 124–141.

Levitt, B. and March, J. G. (1988) Organizational learning. *Annual Review of Sociology*, 14: 319–340.

Luo, Y. (2000) Dynamic capabilities in international expansion. *Journal of World Business*, 35 (4): 355–378.

Luo, Y. and Tung, R. L. (2007) International expansion of emerging market enterprises: A springboard perspective. *Journal of International Business Studies*, 38 (4): 481–498.

Mathews, J. A. (2006) Dragon multinationals: New players in 21st century of globalization. *Asia Pacific Journal of Management*, 23: 5–27.

Mathews, J. A. and Zander, I. (2007) The international entrepreneurial dynamics of accelerated internationalization. *Journal of International Business Studies*, 38 (4): 387–403.

Matsuno, K., Mentzer, J. T., and Özsomer, A. (2002) The effects of entrepreneurial proclivity and market orientation on business performance. *Journal of Marketing*, 66 (July): 18–32.

McDougall, P. P., Shane, S., and Oviatt, B. M. (1994) Explaining the formation of international new ventures: The limits of theories from international business research. *Journal of Business Venturing*, 9 (3): 49–487.

Moen, O. and Servais, P. (2002) Born global or gradual global? Examining the export behavior of small and medium-sized enterprises. *Journal of International Marketing*, 10 (3): 49–72.

Oviatt, B. and McDougall, P. (1994) Toward a theory of international new ventures. *Journal of International Business Studies*, 25 (1): 45–64.

Oviatt, B. and McDougall, P. (2005) Defining international entrepreneurship and modeling the speed of internationalization. *Entrepreneurship: Theory and Practices*, September: 537–553,

Qiu, Y. (2005) Personal networks, institutional involvement, and foreign direct investment flows into China's interior. *Economic Geography*, 81(3): 261–281.

Rialp, A., Rialp, J., and Knight, G. A. (2005) The phenomenon of early internationalizing firms: What do we know after a decade (1993–2003) of scientific inquiry? *International Business Review*, 14: 147–166.

Sapienza, H. J., Autio, E., George, G., and Zahra, S. A. (2006) A capabilities perspective on the effects of early internationalization of firm survival and growth. *Academy of Management Review*, 31 (4): 914–933.

Sapienza, H. J., De Clercq, D., and Sandberg, W. 2005 Antecedents of international and domestic learning effort. *Journal of Business Venturing*, 20: 437–457.

Shane, C., and Venkataraman, S. (2000) The promise of entrepreneurship as a field of research. *Academy of Management Review*, 25 (1): 217–226.

Sharma, D. D., and Blomstermo, A. (2003) The internationalization process of born globals: A network view. *International Business Review*, 12 (6): 739–753.

Sol, P. D., and Kogan, J. (2007) Regional competitive advantage based on pioneering economic reforms: The case of Chilean FDI. *Journal of International Business Studies*, 38: 901–927.

Welch, L. S. and Luostarinen, R. (1993) Inward and outward connections in internationalization. *Journal of International Marketing*, 1 (1): 46–58.

Wong, P., and Ellis, P. D. (2002) Social ties and partner identification in Sino-Hong Kong international joint ventures. *Journal of International Business Studies*, 33(2): 267–289.

Wright, M., Filatotchev, I., Hoskisson, R. E., and Peng, M. (2005) Strategy research in emerging economies: Challenging the conventional wisdom. *Journal of Management Studies*, 42 (1): 1–33.

Yamakawa, Y., Peng, M. W., and Deeds, D. L. (2008) What drives new ventures to internationalize from emerging to developed economies? *Entrepreneurship Theory and Practice*, January: 59–82.

Yen, D. A., Yu, Q. and Barnes, B. R. (2007) Focusing on relationship dimensions to improve the quality of Chinese-Western business-to-business exchanges. *Total Quality Management*, 18 (8): 1–11.

Yin, R.K. (1994) Discovering the future of the case study method in evaluation research. *Evaluation Practice*, 15, 283–290.

Yin, R. Y. (1989) *Case Study Research: Design and Methods*, second edition, Sage: Beverly Hills, CA.

Yiu, D. W., Lau, C. M., and Bruton, G. D. (2007) International venturing by emerging economy firms: The effect of firm capabilities, home country networks, and corporate entrepreneurship. *Journal of International Business Studies*, 38 (4): 519–540.

Young, S., Huang, C-H., and McDermott, M. C. (1996) Internationalization and competitive catch-up processes: Case study evidence on Chinese multinational enterprises. *Management International Review*, 36 (4): 295–314.

Zaheer, S. (1995) Overcoming the liabilities of foreignness. *Academy of Management Journal*, 38 (2): 341–363.

Zahra, S. A. (2005) A theory of international new ventures: A decade of research. *Journal of International Business Studies*, 36: 20–28.

Zahra, S. A. and George, G. (2002) International entrepreneurship: Research contributions and future directions. In M. A. Hitt, R. D. Ireland, S. M. Camp, and D. L. Sexton (Eds.), *Strategic Entrepreneurship: Creating a New Mindset* (pp. 255–288). Oxford: Blackwell Publishers.

Zahra, S. A., Ireland, R. D., and Hitt, M. (2000) International expansion by new venture firms: International diversity, mode of market entry, technological learning, and performance. *Academy of Management Journal*, 43 (5): 925–950.

Zahra, S. A., Sapienza, H. J., and Davidsson, P. (2006) Entrepreneurship and dynamic capabilities: A review, model and research agenda. *Journal of Management Studies*, 43 (4): 917–955.

Zahra, S. A., Zheng, C., Yu, J., and Yavuz, R. I. (2006) Learning advantages of newness: An analysis, critique, and assessment of its antecedents. *Proceedings of the 48th Annual Meeting of the Academy of International Business*, Mary Ann Von Glinow and Tunga Kiyak, eds., Beijing, China.

Zain, M. and Ng, S. I. (2006) The impacts of network relationships on SMEs' internationalization process. *Thunderbird International Business Review*, 48(2): 183–205.

Zhang, C., Cavusgil, S. T., and Roath, A. S. (2003) Manufacturer governance of foreign distributor relationships: Do relational norms enhance competitiveness in the export market? *Journal of International Business Studies*, 34: 550–566.

Zhang, Z., To, C., and Cao, N. (2004) How do industry clusters succeed: A case study in China's textiles and apparel industries, *Journal of Textile and Apparel Technology*, 4(2): 1–10.

Zhejiang Statistics Bureau. (2007) *Zhejiang Yearbook of Statistics*. China Statistics Publishing, Zhejiang.

Zhou, L. (2007) The effects of entrepreneurial proclivity and foreign market knowledge on early internationalization. *Journal of World Business*, 42: 281–293.

Zhou, L., Barnes, B., and Lu, Y. (2010) Entrepreneurial proclivity, capability upgrading and performance advantage of newness among international ventures. *Journal of International Business Studies*, 41 (5): 882–905.

Zhou, L., Wu, W. P., and Luo, X. (2007) Internationalization and the performance of born-global SMEs: The mediating role of social networks. *Journal of International Business Studies*, 38: 673–690.

Zucchella, A., Palamara, G., and Denicolai, S. (2007) The drivers of the early internationalization of the firm. *Journal of World Business*, 42 (3): 268–280.

# 7
## Does Social Capital Always Create Value for Firm Internationalization?

The Case of Chinese Automakers in Russia

*Zejian Li and Yue Wang*

### Introduction

An increasing number of firms from emerging markets are joining the global competition for consumers. To understand how these emerging-market firms compete for global consumers given their inherent disadvantages in brand recognition, proprietary technology and international management capabilities, existing studies have emphasized the positive role of social capital in their internationalization process. The literature on firm internationalization generally holds that social capital has a positive influence on firms' international expansion, especially for emerging-market firms with weaker firm-specific core competencies. The study featured in this chapter argues that social capital as a firm resource does not have an ongoing positive influence. Beyond a certain point, the continuous over-reliance on social capital after the initial foreign entry might negatively affect the marketing of emerging-market firms' products overseas. Based on a case study of independent private Chinese automakers' dramatic rise and fall in the Russian market over the 2004–2009 period, this study demonstrates that while social capital in the form of business ties played a crucial role in facilitating Chinese automakers' initial entry into the Russian market, the over-reliance on the same business ties also contributed significantly to the subsequent failure of these firms' products in, and (in some cases) the eventual withdraw from, the Russian market. Theoretically, this study contributes to the literature on firm internationalization by highlighting the contingency value of social capital in the different stages of a firm's internationalization process under the various demand conditions of the host market. Empirically, it adds to the scant literature on the internationalization behavior of rapidly growing Chinese independent automobile manufacturers.

## Literature review: The role of social capital in Chinese firms' internationalization

Multinational enterprises (MNEs) compete for consumers around the world. The 1980s and 1990s were a great time for established Western and Japanese MNEs as billions of new consumers entered the global market following the opening up of countries such as China and Russia to foreign businesses. In the 2000s while the dominance of Western MNEs in the global competition for consumers continues, the accelerated internationalization of emerging market MNEs added to the tension (Bonaglia, Goldstein and Mathews, 2007). It can no longer be assumed that Western firms will comfortably win over consumers in emerging markets based on their brand reputation and technical prowess. New competitors from emerging markets are increasingly aggressive in the battle for global consumers. As a result, there has been growing interest in the internationalization behavior of emerging-market firms. However, the literature suffers from two problems. First, traditional internationalization theories, such as monopolistic advantage theory (Hymer, 1976), stages theory (Johanson and Vahlne, 1977) and internalization theory (Buckley and Casson, 1976), are ill equipped to examine the antecedents to the internationalization of emerging-market firms that typically lack the product technologies and marketing capabilities exercised by Western MNEs, and thus face significant barriers when trying to sell their products overseas. Second, on the empirical side, most existing studies have focused on emerging-market firms' attempts to sell their products in developed Western markets, which can lead to their neglecting their internationalization experience in other emerging markets (Mathews and Zander, 2007). This further inhibits the development of knowledge regarding the internationalization behavior of emerging-market firms.

Recently, ideas and concepts from social capital theory have been used to offer new insights into what drives the international expansion of emerging-market firms (Chetty and Agndal, 2007; Zhou, Wu, and Luo, 2007). The literature generally holds that social capital, often in the form of the external network relationships of emerging-market firms, can effectively attenuate the risks of overseas operations and hence ease foreign entry (Coviello and Munro, 1997; Coviello, 2006).

Social capital is defined as the actual and potential resources available to a firm through its network of relationships (Nahapiet and Ghoshal, 1998), and plays an important role in firm internationalization (Chetty and Agndal, 2007). An effective way for emerging-market firms to develop international markets is to acquire reliable access to resources through business networks (Ellis, 2000), rather than trying to secure resources through internalization (Oviatt and McDougall, 1994). For Chinese private firms, the social capital embedded in business and political ties (Peng, 1997; Peng and Luo, 2000) plays a crucial role in their internationalization efforts. Both sets of ties enable firms to access and acquire the complementary resources held by network partners, and can become valuable and non-imitable resources in their own right during the internationalization process.

Despite the rapid overall development in the past decade, Chinese private firms are often at a competitive disadvantage within the Chinese market. They lack the proprietary product and process technologies that the Western MNEs' Chinese subsidiaries possess and the financing, marketing and distribution capabilities to compete against large Chinese state-owned enterprises (SOEs) with strong government support. In some cases, private Chinese firms face even higher transaction costs and risks when expanding across regions/provinces within the domestic marketplace than when they expand across national borders into overseas markets with more stable institutional environments. This can result in the choice of international expansion as a strategic exit from China (Cui and Jiang, 2012).

Chinese private firms' internationalization attempts, however, are impeded by their lack of hard technological and marketing capabilities. Their primary competitive advantage overseas rests in exploiting the networks of external relationships to mitigate the risks associated with entering international markets (Mathews and Zander, 2007), and their internationalization efforts can be largely viewed as a process of developing and accessing social capital (rather than hard technologies) as they establish and deepen network relationships (Johanson and Vahlne, 2006).

Social capital in network relationships can be built by creating new relationships in unexplored foreign markets or by identifying links with target markets within a firm's existing networks. Establishing links with various overseas stakeholders helps Chinese firms without international experience to build an initial base of creditability and trust in a new market. Relationships with local suppliers allow a firm to acquire quality inputs and timely delivery, relationships with buyers may spur customer loyalty and sales volume, and links with competitors may facilitate interfirm collaboration and implicit collusion (Peng and Luo, 2000). Ties within a firm's existing network in its domestic market may also facilitate indirect relationship-building with foreign markets through mutual network partners (Yiu et al., 2007). For example, Zhou et al. (2007) show that locally based social networks within the Chinese domestic setting can be successfully extended during the early internationalization of Chinese firms. Whether creating new networks or exploiting existing networks, the social capital embedded in network ties enables Chinese firms to learn and create new knowledge about overseas markets and helps them to acquire competitive advantages through international growth (Chetty and Agndal, 2007).

This study confirms the literature, which suggests that social capital in the form of network ties enables Chinese firms to learn and create new knowledge about overseas markets in addition to generally facilitating their internationalization attempts. However, the value of social capital cannot be assumed to always be positive, and the same source of social capital may play different roles in the internationalization process. In particular, when Chinese firms try to enter other emerging markets where both institutional and business environments are also undergoing significant and constant changes, it is quite possible that the same business and political ties will not have the same weight of influence during the different stages of internationalization, as the regulatory and market conditions in the host country evolve continuously. In addition, possessing social capital may contribute to the initial entry into foreign markets but may not help firms to acquire sustainable competitive advantages that would allow them to survive in the host market in the long term. As the host country's institutional environment continues to evolve, some network ties that helped firms to enter the target market may prove to be counterproductive in a changed environment. As Peng (2003) notes, the value of social capital in reducing the transaction costs of doing business in emerging markets changes during the institutional transitions of those countries.

To fully understand the value of social capital in firm internationalization, it is therefore important to specify what type of social capital will have a positive (or possibly negative) effect on firms' internationalization, and under what conditions. The remaining sections of this chapter provide a real-world account of the role of social capital in the dramatic rise and fall of independent private Chinese automakers' exports to the

Russian market during the 2004–2009 period and discuss the theoretical and managerial implications of the case.

## Background: The rise and fall of Chinese automobile export to Russia

China's entry into the World Trade Organization in 2001 led to an increase in automobile imports and exports, but automobile exports proliferated at a rate exceeding that of imports and, beginning in 2005, China became a net automobile-export country.[1] By 2008, Chinese cars were exported to more than 190 countries around the world, reaching a record of 680,000 units.[2] While the state-owned manufacturers focus overwhelmingly on China's domestic passenger car market, the independent private Chinese automobile manufacturers take a leading role in the nation's automobile export and have engaged in overseas expansions, including finished car exports and onsite knock-down (KD) assembly of not just passenger vehicles but also lightweight trucks.

The early destinations for Chinese automobile exports were mainly in the Middle East and Southeast Asia, and lightweight trucks (including pickup trucks and minibuses based on Chinese Statistical Standards) were the most exported Chinese vehicles. For example, as early as 2003, Changan Auto started to export lightweight trucks to Vietnam and Pakistan; JAC Motors started to export CKD lightweight trucks to Vietnam, Malaysia and Indonesia; and Zhong Xing Auto (ZX Auto hereafter) began to export pickup trucks to the Middle East.[3]

The most dramatic increase in Chinese automobile export was seen in Russia. In 2003 there were only 77 Chinese-made vehicles exported to Russia.[4] Since then a number of Chinese automakers, such as ZX Auto, Chery and Geely, have begun to export their vehicles to Russian markets and the number of Chinese automobiles exported to Russia increased sharply from 543 units in 2004 to 7,730 units in 2005 and 36,809 units in 2006.[5] Other private Chinese automobile manufacturers, such as Great Wall and BYD, followed quickly, resulting in a dramatic increase in the total number of Chinese vehicles exported to Russia, reaching 107,744 units in 2007, suddenly making Russia the top destination for Chinese automobile exports.[6] However, in 2008, the number of Chinese cars sold in Russia, which had until then continued to increase at a steady rate, suddenly began falling and in 2009 it showed a significant drop with only 1,834 vehicles exported to Russia, prompting some Chinese automakers, such as ZX Auto, to withdraw completely from the Russian market.[7]

What exactly happened in the Russian market and what does the dramatic rise and fall of Chinese automobile exports to Russia indicate about the internationalization strategies of independent private Chinese automobile manufacturers? These questions define the starting point for this case study. The Russian market was once the most significant target for Chinese automobile export, and Chinese automakers' experience in Russia is a representative case that can reveal details about the general characteristics of the internationalization behavior of private Chinese automobile manufacturers. More importantly, through careful observation and detailed analysis of the experiences of multiple Chinese automakers in Russia (including ZX Auto, Chery and Geely), the case study reported in this chapter sheds important light on the role of social capital in the sudden increase and dramatic decline in Chinese automobile exports to Russia during the 2004–2009 period.

## Case study: What led to the rise and fall of Chinese automobile exports to Russia?

To better understand the rise of Russia as the most important foreign market for Chinese automobile export, this study begins with a brief examination of some of the Russian automobile market's background characteristics. First, following the 1998 financial crisis, the Russian economy consistently maintained a growth rate of around 5% from 2001.[8] The per-capita gross domestic product was $4,104 in 2004, but in just three years it doubled and reached $9,103.[9] This sustained economic growth contributed to the increasing demand for automobiles. Second, in the years following the collapse of the Soviet Union, the average age of cars increased due to the worsening economic situation and a drastic increase in used car imports, with the majority of passenger cars being more than ten years old. As of October 2008, for example, in Vladivostok (the city with the largest number of used passenger cars), vehicles more than ten years old accounted for 80% of the total number of passenger vehicles and the same statistics for Moscow and St Petersburg were 37% and 38%, respectively.[10] There was a strong potential demand for replacements. Thus, coupled with the gradual increase in personal incomes, the Russian market came to be regarded as a promising one for inexpensive new cars in the mid-2000s.

However, following some rapid market expansion for new car sales starting in 2002, the Chinese market cooled down drastically in 2004 due to monetary tightening policies that resulted in excessive capacity built up during the previous boom period. To streamline their operations and solidify their market positions in China, almost all of the state-owned automakers established joint ventures with the world's major automakers to produce foreign brand-name car models for the Chinese market, and their continuous focus on serving the Chinese customers led to an ever more competitive domestic market for the independent private Chinese automobile manufacturers, who began paying serious attention to exports as a strategy to diversify away from China's huge but highly competitive domestic market. Consequently, the drastic increase in Chinese automobile exports since 2004 was caused mainly by exports from independent private manufacturers.

### The expansion of Chinese automakers' exports to Russia

Thus far, the question of why many independent private Chinese automobile manufacturers were able to expand quickly into Russia remains unanswered. In short, this occurred as a result of the emergence of a powerful "middle man" specializing in automobile exports, with wide-ranging personal connections in both China and Russia to help companies such as ZX Auto, Chery and Geely successfully export their vehicles to Russia.

The middle man is Mr Zhu Jingcheng, a former Chinese diplomat in Russia. Having lived in Russia for more than ten years, he sensed the opportunities for introducing inexpensive Chinese-made vehicles to Russia. With the growing Russian economy and the implementation of the Russian government's used car regulation in 2002, the demand for used cars began to shrink and the demand for new cars began to increase. At the time, a used 1998 Toyota pickup sold for $16,000 in Russia, and a new Mitsubishi sold for the much higher price of $22,300–$28,500.[11] In 2003, after seeing a pickup truck by ZX Auto on display in Beijing, Zhu was convinced that he could sell ZX's pickup trucks priced at around RMB100,000 ($15,000) in Russia. He started a discussion with ZX about the possibility of exporting pickup trucks to Russia. Facing the increasingly competitive domestic market and sensing the potential in Russia, ZX Auto began considering the proposal seriously.

### *ZX Auto's expansion into Russia*

ZX Auto was established in 1949 as Baoding Auto Manufacturing, located in Baoding city in Hebei province, known in China for pickup truck production. The company was later reorganized into a SOE, then, 1999, Brilliance Auto provided capital to restructure the loss-making SOE into a joint venture called Hebei ZX Auto Manufacturing Co., Ltd.[12] In 2002, Brilliance Auto's business began to decline and entered into the protection of the Zhejiang Huaxiang Group, when the group assumed the majority of ZX Auto's shares. In 2003, ZX Auto acquired the right to manage itself independently of the Huaxiang Group and continued to operate its business with a focus on pickup trucks (ZX Auto became famous in 1992 for selling the first pickup truck in the Chinese market).[13]

ZX Auto started conducting exports earlier than most other Chinese automakers. In 2000 the company began by exporting 500 vehicles to Iraq, and went on to develop new export markets in Egypt, the UAE and Vietnam.[14] Not only did the company achieve a record sale of 28,701 units in 2003 but it also became China's top automobile exporter that year, with 7,126 units sold overseas.[15] When Zhu visited Baoding in May 2013, ZX Auto did not hesitate in signing a contract with the former Chinese diplomat to export ZX's Admiral pickup trucks to Russia. In 2004, Zhu established a company specializing in automobile exports known as Siberian Automobile Export (Beijing) Co., Ltd. (hereafter Siberian), and started to work with a Russia dealer who had been importing used Japanese and German-made cars into Russia for many years. In November 2004, a pickup truck by ZX Auto became the first Chinese car successfully sold in Russia (for $16,900) by a Chinese automobile manufacturer.[16]

*The role of middle man*

It should be noted that Mr Zhu and his automobile trading company, Siberian, played a crucial role, not just in bridging the buyers and sellers but more importantly in helping Chinese automobile manufacturers to overcome significant institutional barriers and acquire legitimacy in their initial expansion into the Russian market. Siberian acted effectively as a bridge to reduce the information costs between Chinese and Russian automakers and distributors. Until the early 2000s, few Chinese automakers saw Russia as a promising market. The broader relationship between the two countries' people could be characterized as psychologically distant and mutually mistrusting. In general, the effect of the ideological conflicts that had occurred in the Soviet period still lingered. The Russian language and education had been declining in China since the economic reform. The Chinese business cycle in general and the automobile sector in particular had little knowledge about the state of the Russian market. The establishment of Siberian, however, significantly changed Chinese automakers' perceptions of the Russian market. The successful exports to Russia by ZX Auto, reports from the Russian mass media about the expansion of Chinese cars, and information about the Russian market all reached China through the window of Mr Zhu's Siberian company, arousing great interest among other independent Chinese automobile manufacturers who were facing tough competition at home.

Siberian played a crucial role in helping Chinese automakers acquire badly needed legitimacy in a market that is negative and hostile toward Chinese cars. In Russia, the image of Chinese industrial development has not changed for decades despite China's rapid economic reform in the 1980s and 1990s. This outdated notion was a major cause of the obstacles in automobile trade between the two countries. In Russia, the Chinese were ridiculed with statements such as "The Chinese are going to the moon on a bicycle; since all they can make is bicycles, they have no choice but to use bikes no matter where they go." Russians mistrusted not only the quality of Chinese cars but also the testing and certification capacity of the Chinese system. In fact, model certification was regarded as the number-one barrier when Siberian was trying to export ZX's pickup trucks to Russia. With regard to the model certification of imported automobiles, at the time Russia continued to use a multinational agreement approved in 1958, the "Agreement on Uniform Technical Prescriptions for Vehicles" from the United Nations/Economic Commission for Europe. However, as China was not affiliated with this "1958 agreement," as it was popularly called, the Russians refused to accept the automobile inspection test approval certificates issued by China, insisting that when Chinese cars were imported, all certification inspections had to be conducted at the Russian National Automobile Standards Certification Centre.

For the pickup trucks made by ZX Auto to pass Russia's export certification inspections, Siberian went to great trouble, providing translated materials, explaining circumstances and so on, and the certification was issued after 18 months. The experience made Mr Zhu realize that fully following the process insisted upon by Russia would require enormous time and expense. Likewise, Russia's outdated notions about Chinese industrial capability often forced him to spend extra time and effort explaining the Chinese situation to Russian governmental officials. Thus Zhu concluded that it would be difficult to change the state of affairs unless he could dissolve the Russians' mistrust.

In July 2004, Zhu extended an invitation for personnel from the Russian National Automobile Standards Certification Centre to visit ZX Auto and the Chinese National Automobile Quality Supervision and Inspection Testing Centre. In addition to acting as a bridge between the buyers and sellers, Zhu and his company began devising tactics to get rid of the outdated notions held by the Russians. As a result of Zhu's efforts, the Russian National Automobile Standards Certification Centre accepted the inspection certification results from the Chinese National Automobile Quality Supervision and Inspection Testing Centre, and also consented to proxy applications by Siberian. These efforts by Siberian reduced the time required for the model certification procedure from the original 18 months to 2–4 months, breaking through the most difficult barrier to exporting Chinese cars to Russia.

Finally, as a trading company, Siberian not only mediated transactions by acting as a middle man but also became involved in the Russian domestic distribution business, performing the inventory and transport functions for Chinese independent manufacturers when exporting their vehicles to Russia. In addition, Siberian established two assembly bases of its own in the European and Asian regions and began conducting KD manufacturing of sport utility vehicles (SUVs) branded "Siberian-Dadi" by using imported Chinese parts.

### Chery's expansion into Russia

ZX's expansion into Russia demonstrates that Mr Zhu and his company played a crucial role in initiating the Chinese automobile exports to Russia by helping Chinese automakers overcome information-, institution- and distribution-related barriers. The initial successful expansion into Russia by other independent Chinese automakers followed a very similar pattern to that of ZX Auto's pickup trucks' export and was largely attributed to the same source of social capital that they share – that is, Zhu and his automobile trading company, Siberian. The same middle man's efforts made it possible for many independent Chinese automakers to enter the Russian market beginning in 2004, although Chery's expansion took a different path from that of ZX Auto.

When Siberian introduced Russian buyers to Chinese automakers, Chery Automobile was one of the candidates and its expansion into Russia officially began in April 2004 through an agreement with Siberian to cooperate in developing the Russian market. In 2004 some 476 finished cars were exported and Chery began investigating local production possibilities. In 2005, through Siberian, the Russian business group Avtotor – involved in a diverse range of businesses from agriculture to banking – visited a number of automobile manufacturers in China. In January 2006, Chery signed a contract with Avtotor regarding onsite KD production and in April locally assembled Chery-brand cars were taken offline. Both companies subsequently agreed to use a total of $200 million of additional capital to establish a new factory. With this partnership, Chery Automobile was able to sell 37,000 vehicles in 2007, rapidly increasing its presence in the Russian market.

Compared with ZX Auto, Chery did not rely completely on the export of finished cars and, as a result, it did not overly rely on Siberian as a middle man but was able to maintain a certain degree of independence. After its initial export success, Chery began local production with Avtotor. Vladimir Scherbakov, a deputy prime minister in the former Soviet Union, had gained 100% ownership of Avtotor since 1991 and its choice as a partner was strategic, as Chery understood the importance of legally avoiding customs duties through the privileges enjoyed by Avtotor. Thus, built on the connection provided by Mr Zhu and Siberian, Chery was able to further expand its social capital base in the host market and engage in the local assembly and distribution of its own brand cars. However, the company's strategy did not succeed due to a number of reasons described later.

*Geely's expansion into Russia*

The expansion of Geely Automobile into Russia started with a contract signed in 2007 with the Russian company Rolf, the largest group importing and selling foreign cars in Russia. The deal was also largely facilitated by Mr Zhu and Siberian.

Rolf was involved in importing and selling 13 foreign-branded vehicles including Mitsubishi, Hyundai, Mazda, Ford, Mercedes, Audi and Peugeot, with annual sales of $3 billion in 2007. In the same year, through the Russian Business Society and the Chinese consulate in Russia, Rolf expressed a desire to import $1 billion worth of Chinese passenger vehicles. At first the two state-owned automakers, First Auto Work and Shanghai Automobile Industry Corporation, were mentioned as potential candidates, but Geely Automobile was added to the list on the recommendation of a friend of Mr Zhu. Later, Siberian investigated Geely Automobile on its own, gained confidence in exporting Geely cars to Russia, and then made it the number-one candidate for Rolf. Subsequently, managers from Rolf were invited to visit Geely several times before a deal was reached to export 200,000 units of Geely's cars over five years – $1.5 billion worth of finished cars.

Creating a partnership with a powerful local importer gave Geely a golden opportunity to bypass the many obstacles associated with the initial expansion into Russia that would otherwise be difficult to overcome, such as channel maintenance and the provision of after-sales services. Although Geely's expansion into Russia was still at the stage of exporting finished cars, its internationalization pattern differed from that of ZX Auto in that while ZX left downstream activities such as sales distribution and after-sales services completely to trading companies such as Siberian, Geely exported finished vehicles with full-scale after-sales service benefits from its partnership with Rolf, a local megadealer. As a result, compared with other Chinese-made car models, the export of Geely cars was viewed as the most promising project and the company was in a relatively favorable competitive position in Russia. In this sense, the local social capital brought by Zhu and Siberian was critical to Geely's initial success in the Russian market.

### The fall of Chinese automakers' exports to Russia

Chinese automobile manufacturers' successful expansion into Russia peaked in 2007 with a total of 107,744 units sold, yet the Chinese export phenomenon quickly lost its momentum. The total number of units sold declined to 85,091 in 2008 and fell drastically to 1,834 in 2009. ZX Auto was forced to completely withdraw from the Russian market. What exactly happened and what does the dramatic fall in the Chinese export reveal about the internationalization strategies (if any) of the independent Chinese automakers?

*ZX's decline in Russia*

For ZX Auto, the company focused on exporting highly similar, low-priced pickup trucks and light SUVs. Moreover, the company engaged in a pure "parts trade-based export" strategy with the lowest level of participation in the Russian market. ZX sold CKD parts to Siberian, which would transport the parts to the factories of local Russian manufactures that would then assemble the CKD parts into finished vehicles to be sold as local brands owned by Siberian. In other words, ZX Auto relied completely on Siberian to organize the production and distribution in Russia. Most of the Russian manufacturers that Siberian used for local assemblage were so-called body manufacturers that were even smaller than ZX and lacked the capability to produce quality finished cars.

This method of international expansion relies on low prices as the only competitive weapon, creating an extremely high degree of dependence on trading companies such as Siberian for assemblage, sales, distribution and after-sales service in Russia. If customers had problems with the finished vehicles, local Russian assemblers disappeared as problems arose, leaving the Chinese cars linked to a "cheap but bad" image. Worse still, as ZX did not provide after-sales services in Russia, and Siberian did not have the sufficient technical capability to resolve technical problems, the problems with sold cars had a negative influence on the continuous expansion of all ZX cars. When problems regarding product quality and inadequate after-sales service coupled with the increasing price competition with other Chinese automakers, ZX was forced to withdraw from the Russian market.

*Chery's decline in Russia*

As previously discussed, Chery did not rely completely on Siberian but was able to maintain a certain degree of independence in its expansion. The company realized the importance of local engagement and partnered with a powerful Russian business group (Avtotor) in the joint production and distribution of its own brand of cars in Russia. For example, Chery's Amulet, which sold at $9,000, was once popular due to its value for money. However, the company failed to recognize the importance of product improvement/development in response to the changing market conditions. As the Russian market became less price sensitive and more sophisticated in terms of customers demanding higher-quality cars, Chery (and other Chinese automakers) showed a lack of capability and skills in responding to the market shifts. In 2007 the influential Russian car magazine *AvtoRevu* conducted a crash test of automobiles made by Chery and reported that "the results were the worst seen in the last three years." Making things worse, in March 2008, due to the decline of the dollar (Avtotor's operating currency), the company announced that it was putting a halt to the KD manufacturing of Chery cars and the sales of Chery vehicles fell rapidly in the following years as a consequence.

*Geely's decline in Russia*

As previously discussed, despite its reliance on Siberian as a middle man, Geely's expansion strategy gave the company a relatively favorable competitive position against others, such as ZX. Compared with ZX's "CKD parts trade-based export" pattern, which resulted in a more arm's-length relationship with Siberian, Geely worked closely with the trading company to export original products with full-scale after-sales services and hence was able to accumulate some knowledge in serving the local customers. The company's export performance in Russia also faced serious challenges, partly because the reputation of "cheap and bad" had already been established in relation to Chinese cars in general, and partly due to the worsening relationships with Siberian.

The closer working relationship between Geely and Siberian also prompted a more complex contract. The cooperative relationship functioned well when the market demand was strong but the partnership deteriorated when the market conditions changed. The increasing value that Russian customers placed on quality and service as opposed to price led to the growing pressure on Chinese automakers and Siberian to improve their products and provide more value-added services, which often caused friction between the automakers and trading companies in terms of how they should adapt their respective responsibilities in a changing environment. The original contract signed between Geely and Siberian did not clearly stipulate their respective responsibilities when facing the shifting market conditions. The differences between the two parties' understandings of contract implementation resulted in a definite negative effect on their cooperative relationship. Siberian even brought a lawsuit against Geely regarding the disputes over mediator fees (i.e., the fees Geely should pay Siberian for mediating export contracts with local Russian bulk buyers). In fact, these kinds of dispute started to spread between Siberian and many other Chinese automakers. In 2009, Siberian stopped performing mediation tasks for all 27 Chinese automakers in Russia; instead, the company devoted its attention to lawsuits against these Chinese partners. It is therefore not surprising that the deteriorating relationship(s) between Geely (and other Chinese automakers) and Siberian resulted in the continual decline of Geely's (and other Chinese automakers') sales in the Russian market.

### Institutional factors contributing to the Chinese automobile export decline in Russia

Apart from the above mentioned firm-specific reasons for the failing export performance in Russia, it is worth pointing out some of the broader institutional factors that contributed to the serious legitimacy issues faced by Chinese automobile manufacturers in Russia, which in turn led to the dramatic decline in Chinese automobile exports since 2008.

First, from the beginning, independent Chinese automakers failed to understand that by attracting foreign automobile manufacturers, the Russian government intended to promote the automobile parts industry in its own country. For this reason, there were many cases in which conflicts of interest existed regarding the Russian government's intentions and local production methods or the investment publicity of Chinese independent manufacturers – the image of Chinese automakers ignoring contributions to society through investment and the pursuit of maximum manufacturing scale for minimum investment became entrenched.

Second, some Chinese automakers made the mistake of regarding the positioning strategy of their cars. For example, Chery put its local brand, Amulet, into direct competition with major local Russian manufacturers Avtovaz and Kalina. This reinforced a protectionist view in Russia regarding the "Chinese car threat." Correct or not, the perception that the entrance of Chinese cars contributed nothing to Russian society or the development of the Russian automotive industry, and even caused damage, had become increasingly mainstream.

Third, the Russian manufacturers that Mr Zhu and Siberian used to conduct the local CKD assemblage of Chinese cars were often technologically weak and some were even smaller than the Chinese automakers. They were generally not major Russian manufacturers and they had little interest in protecting the industry of their own country. In addition, because young, small Russian manufacturers obtained separate customs clearance for chassis and bodies through grey imports, they were described by major Russian manufacturers as engaging in "screwdriver assembly."

Due to the abovementioned reasons, over time the export operations of Chinese automobile manufacturers in Russia were increasingly seen as illegitimate by the Russian government and society. In October 2008, a new regulation deliberately designed to eliminate Chinese "screwdriver assembly" by increasing import duties on automobile bodies was issued by the Russian government. The immediate effect of the policy was that the favorable status of Chinese cars in terms of their cost advantage was quickly lost. Some of the Chinese automakers' plans for more local manufacturing (e.g., Chery's partnership with Avtotor for local production) were halted due to the cost increase caused by the amended customs duties. By 2009 the sales of Chinese cars in Russia essentially comprised dealers disposing of stock, with some companies, such as ZX, being forced to withdraw from the Russian market entirely while others struggled.

## Discussion and conclusion

The most recent decade has seen an increasing number of newly internationalized emerging-market firms joining the global competition for consumers. To understand how they compete, given their inherent disadvantages in brand recognition, proprietary technology and international management capabilities, existing studies have stressed the positive role of social capital in the internationalization process. This study argues that social capital can be a double-edged sword for emerging-market firms' international expansion, and that over-reliance on social capital may inhibit emerging-market firms' internationalization after their initial entry into global markets. Using the dramatic rise and fall of Chinese automakers in Russia as a case study, the role of a former Chinese diplomat and his company, Siberian, was analyzed as the most important source of social capital for Chinese automakers' expansion into Russia. The subsequent indication is that the initial success of Chinese automobile products' export to Russia was largely attributed to this business tie possessed by Chinese automakers, and the results suggest that Chinese auto-makers' over-reliance on the same business tie coupled with their subsequent failure to develop other competences in line with the changing consumer demand pattern in Russia resulted in the dramatic decline of Chinese-made vehicles in Russia.

Chinese automakers' experience in Russia offers managerially relevant insights into the role of social capital in emerging-market firms' internationalization process, especially when the host country is another emerging market. First, the same source of social capital does not have an ongoing positive performance effect during the firm's internationalization process. While social capital in the form of network ties generally plays a positive role in the early stage of firm internationalization, its value (relative to the value of other firm resources and capabilities) may diminish quickly in the later stages of the process.

Second, the value of social capital is often subject to the institutional and market environment of the host country, and to the extent that the host countries' environments are constantly changing, the value of a particular source of social capital is also likely to change. Indeed, as the case study shows, although former Chinese diplomat Mr Zhu and his company Siberian played an important and positive role in introducing Chinese-made pickup trucks and other lightweight vehicles to Russia initially, the Chinese automakers made a strategic mistake by continuously relying on the same source of social capital for their further expansion into Russia. The result was a misalignment between the social capital that they possessed and relied on, and the changing institutional conditions in the host country, which turned the same source of social capital into a negative force in the Chinese firms' further expansion into Russia.

Third, the implication for the emerging market firms' managers is that while social capital may be crucial for the initial stage of international expansion as a remedy for the lack of proprietary technologies and marketing capabilities, its value does not last indefinitely. When the same source of social capital (i.e., Zhu and his company in this case) is drawn on by many firms competing in the same industry and in the same market, it can lose its value as a scarce resource and might not be able to provide a substantial competitive advantage for emerging market firms. Fourth, managers of emerging market firms should be alarmed about the potential "trap effect" of social capital – the high level of dependence on a particular social network may increase the likelihood that the firm will interact only with the network partner (Laursen, Masciarelli and Prencipe, 2012). This effect induces an over-reliance on a narrow source of social capital for local opportunities in host countries, and hence limits firms' ability to increase their involvement in foreign markets. In other words, social capital can both help and constrain the abilities of firms to engage in internationalization. To reduce the possibility of experiencing the negative consequences of social capital in relation to internationalization, managers should take deliberate actions to forge links with more distant network partners in international markets (Laursen et al., 2012).

Finally, from a dynamic resource-based view (Helfat and Peteraf, 2003), in addition to new partnerships and networks, firms must develop new resources and capabilities to sustain their performance in the continuing process of internationalization. In particular, a firm's capacity to modify and improve its products is often necessary to satisfy international demand and crucial for its participation in international markets (Patel and Vega, 1999). Unfortunately, some emerging market firms (e.g., those in the case reported in this chapter) have a misconception that product modification and adaption are only essential for servicing customers in developed countries, and tend to take customers in other emerging markets for granted. This study argues, based on the case study, that continuous improvement in product and service quality is also necessary in emerging markets in which the consumer demand patterns and institutional environment governing the business exchanges are changing rapidly. Ultimately for emerging market firms, it is their ability to develop hard, non-imitable competencies in producing quality products and services that will help them to achieve success in their internationalization efforts.

## Notes

1. See China Automotive Information Net (2005).
2. Ibid.
3. See Chen (2007).
4. See China Automotive Information Net (2003).
5. See Association of European Business in the Russian Federation (2008a, 2008b, 2008c, 2008d), Wa (2007), Shi (2007) and Chen (2007).

6. Ibid.
7. See Siberian Automobile Export (Beijing) Co. Ltd. (2007).
8. Ibid.
9. See IMF (2009).
10. See Luo (2008).
11. See Siberian Automobile Export (Beijing) Co. Ltd. (2007).
12. See Economics (2004).
13. Ibid.
14. See Wang (2005).
15. Ibid.
16. See Siberian Automobile Export (Beijing) Co. Ltd. (2007).

## References

Association of European Businesses in the Russian Federation (2008a) Sales of foreign cars and light commercial brands in 2007 in Russia – over 1.6 million vehicles sold, http://www.aebrus.ru/files/File/CommunicationsFiles/PressReleases/AEB_pr_07_06_eng.pdf, date accessed 24 September 2008.

Association of European Businesses in the Russian Federation (2008b) AEB press release, http://www.aebrus.ru/application/views/aebrus/files/pages_files/AEB_pr_07_06_eng_filess_2008_06_19_17_57_09.pdf, date accessed 24 September 2008.

Association of European Businesses in the Russian Federation (2008c) AEB press release, http://www.aebrus.ru/application/views/aebrus/files/pages_files/AEB_pr_6mnths_08_eng_filess_2008_07_11_12_44_41.pdf, date accessed 24 September 2008.

Association of European Businesses in the Russian Federation (2008d) Sales of foreign brands in Russia in November/12 months 2008/2007, http://www.abiz.ru/content_Download.php?rn=Sales_car_12mon2008.pdf&f=1205__Sales_car_12mon2008.pdf, date accessed 24 September 2008.

Bonaglia, F., Goldstein, A., and Mathews, J. (2007) "Accelerated internationalization by emerging markets' multinationals: The case of the white goods sector", *Journal of World Business*, 42 (4), 369–383.

Buckley, P. J., and Casson, M. (1976) *The Future of the Multinational Enterprise*. New York: Holmes and Meier.

Chen, X. (2007) "Automotive industry sees trend toward overseas factories", *China Automobile Report*, 15 April.

Chetty, S., and Agndal, H. (2007) "Social capital and its influence on changes in internationalization mode among small and medium-sized enterprises", *Journal of International Marketing*, 15 (1), 1–29.

China Automotive Information Net (2003) *Imports and Exports*, retrieved from Automotive and Statistics database.

China Automotive Information Net (2005) *Imports and Exports*, retrieved from Automotive and Statistics database.

Coviello, N. E. (2006) "The network dynamics of international new ventures", *Journal of International Business Studies*, 37, 713–731.

Coviello, N. E., and Munro, H. J. (1997) "Network relationships and the internationalization process of the small software firms", *International Business Review*, 6, 361–386.

Cui, L., and Jiang, F. (2012) "State ownership effect on firms? FDI ownership decisions under institutional pressure: A study of Chinese outward investing firms", *Journal of International Business Studies*, 43 (3), 264–284.

Economics (2004) *A Story of Tianye Automobiles (Tianye qiche de tixiao yinyuan)*, 4, 74–75. (in Chinese).

Ellis, P. (2000) "Social ties and foreign market entry", *Journal of International Business Studies*, 31, 443–470.

Helfat, C. E., and Peteraf, M. A. (2003) "The dynamic resource-based view: Capability life cycles", *Strategic Management Journal*, 24, 997–1010.

Hymer, S. (1976) *The International Operations of National Firms: A Study of Direct Investment*. Cambridge, MA: MIT Press.

IMF (2009) *World Economic Outlook Database*, retrieved on 31 January 2013.

Johanson, J., and Vahlne, J. (1977) "The internationalization process of the firm: A model of knowledge development and increasing foreign market commitment", *Journal of International Business Studies*, 8 (1), 23–32.

Johanson, J., and Vahlne, J. (2006) "Commitment and opportunity development in the internationalization process: A note on the Uppsala internationalization process model", *Management International Review*, 46 (2), 165–178.

Laursen, K, Masciarelli, F., and Prencipe, A. (2012) "Trapped or spurred by the home region? The effects of potential social capital on involvement in foreign markets for goods and technology", *Journal of International Business Studies*, 43, 783–807.

Luo, L. 2008. Russian car ownership statistics as a reference for Chinese automakers. Sohu blog, [blog] 9 October, http://luolansohu2007.blog.sohu.com/101560515.html, date accessed 20 October 2008.

Mathews, J. A., and Zander, I. (2007) "The international entrepreneurial dynamics of accelerated internationalization", *Journal of International Business Studies*, 38, 387–403.

Nahapiet, J., and Ghoshal, S. (1998) "Social capital, intellectual capital and the organizational advantage", *Academy of Management Review*, 23, 242–266.

Oviatt, B. M., and McDougall, P. P. (1994) "Toward a theory of international new ventures", *Journal of International Business Studies*, 25 (1), 45–64.

Patel, P., and Vega, M. (1999) "Patterns of internationalization of corporate technology: Location vs. home country advantages", *Research Policy*, 28 (2/3), 145–155.

Peng, M. W. (1997) "Firm growth in transitional economies: Three longitudinal cases from China, 1989–96", *Organization Studies*, 18, 385–413.

Peng, M. W. (2003) "Institutional transitions and strategic choices", *Academy of Management Review*, 28 (2), 275–296.

Peng, M., and Luo, Y. (2000) "Managerial ties and firm performance in a transition economy: The nature of a micro-macro link", *Academy of Management Journal*, 43 (3), 486–501.

Shi, B. (2007) "Chinese car business defeated in Russia due to internal factors causing trouble abroad", *21st Century Economic Report*, 5 August (in Chinese).

Siberian Automobile Export (Beijing) Co. Ltd. (2007) *The Path of Chinese Automobiles into Russia*, unpublished.

Wa, X. (2007) "Chinese vehicles march on into Russia: Past and future", *Automobiles and Parts*, 50, 38–41.

Wang, D. (2005) *ZX Auto: From the Middle East to South America* (Zhongxing Pika: Cong Zhongdong Shixiang Nanmei), http://www.ycwb.com/gb/content/ 2005–02/07/content_847438.htm, date accessed 24 September 2008.

Yiu, D. W., Lau, C. M., and Bruton, G. D. (2007) "International venturing by emerging economy firms: The effects of firm capabilities, home country networks, and corporate entrepreneurship", *Journal of International Business Studies*, 38, 519–540.

Zhou, L., Wu, W., and Luo, X. (2007) "Internationalization and the performance of born-global SMEs: The mediating role of social networks", *Journal of International Business Studies*, 38, 673–690.

# 8
## Multinational Enterprise Strategy, Institutions, State Capacity and Inward Foreign Direct Investment into the ASEAN Countries

*Greg Mahony, Bilal Rafi and Chris Sadleir*

## Introduction

The role played by institutions in the closely related fields of international business and strategy has attracted increasing attention, with much of the motivation for such interest coming from the engagement of multinational enterprises (MNEs) in the diverse institutional environment of emerging economies from the Asia Pacific region (Peng et al., 2008; Chan et al., 2008; Rodriguez et al., 2005). Managers' strategic decisions regarding entry mode and the associated foreign direct investment (FDI) are influenced by a range of institutional factors, including culture, legal certainty, political stability, governmental and market roles, treatment of property rights and degrees of perceived corruption. Strategic decision-making in unfamiliar and diverse environments is of central importance to MNEs investing in Asia, whether their motivation is the extension of global and regional supply chains or the desire to sell to consumers in the region. For MNEs, the region's potential in both of these dimensions of inward investment is underpinned by the tension surrounding the contrasting attraction of a large population offering a workforce with relatively low wage costs in the midst of rising incomes for increasing numbers of consumers. MNEs compete in an environment of rivalry between regional states to attract FDI. The competition not only takes the form of overt incentives linked to location but is also, more subtly, a competition based on relative institutional strength and the soundness of institutional capacity in each country (Buckley, 2009; Dunning and Zhang, 2008; Peng et al., 2008).

To develop and implement strategies in Southeast Asia, MNEs from Europe, North America, Japan and Australasia not only need to adapt the practices used in their home countries but also must be cognizant of the considerable differences within the region. This is especially pertinent with regard to entry modes entailing inward FDI because the MNE finds itself in close proximity to the state and reliant on the host nation's administrative and bureaucratic capacities to facilitate or hinder its subsidiary operations in that location. Likewise, the MNE's organizational management often faces demands for which it may be quite unprepared. The organization's ability to deal with the various legal, administrative and bureaucratic procedures of the host country, where the social norms are so different, tests the internal capacity of that organization in ways that are not easily predicted.

The remainder of this chapter is organized as follows. The next section discusses the treatment of institutions and MNE strategy in the strategy and international business literature, followed by a section that examines the relationship between FDI and institutional capacity. Recent trade and investment trends among the countries belonging to the Association of South East Asian Nations (ASEAN) are then outlined and an analysis of FDI and capacity in the five major ASEAN countries is undertaken. The methodology of the empirical work is then explained and the results displayed and discussed, before concluding remarks are made.

## Institutions and MNE strategy

National institutional frameworks include the formal and informal rules under which firms interact (North, 1989), and these can differ between home and host country, which makes them an important influence on MNE strategy (Estrin et al., 2009). Institutional effects greatly increase the complexity of MNEs' strategy formulation, demanding that strategy theorists take a nuanced approach. The institutional framework of the wider market must be reconciled with institutions internal to an MNE, such as its organizational culture and human resource practices. Strategies that effectively reconcile external and internal institutional contexts enable an MNE to create value in that market. The ability to apply home-country polices and strategies at the foreign subsidiary level depends greatly on the level of similarity in the institutional and cultural environments that exist between the home and the host environments (Stepien, 2009).

MNEs must manage two sets of institutional norms. How MNEs react to changes in and interactions between these sets is an underexplored area of the international business literature (Peng and Chen, 2011). The mediation of both home and host institutional environments greatly enhances the complexity of strategy formulation while increasing the variety of possible strategic responses to any given market situation. For example, the presence of institutional norms, such as corruption in a host market, affects the external and internal legitimacy of MNE subsidiaries, so the examination of the "broader institutional environment" is crucial (Rodriguez et al., 2005). Rodriguez et al. (2005) argue that the prevalence of corruption in transition economies influences MNE behavior by modifying entry mode choices. It is the state that can mitigate some of this complexity. The state apparatus can act as an institutional entrepreneur "shaping and crafting the necessary institutional infrastructure in order to capitalise on and exploit international market opportunities" (Nasra and Dacin, 2010: 584). By adopting an effective regime of incentives and upgrading institutional quality, government institutions can send the right signals to MNEs to influence their strategic decision to invest or to increase the scale of any planned investment.

Late in his career, John Dunning (2006) acknowledged the importance of institutions and their relative neglect in international business research. Scholars have perhaps become aware that a finely grained appreciation and accommodation of institutions is necessary to address the contemporary dynamics of private actors and states in the area of FDI. Institutional strength and infrastructure might be considered among the most important factors in the competition for inward FDI, as resources were in the past (Lall, 2002; Buckley, 2009; Dunning, 2006). An institution-based view of international business can be seen as the third leg of the strategy tripod, complementing the resource- and industry-based views (Peng et al., 2008). The twenty-first century has seen increased pressure on states to enable regional integration and support the flow of capital as part of the "global factory" construct (Buckley, 2009). It is the quality of domestic capabilities and institutions that is becoming a prime determinant in the pattern of FDI (Lall, 2002).

Mike Peng's comparison of North American and Asian approaches to understanding the effects of institutional capacities, or governance frameworks, on the practice of MNE business suggests the benefits of a rich research program into how institutions matter (Peng et al., 2008: 921) in relation to international business practice and theory. Thus it is important to closely explore the nature of state capacities and their relationship to business strategies. Such an exploration invites the detailed analysis of decision-making at the firm level and of the influence of incentives and disincentives, including regulation, as administered by the state. Arslan's (2012) stress on the relevance of institutions, such as the bureaucracy for strategic decisions (e.g., entry mode choice) is appropriate. Institutions help to shape regulatory behavior (Jansson, 2008). The legal, political and administrative systems in a host country are immobile factors. An MNE's capacity to address these factors determines the relative viability of the host economy for that firm. In this way the institutional context influences the transaction and coordination costs of production and ownership for an MNE in a host economy.

Yin-Li Tun et al. (2012) explore the manner in which institutional quality matters in relation to FDI by testing the hypothesis of a positive correlation between institutional quality and the level and extent of FDI. They identify three factors that explain the relationship:

- good institutions raise productivity and attract foreign investors;
- poor-quality institutions (e.g., in which corruption is significant) can increase the cost of doing business;
- inefficient government institutions create uncertainty for FDI, which is characterized by high sunk costs and therefore is especially vulnerable.

Nevertheless, only a partial picture emerges of how a range of such factors interact in conditions specific to regions such as Southeast Asia. We seek to clearly identify the manner in which locations differ (Ricart et al., 2004; Peng et al., 2008). One important element that differentiates locations within the ASEAN grouping is the state capacities, as indicated by bureaucratic quality (BQ) and other characteristics stressed in the public administration literature. This study contributes to the emerging research agenda by concentrating on one important subset of the host country's institutional framework: the bureaucratic apparatus. This study explores the extent to which variations in BQ within the five senior ASEAN members explains variations in inward FDI among these countries. Such a relationship, by extension, has important implications for MNE strategy. We concentrate on Singapore, Malaysia, Indonesia, Thailand and the Philippines as they account for the vast majority of gross domestic product (GDP) and inward FDI flows into the ASEAN. Furthermore, gaps in the available data sources prevent the inclusion of the other member states in this analysis.

## FDI and institutional capacity

The pursuit of strategies by MNEs focused on emerging economies confronts the challenge of adapting to the new institutional conditions associated with the governance of international business practices. Such conditions shape the modes of interaction between businesses and the state, and influence the outcomes for inward FDI. The role of the state has generally been considered as important in attracting FDI in East Asia and in the managerial decision-making related to these flows (White and Wade, 1984; Amsden, 1992; Weiss, 2003). With the exception of Singapore, the ASEAN countries have not used the strong state policies found in East Asia. However, all of them work to attract FDI while remaining cautious in their mediation and screening of these potential flows. The states in the majority of ASEAN countries can be characterized as having weak apparatuses, certainly if strength is considered in terms of capacities and capabilities.

Faced with the complexity of factors underpinning the strategic investment decisions of firms and the apparent opaqueness of much of the interaction between states and private sectors, research in international business is characterized by a pragmatic methodology. This pragmatism is also driven by the expense and difficulties related to standardizing micro-level data sources. Broad indicators collected for other purposes, such as corruption indices, are used as proxies for institutional strength and may well conceal much diversity in countries' institutional capacity in specific areas, such as the regulation of FDI. More finely grained data are desirable to better understand the interaction between MNE strategy and state capacity.

The absence of a textured and refined understanding of the state means that it is difficult to determine whether the state is an inhibitor or an enabler of private sector activity. For example, governments are active in providing state aid (such as financial incentives, tax holidays, providing infrastructure or trained workforces) and arrangements such as bilateral investment treaties that may be seen as favorable for inward FDI. Exploring governmental capacity is increasingly part of the project to better understand the nature of governance in international business (Chhotray and Stoker, 2008). Many possible configurations of state–society relationships are possible, including the private and public capacities to enable regulation in different forms, from self-regulation to strongly interventionist laws created and executed by the government. It is this type of emergent challenge that offers new MNE strategy opportunities.

A key variable in seeking a better understanding of state capacity through state behavior, and a possible focus for international business research, is a government's unique ability to successfully exert its influence in the area of FDI regulation. The need for a focus on governmental skills and capacities is recognized in the globalization and political science literature. For example, governmental capacities such as institutional arrangements may be ill-matched to work with the strategies of global businesses (Cherry, 2012). For example, government may offer strong protections in response to the concerns or fears that inward FDI generates in domestic cultures and business practices but be weak in enabling effective engagement with MNEs. This mismatch highlights the difficulties with the concept of governmental capacity – in particular, how this concept is defined and operationalized. The term "capacity" when applied to the state refers to the latter's ability "to act effectively on a sustained basis in pursuit of its objectives" (Polidano, 2000: 808). This implies both the capacity of the state itself as an organizational or institutional entity and the administrative or bureaucratic machinery of government to ensure effective policy development and implementation. Being aware of and responding to the challenges of various governance regimes is integral to MNEs developing successful strategies. This applies to both MNE inward investment strategies and modes of operational management in a host country.

Polidano (2000) goes further and argues that more emphasis should be given to examining specific public administrative capacities within states as a key explanatory variable in exploring state responsiveness to change. He emphasizes three areas in which administrative capacity is critical for effective government: policy capacity such as the ability of the bureaucracy to gather information, expertly analyze it and present findings in the form of policy proposals to government; the authority of the bureaucracy in implementing government policy; and the operational efficiency in terms of costs and quality in delivering or enabling government policy (Polidano, 2000: 819). Such work is consistent with others who have sought to better define and emphasize the importance of governmental capacity in enabling the successful engagement of nation states in globalization (Welch and Wong, 2001; Knill and Lehmkuhl, 2002; Sadleir and Mahony, 2009; Mahony and Sadleir, 2011).

## Recent trade and investment trends among the ASEAN countries

While MNEs face the challenge of determining an appropriate strategy to adopt for the countries of Southeast Asia, the capacities and skills of the countries in the region are tested by the inward FDI that is integral to such strategies. It is useful to explore the experiences of these countries, which have a history of pursuing stronger integration and an explicit policy of attracting MNEs and FDI. The working assumptions, in the case of the ASEAN, are that intraregional engagement and the development of state capacities will be closely related. Such capacitates may be attuned to and effectively mediate FDI from within and outside the region.

Despite a general recovery from the 1997 financial crisis, investment levels in the region struggled to return to their pre-1997 levels before the 2008 global crisis further influenced inward FDI. In 2011, global flows of FDI exceeded the pre-2008 crisis level. However, East and Southeast Asia saw only an 11% increase in that year – much less than the 35% increase recorded in South America (UNCTAD, 2012). Members of the ASEAN face considerable challenges in maintaining flows of FDI in terms of both level and share within the broader area of Asia, and all ASEAN inflow in 2011 was a mere USD76.2 billion of the USD1.5 trillion globally. A declining share of global flows within the Asia Pacific region highlights the need to revisit the domestic factors affecting FDI, including the relevance of government policy and individual state capacities. What is sought is a greater or more effective capacity to engage with international capital in relation to governmental policy development, implementation and regional engagement while mediating domestic opposition and other sectional interests.

Despite the uncertainty caused by the global financial crisis, it is clear that FDI inflows into the ASEAN have increased in recent years. Recent data (HSBC, 2013) suggest that Southeast Asia's share of the global FDI (7.6%) is not much less than China's (8.1%). Clearly there are attractive opportunities in the South East Asia region, as MNEs face higher wage costs in China, turn to newer markets and tap into new resource pools. Table 8.1 also illustrates how intra-ASEAN FDI continues to feature prominently in FDI inflows, followed by the two traditional MNE cohorts from Europe and the United States.

MNEs respond to evolving market opportunities and it can be argued that the level and scope of their involvement, hence the level of FDI into

*Table 8.1*   Major sources of FDI inflows into ASEAN (USD millions)

| Country or region | 2009 | 2010 | 2011 | 2009–2011 |
|---|---|---|---|---|
| ASEAN | 6,300 | 14,323 | 26,271 | 46,894 |
| European Union | 8,063 | 17,012 | 18,240 | 43,316 |
| Japan | 3,790 | 10,756 | 15,015 | 29,561 |
| China | 1,853 | 2,785 | 6,034 | 10,672 |
| United States | 5,704 | 12,772 | 5,783 | 24,259 |
| Hong Kong | 5,667 | 344 | 4,096 | 10,107 |
| Top ten sources | 35,705 | 68,600 | 83,449 | 187,754 |
| Others | 11,192 | 23,679 | 30,662 | 65,532 |

*Source*: Data from ASEAN (2013).

the region, can be amplified or mitigated by the presence or absence of strong institutional frameworks.

ASEAN has been a focus for cooperation and the opening of the region to trade and investment. However, despite ongoing discussion, good intentions and agreements, the slow growth of intra-ASEAN trade continues to attract attention in contrast with the reliance of countries on trade relationships with the rest of the world (Green, 2007). The rise of China since the early 1990s has only added to this dilemma (Jarvis, 2004, 2012). Intraregional trade is highly reliant on supply chains that are focused on delivery to China and thus the trade pattern is largely mirrored in flows of investment. China's influence has been no less evident in the pattern of FDI than in trade since the mid-1990s, although the attractions of the Chinese market have reflected a deterioration in the performance of the ASEAN group in terms of shares, thus undermining a key source of growth for the region. For example, the ASEAN attracted 50% of region-wide FDI in 1990 and saw its share decline to less than 20% over the next 15 years (Jarvis, 2012).

In light of the decades of regional cooperative efforts, it is reasonable to think that the liberalization of FDI would be well advanced in the ASEAN. However, Jarvis' (2012: 224) assessment is discouraging, with progress still needed in four areas:

(1) absolute reductions in national autonomy in relation to investment screening and conditionality provisions; (2) increased transparency in respect to member states' national investment regimes; (3) enhanced standardisation and codification of regulatory standards governing investment-related provisions across member

states; and (4) enhanced centralised coordination and decision making in respect to investment governance.

In all four of the abovementioned areas, Jarvis finds that there is currently little that is satisfying. The picture that emerges from his analysis is one of high-minded intent regarding investment liberalization being constantly stymied by vested interests in several countries. Investment nationalism persists within the grouping and there seems little prospect of it abating and allowing even ratified treaties to be implemented effectively. Average tariff levels are reported as falling to quite low levels while the exemptions allow the tariffs that do influence traded goods to be considerably higher. The "noodle bowl" of bilateral and regional trade agreements adds further complexity to trade and investment relations in this region (Dent, 2010).

While Jarvis (2012) offers a pessimistic picture, it is of considerable import to this study. His political economy analysis seems accurate. However, little mention is made of the bureaucratic capacity within the ASEAN countries aside from the observation that there are "pitfalls of dissimilar national institutional capacity" (Jarvis, 2012: 235) and, later, that "For the vast majority of ASEAN states, however, lower levels of economic development and poor levels of institutional and infrastructural capacity limit their ability to absorb investment flows on a scale that would significantly change current investment patterns" (Jarvis, 2012: 339).

## Analysis of FDI and capacity among the ASEAN

To explore the effect that institutional factors have on inward FDI among the ASEAN countries, this empirical analysis uses publically available indicators to create proxies for state capacity. The factors affecting FDI flows have long attracted attention in international business studies. While macroeconomic factors have often been found to be significant in similar studies, attention is also drawn to culture and to institutional strength. In a sense, this empirical analysis is a "first pass" at measuring state capacity as a determinant of inward FDI.

In doing so, this study draws on the work of Grosse and Trevino (2009), which provides a useful model for this approach to assessing experience among the ASEAN. They use aggregate data to explore the relationship between FDI flows and governmental regulatory regimes and institutions, as experienced in several of Eastern Europe's transitional economies. While their primary concern is the effects of bilateral investment, their focus is on the institutional strength of transitional economies, which offers us an interesting point of departure.

## Methodology

Following Grosse and Trevino (2009), this study uses panel data estimation techniques, such as pooled ordinary least squares (OLS) and fixed and random effects models, to estimate the marginal effects of bureaucratic quality (*BQ*), corruption (*Cor*), investment profile (*IP*), level of aggregate output (*GDP*), inflation (*Inf*) and exchange rates (*exrate*) on FDI inflows (*FDI_in*). The standard pooled multiple linear regression over time *t* is represented by

$$FDI\_int = \beta 1 + \beta 2 BQt + \beta 3 Cort + \beta 4 IPt + \beta 5 GDPt + \beta 6 Exratet$$
$$+ \beta 7 inflt + \varepsilon t, \tag{1}$$

where $\varepsilon t$ is a random error term with a mean of zero and a constant variance.

The use of pooled multiple linear regression in isolation is far from ideal as it is based on the rather simplistic assumption that the behavior of these ASEAN countries is identical and that factors influencing FDI inflows are identical across countries. In reality, this is far from the truth. Each country in the ASEAN has its own idiosyncratic set of factors that are likely to influence investment flows. It would be prohibitively time-consuming to identify and include all of these variables to control for their influence. However, in the absence of incorporating these unknown variables, pooled OLS estimation is likely to suffer from omitted variable bias.

To address these problems, fixed and random effects estimation can be used. Adkins (2010) provides a concise operational treatment of fixed and random effects models for practical estimation using the popular open source econometric package GRETL. Operationally, the fixed effects model specification for N = 5 original ASEAN countries can be represented as

$$FDI\_init = \beta 1 + \beta ind + \beta mal + \beta phl + \beta thl + \beta 2 BQit + \beta 3 Corit + \beta 4 Iit$$
$$+ \beta 5 GDPit + \beta 6 Exratit + \beta 7 infit + \varepsilon it. \tag{2}$$

The fixed effects model is also known as the least squares dummy variable model because it includes N − 1 country dummy variables that allow the intercept of the estimated equation to vary for each country. The dummy variables control for country-specific variations in FDI inflows and are an example of individual one-way fixed effects, as it is still assumed that the intercepts for individual countries are time invariant.

Random effects models, in contrast, do not estimate individual fixed effects for each observational unit. Instead, an overall average intercept is estimated and the regression function for individual countries is then expected to randomly vary around this overall average intercept. According to Adkins (2010), the variability of the random effect is captured by a new parameter, $\mu i$, such that the random effects model can be specified as

$$FDI\_init = (\beta 1 + \mu i)) + \beta 2 BQit + \beta 3 Corit + \beta 4 Iit + \beta 5 GDPit$$
$$+ \beta 6 Exratit + \beta 7 infit + \varepsilon it. \tag{3}$$

The variance $(\sigma^2_{\mu i})$ of $\mu i$ can be used to determine the presence of random effects through a Breusch-Pagan test. If the null hypothesis of $\sigma^2_{\mu i} = 0$ can be rejected against the alternative that $\sigma^2_{\mu i} > 0$, then random effects estimation can be used. Similarly, the consistency and non-correlation of the random effects with the other explanatory variables can be established by using a Hausman test.

### Variable definitions and data treatment

FDI inflows (dependent variable) – billions of current US dollars are used in level form and FDI inflows were obtained from the UNCTADstat online database.

*Bureaucracy quality* is a measure that assesses where the bureaucracy has the strength and expertise to govern without drastic changes in policy if government services are interrupted. It is an index constructed by the Political Risk Services International Country Risk Group (ICRG) database using the subjective evaluation criteria.

*Corruption* is a measure of corruption in the political system. It is an index constructed by the ICRG database using the subjective evaluation of country criteria.

*Investment profile* is a measure of the government's attitude toward inward investment. It includes assessments of contract viability, profits repatriation and payment delays. It is an index constructed by the ICRG database using the subjective evaluation of country criteria.

*GDP* is measured in billions of current US dollars and obtained from the UNCTADstat online database.

*Inflation* is measured by a consumer price index for each country with 2005 as the base year (100). Measures of inflation were obtained from the World Bank, World Development Indicators database.

*Exchange rate* is measured by the nominal average annual exchange rate between the local currency unit and the US dollar. Data on this variable were obtained from the World Bank, World Development Indicators database.

We originally estimated the marginal effects of the explanatory variables on FDI inflows for the five original ASEAN member countries from 1985 to 2010 for a total of 130 observations. However, the scope of the analysis has been expanded to include the junior ASEAN members: Brunei, Myanmar and Vietnam (referred to as the ASEAN 8). The authors were unable to include Cambodia and Laos in this estimation due to the unavailability of data on the corruption and investment profile variables for these two countries. Consistent data on the junior members is only available from 1995 onwards, thus the estimation of the ASEAN 8 models is over a restricted timespan of 1995–2010 for a total of 120 observations. Random effects estimation for the senior ASEAN member countries (ASEAN 5) was not possible due to insufficient degrees of freedom. To test the consistency of the random effects generalized least squares (GLS) estimates, a Hausman test must be conducted, which is not possible for the ASEAN 5 as the number of cross-sectional units (five) is less than the number of explanatory variables (six, excluding the intercept and random effect parameters). Furthermore, given the long timespan of the data, non-stationarity is a problem. The Levin-Lin-Chu unit root test for panel data was used to test for stationarity, and in the presence of non-stationarity the variables were transformed by first differencing the variable series prior to estimation.

## Results

Estimation results are presented in Table 8.2. The White test for heteroskedasticity was used to test for inconstant error term variance and the standard errors reported in Table 8.2 are robust to heteroskedasticity. For the ASEAN 5 the fixed effects model wields the highest explanatory power, whereas for the ASEAN 8, as per the Hausman test, the GLS estimates for the random effects are consistent. Thus the marginal effects estimated by model 5 are also valid for analysis.

The coefficient estimates for models 4 and 5 are approximately similar, barring bureaucracy quality. While the marginal effect and statistical significance of bureaucracy quality varies considerably across the

Table 8.2 Marginal effects of FDI inflows into ASEAN countries

| Variable | Model 1 | Model 2 | Model 3 | Model 4 | Model 5 |
|---|---|---|---|---|---|
| | Pooled OLS | Fixed effects | Pooled OLS | Fixed effects | Random effects |
| | ASEAN 5 | ASEAN 5 | ASEAN 8 | ASEAN 8 | ASEAN 8 |
| Intercept | −11.5 (4.01)*** | −4.62 (3.19) | −7.34 (4.58) | 1.76 (4.57) | −1.99 (4.05) |
| Bureaucratic quality | −0.36 (0.58) | −1.62 (0.46)*** | −0.03 (1.30) | −2.52 (1.30)* | −1.40 (1.29) |
| Corruption | 1.17 (0.49)** | 0.12 (0.33) | 3.27 (0.97)*** | 1.18 (0.22)*** | 1.40 (0.55)** |
| Investment profile | 1.75 (0.54)*** | 1.52 (0.50)*** | 0.37(0.37) | 0.66 (0.17)*** | 0.71 (0.27)*** |
| GDP | 0.03 (0.02) | 0.04 (0.02)** | 0.06 (0.03)* | 0.06 (0.03)** | 0.06 (0.01)*** |
| Exchange rate | −0.0004 (0.0001)*** | −0.0005 (0.00008)*** | 0.001 (0.0009) | 0.002 (0.0009)** | 0.002 (0.001)* |
| Inflation | 0.02 (0.140) | 0.34 (0.06)*** | 0.07 (0.06) | 0.08 (0.05)* | 0.07 (0.06) |
| Adjusted R square | 0.43 | 0.56 | 0.39 | 0.69 | – |

*Note*: ***significant at 1%, **significant at 5%, *significant at 10%.

model specifications, the negative sign on the coefficient is unexpected. This suggests that an increase in bureaucracy quality has a detrimental effect on FDI inflows. However, a more logical and reasonable interpretation, especially given the low levels of statistical significance for this variable, is that the Political Risk Services (PRS) Group's (2007) measure of bureaucracy quality is not a particularly good one with respect to explaining FDI inflows. Reductions in corruption, improvements to a country's investment profile, and to a somewhat lesser extent, the level of aggregate development (GDP) have statistically significant positive marginal effects on FDI inflows.

The effect of exchange rates on FDI inflows has the correct expected sign (and is also the most statistically significant) in models 1 and 2. However, as the magnitude of the coefficient estimates reveals, the effect of exchange rates on FDI inflows is quite limited. This finding should be treated with caution and warrants further investigation. Similarly, higher inflation levels (leading to higher interest rates) show a positive relationship with FDI inflows, but this variable is only statistically significant in models 2 and 4. Given the mixed nature of the marginal results for these two financial variables, it is hypothesized that there may be a time lag with respect to the timing of FDI, such that these variables or the FDI inflows among the ASEAN were motivated by long-term strategic implications rather than by year-on-year exchange rate and price movements. These hypotheses should be tested in future research.

## Discussion

In the context of this study the critical variable is BQ. In particular, the focus is on the bureaucratic capacity, which contributes to the state's ability to exert its influence over inward foreign investment processes. The state's intent is to influence MNE strategies in relation to such investments. Focusing on the BQ of government institutions allows a previously tested set of variables to be used, as developed by Welch and Wong (2001), who examined the responsiveness of national bureaucracy to the pressures of globalization. The five variables identified by Welch and Wong are bureaucracy, structure, size, scope, autonomy and accountability. Each of these is described further in Table 8.3.

More broadly, "bureaucratic capacity" has been interpreted as indicative of a nation state's ability to respond to political complexity. We argue for the adoption of bureaucratic capacity as a variable for use by international business scholars. The hypothesis is that it should help the assessment of a particular state's effectiveness to regulate or at

*Table 8.3* Bureaucratic capacity variables

| Variables | Description |
| --- | --- |
| *Structure* | Level of centralization or decentralization of the bureaucracy. |
| *Size* | Extent of resources (human, financial or natural) used by the bureaucracy. |
| *Scope* | The range of services for which a bureaucracy is responsible. |
| *Autonomy* | The ability or power of the bureaucracy to make independent policy decisions. |
| *Accountability* | Mechanisms that hold government responsible to citizens and stakeholders for their actions. |

*Source*: Welch and Wong (2001: 377–378).

least make decisions on investment proposals associated with specific instances of inward FDI, such as for cases in which a government seeks to influence the kinds of investment and the mixture of foreign and domestic ownership in an industry. This includes the form of controls on the level of firm ownership and the openness to various modes of entry, perhaps favoring joint venture arrangements over foreign-owned subsidiaries.

To this end, BQ is employed as a proxy for bureaucratic capacity and its characteristics in terms of types and numbers of bureaucratic resources; that is, the number of bureaucrats working on regulating FDI and their education and skill levels, experience and motivations. Such capacity is fundamental to any national government's ability to both project its particular policy stance and carry through such commitments in enabling or restricting inward FDI. Thus, the bureaucratic capacity to engage with MNEs as investors, to recognize and understand the strategic intent of such investors and to look for an accommodation within the policy and regulatory controls is fundamental to patterns of successful industry investment. In turn, bureaucratic capacity, either in better enabling or restricting foreign investment through MNEs, is fundamentally important in implementing a governmental regime's approach to inward FDI. For MNEs, such a factor should be seen as a significant variable in the realization of strategic intent when seeking engagement with a host country's markets or industry.

This view is set out in Figure 8.1 and shows the significance of bureaucratic capacity in mediating FDI flows and codifying and operationalizing institutional norms. According to the diagram, the first order of engagement is between an MNE's strategy and decisions to directly invest in a host country market or industry, emphasizing the

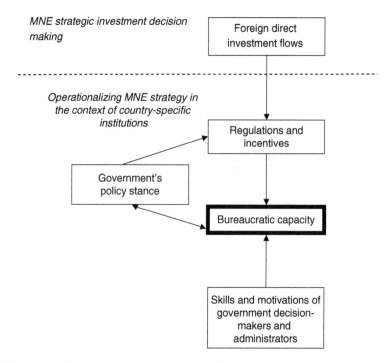

*Figure 8.1*   Schematic situating government bureaucratic capacity in FDI flows

former's perceptions as a foreign investor. In doing so, the focus for the MNE is on the opportunity the host country market or industry offers, the perceptions of the government's policy stance (open or closed to inward FDI), incentives for or barriers to entry and the skills and motivations of government decision makers and administrators in terms of ease of doing business. Thus, the diagram illustrates how bureaucratic capacity, which serves government and enables engagement with foreign investors, is fundamental to the achievement of both the investor's objectives and those of the host government. Such bureaucratic capacity enables the mobilization of state institutional norms and resources to be directed toward engaging with investment flows.

However, the results show that using the PRS data set, "bureaucracy quality" performs poorly. Across all five models, "bureaucracy quality" shows a negative correlation while the corruption proxy tends to show a result more consistent with the expectation that institutional capacity is an important determinate of inward FDI flow. Although the poor fit of the BQ variable is unexpected, the better fit of corruption is consistent with research suggesting that corruption, as a form of institutionalism, captures forms of state and bureaucratic behavior, which also significantly affect MNE strategy and decision making on the location and type of direct investment in host countries (Peng, 2008; Wei, 2000; Jansson, 2008).

The counter-intuitive result in relation to BQ is probably due to the weakness of the chosen measure; that is, BQ as a stand-alone measure of institutional strength. It might also reflect idiosyncrasies in the data over the period. The improved BQ ranking of Indonesia in the post-Suharto period was also during the time of declining FDI flows in the wake of the 1997 Asian Crisis. Furthermore, these data do not allow for other explanations as to why higher levels of BQ would lead to less certainty in FDI regulation for international businesses. For example, decline in FDI since the Asian Crisis of 1997 has seen an increase in state capacities for regulation; however, such a trend is difficult to disaggregate in the PRS measure of BQ. The performance of BQ may reflect the difficulty in using only one component from a larger PRS index of political risk. The PRS acknowledges the limitations of the individual components, but holds the view that on balance these limitations are less significant in the case of their aggregate index data. Evidently, researchers face substantial limitations in finding valid measures for institutional strength that are sufficiently robust to allow for the analysis of state administrative capacity. Likewise, MNE management is also constrained in their knowledge of and ability to develop and implement strategies in the ASEAN countries. The existence of heterogeneous bureaucratic capacity between ASEAN states indicates that MNEs must adapt their processes and internal management or work to influence the extant capacity they confront in each state.

A research program may need to be strongly qualitative while surveying and analyzing the experience of MNEs across national borders. Further data collection needs to focus on the MNEs' leveraging of subsidiary experience. From the perspective of MNEs, individual firms will need to gather data on a case-by-case basis for the institutions that concern them in the pursuit of their strategies and where such strategies engage with state or government institutions. To date, measures such as BQ are purely subjective, whereas ideally measures would contain a large objective component (Lall, 2002). In turn, such limits to data restrict likely methodological responses to Peng's challenge to explore and build the third leg of the "strategy tripod." Nevertheless, there are guides, such as from those who are investigating the workings of government institutions (Polidano, 2000) and engagement with international businesses (Jansson, 2008). Such objective measures might be found in the form of staff expertise within the state bureaucracy, internal compliance, cost and efficiency of government services and service quality.

## Conclusion

This chapter contributes to the emerging research on the role of institutions in MNE strategy by exploring the role of state capacity and specifically the quality of the bureaucracy in attracting inward FDI. Recent attention to institutions in the strategy and international business literature is to a significant extent due to the experience of MNE activity in Asia and the diverse cultural and institutional environment represented by regions such as Southeast Asia. Such diversity has demonstrated the limited efficacy of traditional theories that focus on industry- or resource-based views of international firms. Attempting to develop a third leg for the "strategy tripod" presents challenges of both a conceptual and an empirical nature, all of which have been outlined in this chapter. The focus on the ASEAN 5 is motivated by the challenges such countries face in establishing adequate institutional capacity.

This research was prompted by increasing interest in international business with institutions as a key variable in explaining FDI flows. This is explored by investigating the experience of ASEAN member countries and we find that reliance on broad indicators of institutional strength are of limited utility. This is both a problem of the manner in which institutions such as a government's administrative capacity are conceptualized and a problem of data. Dunning (2006), Buckley (2009) and Lall (2002) all identify institutional strength as a theoretical blind spot. Similarly, Rodriguez et al. (2005), Jansson (2008) and Arslan (2012) all point to the importance of institutions for MNE strategy. The understanding of institutions needs considerable refinement, and challenges us to develop better ways to portray and measure institutional capacity.

As the discussion of the empirical results reveals, it is important to conceptualize state capacity as a subtle entity that needs to be specifically measured rather than incorporated into a general notion of "institutional strength" where it can be subsumed into the empirical work by commonly available proxies. More bespoke measures of state capacity and BQ are needed to advance this third leg of the strategy tripod. Thus we suggest the adoption of public administration and political science approaches to reconceptualize the problem. While data limitations remain, a route that incorporates a more nuanced treatment of government and state capacity offers the way forward.

## References

Adkins, L.C. (2010) *Using GRETL for Principles of Econometrics*. Stillwater: Oklahoma State University.

Amsden, A. H. (1992) *Asia's Next Giant: South Korea and Late Industrialization*. Oxford: Oxford University Press.

Arslan, A. (2012) Impacts of institutional pressures and the strength of market supporting institutions in the host country on the ownership strategy of multinational enterprises: Theoretical discussion and propositions. *Journal of Management and Governance*, 16 (1), 107–124.

Association of Southeast Asian Nations (2013) Foreign direct investment statistics, http://www.asean.org/news/item/foreign-direct-investment-statistics, date accessed 25 February 2013.

Buckley, P. (2009) The impact of the global factory on economic development. *Journal of World Business*, 44 (2): 131–143.

Chan, C. M., Isobe, T., & Makino, S. (2008) Which country matters? Institutional development and foreign affiliate performance. *Strategic Management Journal*, 29: 1179–1205.

Chhotray, V., & Stoker, G. (2008) *Governance Theory and Practice: A Cross-Disciplinary Approach*. New York, NY: Palgrave Macmillan.

Cherry, J. (2012) Upgrading the "software": The EU-Korea Free Trade Agreement and sociocultural barriers to trade and investment. *The Pacific Review*, 25 (2): 247–268.

Dent, C. (2010) Free trade agreements in the Asia-Pacific a decade on: Evaluating the past, looking to the future. *International Relations of the Asia-Pacific*, 10 (3): 201–245.

Dunning, J. H. (2006) Towards a new paradigm of development: implications for the determinants of international business. *Transnational Corporations*, 15 (1): 174–227.

Dunning, J.H., & Zhang, F. (2008) Foreign direct investment and locational competitiveness of countries. *Transnational Corporations*, 17 (3): 1–30.

Estrin, S., Baghdasaryan, D., & Meyer, K. E. (2009) The impact of institutional and human resource distance on international entry strategies. *Journal of Management Studies*, 46 (7), 1171–1196.

Green, D.J. (2007) Bridging the ASEAN development divide: A egional overview. *ASEAN Economic Bulletin*, (24): 15–34.

Grosse, R., & Trevino L.J. (2009) New institutional economics and FDI in Central and Eastern Europe. In K.P. Sauvant & Sachs, L.E. (Eds.) *The Effect of Treaties on Direct Investment*. Oxford: Oxford University Press.

HSBC (2013) *The Great Migration. How FDI is Moving to ASEAN and India*. Asian Economics, Business Research. The Hong Kong and Shanghai Banking Corporation (HSBC) Ltd.

Jansson, H. (2008) *International Business Strategy in Emerging Country Markets: The Institutional Network Approach.* Cheltenham: Edward Elgar Publishing.

Jarvis, D. (2004) *The Changing Economic Environment in Southeast Asia: ASEAN, China and the Prospects for Enhanced Cooperation.* Tokyo: Ministry of Finance, Japan.

Jarvis, D. (2012) Foreign direct investment and investment liberalisation in Asia: Assessing ASEAN's initiatives. *Australian Journal of International Affairs,* 66 (2): 223–264.

Knill, C., & Lehmkuhl, D. (2002) Private actors and the state: Internationalization and changing patterns of governance. *Governance: An International Journal of Policy, Administration, and Institutions,* 15 (1): 41–63.

Lall, S. (2002) Linking FDI and Technology development for capacity building and strategic competitiveness. *Transnational Corporations,* 11 (3): 40–88.

Mahony, G., & Sadleir, C. (2011) Metagovernance and the role of cultural norms in the regulation of foreign direct investment: Trans-Tasman FDI regimes. *Asia Pacific Journal of Public Administration,* 33 (1), 77–92.

Nasra, R., & Dacin, M. T. (2010) Institutional arrangements and international entrepreneurship: The state as institutional entrepreneur. *Entrepreneurship: Theory & Practice,* 34 (3), 583–609.

North, D. (1989) Institutions and economic growth: An historical introduction. *World Development,* 17 (9): 1319–1332.

Peng, M. W., Wang, D. Y., & Jiang, Y. (2008) An institution-based view of international business strategy: A focus on emerging economies. *Journal of International Business Studies,* 39 (5), 920–936.

Peng, M. W., & Hao, C. (2011) Strategic responses to domestic and foreign institutional pressures. *International Studies of Management & Organization,* 41 (2), 88–105.

Polidano, C. (2000) Measuring public sector capacity. *World Development,* 28 (5): 805–822.

Political Risk Services Group. (2007) *The Handbook of Country and Political Risk Analysis,* 4th ed. L.D Howell (Ed.). East Syracuse, New York: PRS Group.

Ricart, J. E., Enright, M. J., Ghemawat, P., Hart, S. L., & Khanna, T. (2004) New frontiers in international strategy. *Journal of International Business Studies,* 35 (3): 175–200.

Rodriguez, P., Uhlenbruck, K., & Eden, L. (2005) Government corruption and the entry strategies of multinationals. *Academy of Management Review,* 30 (2), 383–396.

Sadleir, C., & Mahony, G. (2009) Institutional challenges and response in regulating foreign direct investment to Australia. *Economic Papers,* 28 (4): 337–345.

Stępień, B. (2009) Host country effects in multinational companies' performance – empirical evidence from Polish subsidiaries. *Poznan University of Economics Review,* 9 (2), 57–77.

UNCTAD. (2012) *Global Investment Trends Monitor* No. 8. 24 January.

Wei, Shang-Jin. (2000) How taxing is corruption on international investors? *Review of Economics and Statistics,* 82 (1): 1–11.

Weiss, L. (Ed.). (2003) *States in the Global Economy: Bringing Domestic Institutions Back in.* Cambridge University Press.

Welch, E.W., & Wong, W. (2001) Effects of global pressures on public bureaucracy: Modeling a new theoretical framework. *Administration & Society,* 33 (4): 371–402.

White, G., & Wade, R. (1984) Developmental states in East Asia: Editorial introduction. *IDS Bulletin,* 15 (2), 1–3.

Yin-Li Tun, W.N.W. Azman-Saini, & Siong-Hook Law (2012) International evidence on the link between foreign direct investment and institutional quality. *Engineering Economics,* 23 (4), 379–386.

# Part III

# Marketing and Consumer Behavior

# 9
## Cross-Cultural Research on Consumer Responses to Service Failure: A Critical Review

*Lisa C. Wan and Maggie Y. Chu*

### Introduction

The service industry contributes significantly to global economic development and there has been a strong research effort to understand consumers' perceptions of service quality and satisfaction. Although service performance is pivotal to consumer satisfaction in the service-delivery process, it is characterized by heterogeneity (Zeithaml, Parasuraman and Berry, 1990). Given this inherent variability, researchers have recognized that service failures are almost inevitable. Therefore understanding how consumers react to service failures, including what factors mitigate their dissatisfaction, has important theoretical and managerial implications for the service industry. Not surprisingly, issues of service failure and recovery have received considerable research attention in the service marketing field (e.g., Choi and Mattila, 2008; Hess, Ganesan and Klein, 2003; Kalamas, Laroche and Makdessian, 2008; Mattila, 2001; Mittal, Huppertz and Khare, 2008; Smith and Bolton, 2003; Smith, Bolton and Wagner, 1999; Witz and Mattila, 2004).

Characterized by an intense amount of social interaction between the service provider and customers, service encounters are highly vulnerable to cultural influences. Evidence pointing to culture's influence on consumers' responses to service failure and recovery efforts has been accumulating in recent years (Chan and Wan, 2008; Chan, Wan and Sin, 2009; Liu and McClure, 2001; Hui and Au, 2001; Hui, Ho and Wan, 2011; Mattila and Patterson, 2004a, 2004b; Patterson, Cowley and Prasongsukarn, 2006; Wan, 2013; Wong, 2004). The global expansion of service industries indicates a pressing need for more cross-cultural research to advance the knowledge about consumer reactions to service failure.

This chapter provides a brief review of the recent cross-cultural research in the area of consumer reactions to service failure, to identify future research directions. There are two major themes in cross-cultural research: consumer reactions to service failure and consumer preference for different types of service recovery. The former has focused on investigating how culture influences consumers' level of dissatisfaction with service failures and their tendency to complain, switch or spread negative word-of-mouth. Attribution theory has been employed in some of these studies to explain the cross-cultural difference. The consumer preferences examined have highlighted specific service-recovery types, such as apology, compensation and speed of recovery. Justice theory is the key theoretical framework applied to explain the cross-cultural differences in consumers' responses to service-recovery efforts (see Figure 9.1 for the conceptual framework of the review).

The majority of cross-cultural studies have used Hofstede's (1980, 1991) individualism vs. collectivism cultural dimension to explain consumer reactions to service failures. Relatively few studies have employed other cultural dimensions (e.g., power distance, uncertainty avoidance) to examine such cross-cultural differences. More recently, a few researchers have used other cultural values, such as face

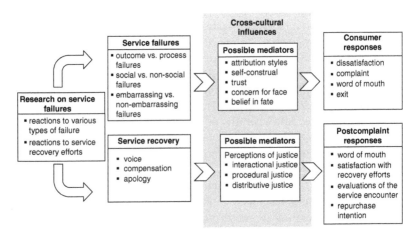

*Figure 9.1*   An overview of cross-cultural research on consumers' responses to service failure

concern and fate belief, to investigate the cross-cultural differences in consumers' reactions to service failure (e.g., Chan, Wan and Sin, 2009).

Previous cross-cultural research has focused on investigating the cognitive aspect of consumer reactions to service failure, such as satisfaction (a comparison between expected and actual performance) and complaint intention. Very scant attention has been paid to the emotional aspect of consumers' reactions to service failure (e.g., anger, fear, regret, embarrassment) across cultures. This observation suggests avenues for future investigation.

This chapter is divided into three major sections. First, a general introduction is provided for some of the key cultural constructs used in the previous service-failure literature, including a description of the characteristics of individualism vs. collectivism and two other cultural values: concern for face (CFF) and belief in fate (BIF). Second, the literature on the differences in Asian and Western consumers' reactions to service failure and recovery is reviewed. Finally, possible future directions for cross-cultural service-failure research are discussed.

## Culture

### Culture: Individualism vs. collectivism and self-construal

One of the most widely cited constructs used to compare cross-cultural consumer differences is individualism vs. collectivism (e.g., Chan and Wan, 2008; Liu, Furrer and Sudharshan, 2001; Laroche, Ueltschy, Abe, Cleveland and Yannopoulos, 2004; Mattila and Patterson, 2004a). Individualism vs. collectivism is the extent to which an individual views themselves as an individuated entity or in relation to others, and these two aspects of self-view constitute an independent and an interdependent self-construal, respectively (Markus and Kitayama, 1991). People with independent self-construal regard themselves as individuated entities; the self is defined by unique attributes and the separateness of people is emphasized. People with an interdependent self-construal define themselves in relation to others, which highlights the importance of relationships and social connectedness. In general, independent self-construal is more prevalent among the individualist cultures, such as that of the United States. The pursuit of personal goals and self-interests are encouraged in these societies and people are more inclined to strive for individual accomplishments. In collectivist cultures such as that of China, the interdependent self-construal predominates. The fulfillment of one's social obligations is more important than satisfying one's own desires. People pursue collective goals and strive to preserve social harmony. As one's culture is closely tied to a particular self-construal, self-construal plays a crucial role in explaining the cross-cultural difference observed in service-failure and recovery research.

Recent research has found that a particular self-construal can be made temporarily accessible through primes even if it is inconsistent with the chronic self-construal (e.g., an interdependent self can be temporarily made accessible in Americans). For example, Aaker and Lee (2001) used a situational prime (i.e., a website with wording that primed either an independent or an interdependent self) to manipulate the two self-construals in both Chinese and American participants, with the chronic self-construal being either consistent or inconsistent with the primed self-construal. They found that the participants who were exposed to the chronically inconsistent prime behaved in ways that were consistent with the primed self-construal rather than with the chronic self-construal (e.g., American participants who were exposed to the interdependent primes acted in ways that were consistent with the interdependent self-construal). In other words, while cultures may chronically activate a particular self-construal, priming can temporarily activate the other self-construal to make the corresponding set of knowledge temporarily more accessible.

Because the independent vs. interdependent self-construal is an individual-level extension of the individualism-collectivism cultural dimension (Markus and Kitayama, 1991; Singelis, 1994), the following review includes research findings about consumer reactions to service failure that used priming to temporarily activate consumers' self-construals.

### Face concern and fate belief

In addition to the well-known individualism-collectivism construct, some researchers have recently advocated two cultural values – face concern and fate belief – to examine consumers' reactions to service failure (e.g., Chan, Wan and Sin, 2009; Wan, 2013). The concept of face is rooted in people's innate need for social acceptance. According to Goffman (1967), face is a favorable public self-image that an individual seeks to maintain – a perceived image of self that is affirmed through interaction with others. One's face can be enhanced, maintained or lost through social interactions, thus it represents a dynamic aspect of the self-concept. Building on Goffman's works, Chan, Wan and Sin (2009) defined CFF as "the extent to which an individual shows regard for and is interested in the protection and enhancement of face in social interactions." Because Asians hold a socially defined interdependent self-view, they generally have greater CFF than Westerners.

Across cultures, individuals frequently invoke the notions of fate and luck to interpret unexpected events or outcomes. Fate represents the mysterious impersonal power that brings about positive and negative events. The assignment of events can be based on a predestined order or determined transitorily by the luck or bad fortune of a person in a particular situation. Chan, Wan and Sin (2009) further defined "BIF" as "the extent to which an individual believes in fate/luck as a powerful force shaping events and outcomes." Note that impersonal transcendental laws are commonly found in the faith traditions held by Asians. In contrast, science and rationality take precedence over mystical convictions in Western societies. Asians therefore tend to hold a stronger BIF.

### Consumer reactions to service failure across cultures

The process of service production, delivery and consumption involves considerable human interaction. A high level of human involvement is often necessary for service providers to satisfy customers with varying needs (e.g., a haircut or a spa treatment), but such involvement can be failure prone. Within the stream of service-failure research, there emerge some typologies that categorize service failures of various natures. These distinctions provide substantial implications for the cross-cultural study of consumers' responses to service failure. In the following, these typologies are delineated and how Western and Asian consumers differ in their relative responses is discussed.

### Service failures

Service failures occur when customers experience dissatisfaction as a result of the actual service performance not meeting expectations. The service literature defines service quality according to two aspects: the outcome and process qualities (Grönroos, 1984). The outcome quality is the impersonal aspect of services and centers on the core service that consumers receive (also known as the "what" component), whereas the process quality is the interpersonal aspect of services and centers on the manner in which the core service is delivered (also known as the "how" component). Based on this distinction, service failures are further dichotomized into outcome and process failures. An outcome failure is a situation in which some aspect of the core service is not delivered. For example, the flight is delayed. A process failure occurs when the service is delivered in a deficient manner. For example, the flight attendant is inhospitable. An outcome failure can also be regarded as a non-social failure, as the consumers mainly suffer from a loss of economic resources (such as time and money). However, when a process failure occurs, consumers' status or esteem is threatened (i.e., social resources) and thus the failure is social (Chan, Wan and Sin, 2009). The outcome-process or social–non-social distinction is the cornerstone to investigating cross-cultural differences in responses to service failure.

Wan (2013) enriched the conceptualization of service failures by considering the presence and absence of other consumers. When service failure occurs in the presence of other consumers, much embarrassment is provoked (i.e., embarrassing failure). For example, a waiter could accidentally spill soup on a customer and other customers witness the entire process. The target customer is likely to experience more embarrassment than if the restaurant had been empty and there had been no witnesses. In this situation, their desired social identity is threatened. In contrast, when the failure occurs in a private context (i.e., non-embarrassing failure), consumers' social images remain intact. Empirical evidence from Wan's study shows that whether the failure occurs in a public or private context determines the strategies that Western and Asian consumers pursue to vent their dissatisfaction.

## Dissatisfaction

Earlier findings have concluded that consumers in collectivist cultures exhibit more tolerance toward service failures than do consumers in individualist cultures (e.g., Liu, Furrer and Sudharshan, 2001; Laroche et al., 2004). However, more recent evidence has shown that given the same failure, Asian consumers can become even more dissatisfied than their Western counterparts. The effect of culture on consumer dissatisfaction with service failure can be contingent on other factors (e.g., Chan and Wan, 2008; Chan, Wan and Sin, 2009) such as attribution tendency, failure types, CFF, BIF and relationship norms.

### Attribution

Attribution theory concerns how one uses information to infer the causes of another party's behavior or events (Folkes, 1988). When a negative incident occurs, people often attempt to make attributions regarding its cause to blame the potential parties. Therefore when a service failure occurs, attribution is a key mediator of consumer dissatisfaction (Bitner, 1990; Oliver and DeSarbo, 1988; Weiner, 2000). There are two general ways in which consumers make attributions: i) they blame the service provider/firm or ii) they blame the situational factors (e.g., bad luck). Consumers are more dissatisfied if they attribute more responsibility to the service provider/firm.

The cultural literature has suggested that individualists are more likely than collectivists to commit the fundamental attribution error – that is, showing a stronger tendency to overestimate personal responsibility and underestimate situational influence for behavior observed in others (e.g., Markus and Kitayama, 1991; Morris and Peng, 1994). Therefore there is a general prediction that individualists (vs. collectivists) would attribute more responsibility to the service provider/firm in service-failure situations and thus become more dissatisfied. Given this differential sensitivity of individualist and collectivist consumers to situational constraints, Mattila and Patterson (2004a) found that a causal explanation of a service failure had a greater effect on i) reducing American (vs. East Asian) consumers' internal attributions (i.e., blaming the service provider) and ii) increasing American (vs. East Asian) consumers' external attributions (i.e., blaming situational factors).

Drawing on the defensive attribution theory, Chan and Wan (2008) argued that collectivists (vs. individualists) would attribute more responsibility to the service provider/firm if they put greater value on the loss of resources involved in the failures. In this regard the service-failure type plays an important role in influencing consumer attribution tendencies and dissatisfaction across cultures.

*Service-failure types*

As previously noted, service failures involve the loss of consumer resources. Specifically, outcome and process failures lead to the loss of economic and social resources, respectively. More importantly, consumers' reactions to the service failure may depend on their preference for these resources. Previous cross-cultural studies have shown that collectivists tend to emphasize social resources (Weber, Hsee and Sokolowska, 1998; Goffman, 1967; Oetzel et al., 2001). This may be due to the prevailing emphasis on interpersonal relationships in collectivist cultures. Social resources are essential to the functioning of many aspects of life and therefore are valued more highly among collectivists. In contrast, individualists attach more value to economic resources. Unlike collectivists, they prefer tangible incentives in work settings (Money and Graham, 1999; Thomas, Au and Ravlin, 2003) and focus more on the economic attributes when evaluating service (Schmitt and Pan, 1994). Based on these premises, Chan and Wan (2008) further proposed that when a process failure occurs (i.e., a loss of social resources), collectivists tend to take it as a more serious offense and become more dissatisfied than individualists. However, an outcome failure (i.e., a loss of economic resources) leads to more dissatisfaction among individualists. This hypothesis generated empirical support in their study.

### Concern for face and belief in fate

As discussed, individualists and collectivists are more dissatisfied with outcome and process failures, respectively. Based on this evidence, Chan, Wan and Sin (2009) identified the two factors mediating the cultural effect and extended their investigation beyond the long-established individualism-collectivism framework by demonstrating the difference between Western and Asian consumers in relation to two other cultural values: concern for face (CFF) and belief in fate (BIF).

Because Asians hold a socially defined interdependent self-view, they generally have a greater CFF than Westerners. In the case of social failure, consumers lose face during the interaction with service providers (e.g., a waiter is rude when taking an order). This poses a severe face threat to the consumer. Asian consumers, who are inherently more sensitive to face issues, are generally more dissatisfied than their Western counterparts. CFF aggravates dissatisfaction – an effect that holds even for non-social failure as long as face issues are salient in the situation (e.g., other consumers are present).

Chan, Wan and Sin (2009) demonstrated that BIF mediates the effect that culture has on consumer dissatisfaction with non-social failure. In the event of non-social failure (e.g., a dish is not cooked properly), there is much ambiguity as to the causes of the failure. For instance, the chef may be sick or the restaurant may happen to run over capacity, which leaves the situation open to mystical interpretations (e.g., "I'm just unlucky today"). Given that Asians hold stronger BIF than Westerners, they are more likely to resort to such fatalistic explanations. As a result, Asian consumers are more tolerant than Western consumers when faced with non-social failure. In Chan, Wan and Sin's (2009) study, this effect still holds even for social failure as long as the situation is fate-suggestive (e.g., a brand name like "Lucky Star" heightened fatalistic thinking).

### Relationship norms

When service failure occurs, are consumers more tolerant if the service provider is a friend? Wan, Hui and Wyer (2011) suggested that this may not be the case. Their results showed that a friendly relationship with the service provider is not always beneficial. In particular, friendships are governed by communal norms (Aggarwal and Zhang, 2006), and the participants in these relationships are supposed to be attentive to the other's needs and are obligated to give benefits in response to such needs (i.e., self-obligation). They also expect that the others will be responsive to their own needs (i.e., other-obligation). Following this logic, Wan, Hui and Wyer (2011) postulated that tolerance of a friend's (i.e., the service provider's) mistake depends on whether the consumers consider their self- or other-obligations. In their study, interdependent and independent self-construal was experimentally induced (Experiment 4) and they found that considering oneself as interdependent with others supports accessible self-obligation. In such a situation, consumers feel that it is their responsibility to empathize with the service provider's difficulty. As a result, consumers react less negatively to the service failure. However, they also identified a boundary condition of this effect. When the service provider fails to deliver an explicit promise, the participants who are primed with interdependent self-construal react even more negatively because an explicit promise makes the other-obligation (i.e., that of the service provider) salient. Breaking such a promise implicates a breach of the communal norms and results in a sense of betrayal that amplifies consumers' negative reactions.

Although Wan, Hui and Wyer (2011) induced self-construal experimentally, it is acknowledged that more chronic cultural differences exist in the disposition to think of oneself as either independent or interdependent (Markus and Kitayama, 1991; Singelis, 1994). Because the interdependent self-construal is chronically more accessible in collectivist cultures, to this extent their results suggest that Asians may be more tolerant than Westerners of service failures that result from the breach of an implicit agreement. However, they may be less tolerant than Westerners of the breach of an explicit promise. The implications of these cross-cultural consumer behavior differences warrant further examination.

### Behavioral responses

When a service encounter does not live up to the consumers' standards, they may engage in different behaviors to express their dissatisfaction. Hirschman (1970) delineated three broad categories of responses to dissatisfaction: i) exit – to terminate the relationship with the service provider or avoid further patronization; ii) loyalty – the opposite of exit; and iii) voice – to complain or disseminate negative word-of-mouth. The voice response can be further classified into three categories based on at whom it is directed (Singh, 1988). Consumers may lodge a complaint directly with the service provider, spread negative word-of-mouth privately or complain to a third party (e.g., consumer agency) for sanctioning the service provider. In general, consumers in collectivist cultures have a heightened concern for social harmony, thus confrontational responses such as direct complaint are less preferable. Instead they are more likely to engage in private responses than are consumers in individualist cultures (Liu and McClure, 2001).

In addition to the abovementioned evidence, Hui, Ho and Wan (2011) investigated the effect of prior relationships with the service provider on the behavioral responses after service failure. Well-established relationships are imbued with trust. As a social resource, trust attenuates the negative effects of process failure (i.e., a loss of social resources) and reduces switching intention across both individualist and collectivist cultures. This effect still holds among the collectivists on outcome failure because in collectivist cultures such as that in China, trust also has instrumental value. Interpersonal relationships or *guanxi* are often viewed as an economic resource that one can use (Park and Luo, 2001). So, in such a context, a trusting relationship can also serve as a remedy to the loss of economic resources (i.e., outcome failure). However, trust has opposite effects on complaint intention across individualist and collectivist cultures. Trust reduces complaint intention in the collectivist culture because direct confrontation is not preferred in these societies, while in individualist cultures a trusting relationship often encourages constructive confrontation, which enables improvement. Therefore Western consumers are more likely to complain if a prior relationship with the service provider exists.

When service failure occurs, the strategies that consumers adopt to vent their dissatisfaction may depend on the presence or absence of other consumers. The recent studies conducted by Wan (2013) provided the first-known evidence in relation to the above inquiry. Drawing on the differences between individualists and collectivists regarding CFF, Wan (2013) postulated that collectivists are sensitive to self-face and other-face while individualists are only sensitive to self-face. A particular service failure may heighten the concern of self-face, other-face or both. Specifically, in the presence of social others, the situation becomes more embarrassing and can result in a significant loss of face, and therefore concern for self-face predominates. Collectivists should engage in a variety of facework remedies to regain their own face, and this is indeed the case. Findings from Wan's (2013) study suggested that collectivists are more likely to complain, switch and spread negative word-of-mouth than individualists when embarrassing failure occurs.

However, in non-embarrassing failures, consumers' desired social image remains unaffected. In this situation, concern for other-face predominates and guides the behavior of collectivists. Hence,they are more likely to engage in avoiding facework and exhibit a stronger intention to switch and spread negative word-of-mouth and a weaker intention to complain than individualists.

### Cultures and service recovery

Service recovery is key to restoring consumer satisfaction after a service failure. There are three common types of complaint-handling strategies: compensation, voice (allowing consumers an opportunity to express dissatisfaction and listening to them) and apology. Tax, Brown and Chandrashekaran (1998) pointed out that consumer evaluations of complaint handling are contingent on the following types of justice: i) distributive (the outcomes they receive), ii) procedural (the procedures used to arrive at the outcomes) and iii) interactional (the nature of the interpersonal treatment during the process). For example, consumers will use distributive justice to evaluate compensation, procedural justice to evaluate voice, and interactional justice to evaluate apology.

Generally speaking, previous cultural findings have suggested that individualists have a greater concern for distributive justice than collectivists, whereas collectivists seem to put greater emphasis on procedural and interactional justice than individualists. For example, Mattila and Patterson (2004b) found that compensation (e.g., offering a discount) was more effective in restoring a sense of justice to American consumers than to their East Asian (Thai and Malaysian) counterparts. Hui and Au (2001) learned that voice had a stronger effect on Chinese than Canadian consumers, whereas compensation had a stronger effect on Canadian than Chinese consumers. Wong (2004) found that although compensation improved consumers' assessments of the service encounter in both Asian and Western countries (i.e., Singapore, Australia and the United States), it only affected American consumers' repurchase intentions and word-of-mouth. Interestingly, an apology improved satisfaction for Singaporean and Australian consumers but not for American consumers.

## Future research directions

This chapter reviews the findings with regard to the cross-cultural differences in consumer responses to service failure. Early work in this research area has focused on investigating how cultures influence consumer dissatisfaction and complaint responses in cases of service failure, and there are some previously overlooked issues that may suggest avenues for future research. First, the cultural dimensions used in the literature are analyzed, followed by some thoughts related to the role of observing consumers in service-failure situations, and finally culture's influence on consumers' emotional responses to service failure are discussed.

### Cultural dimensions and service-failure types

Hofstede's works (1980, 1991) are the most cited in comparing cross-cultural differences in consumer behavior. Although he (1991) suggested five dimensions to conceptualize cross-cultural differences – individualism/collectivism, power distance, uncertainty avoidance, masculinity/femininity and long-term orientation – the majority of previous cross-cultural research has used the individualism/collectivism dimension to investigate consumer reactions to service failures (see Table 9.1). Therefore future research may explore how to use other cultural dimensions to explain and predict consumer reactions to different types of service failure.

For example, power distance is related to how people perceive the power inequalities in a society. People in high power distance societies (e.g., Asians) are more likely to accept a power hierarchy and vertical top-down communication than those in low power distance societies (e.g., Westerners). The former are also more likely to respect people with high social status and exhibit greater tolerance of power and wealth inequalities. Note that in service interactions between consumers and service providers, consumers sometimes exercise greater bargaining power than providers, and in other situations that dynamic is reversed. In the hospitality industry (e.g., restaurants, hotels) the consumer is generally treated as "king" and service providers do their best to satisfy consumers, given the keen competition in the industry. Thus consumers may have more bargaining power than service providers. However, in the professional service industry (e.g., hospitals, law firms), consumers are dependent on the expertise of service providers (e.g., doctors, lawyers) to reduce the perceived risk inherent in the service-delivery processes. In this case, service providers may have more bargaining power than consumers. Because consumers in high (vs. low) power distance societies are more likely to accept a power hierarchy and to respect people with high social status, they may have a higher tolerance level for service failures in professional service

Table 9.1 Summary of the cross-cultural literature on service failures

| Source | Key constructs | Measures of cultural orientation | Samples | Service context | Key findings |
|---|---|---|---|---|---|
| Liu, Furrer and Sudharshan (2001) | Hofestede's five dimensions | Using items adapted from Hofstede (1991) | United States, Switzerland, China, Singapore, South Korea | Banking services | For inferior service, consumers from high-individualism or low uncertainty-avoidance cultures were more likely to engage in negative word of mouth, switching and complaint than those from low-individualism or high uncertainty-avoidance cultures. |
| Liu and McClure (2001) | Hofestede's individualism vs. collectivism; in-group vs. out-group perceptions | Not measured | United States vs. Korea | Retail and restaurant services | In the event of postpurchase dissatisfaction, collectivists were less likely to engage in voice behavior (complain) but were more likely to engage in private behavior (spreading negative comments or exit) than individualists. |
| Hui and Au (2001) | Hofestede's individualism vs. collectivism | Using items adapted from Hui (1988) and Triandis (1988) | China vs. Canada | Hotel services | The effects of the three complaint-handling strategies varied across the two countries. For the Chinese consumers, voice increased fairness perceptions regarding the complaint-handling process whereas compensation enhanced these perceptions among the Canadian consumers. |

*Table 9.1* (Continued)

| Source | Key constructs | Measures of cultural orientation | Samples | Service context | Key findings |
|---|---|---|---|---|---|
| Mattila and Patterson (2004b) | Independent-interdependent self-construal | Using items from Singelis (1994) | United States, Malaysia, Thailand | Restaurant services | The authors compared the effects of compensation and explanation on consumers' fairness perceptions. Offering compensation (e.g., discount and apology) was more effective in restoring a sense of justice among US consumers. East Asian consumers had higher perceptions of interactional and distributive justice than their US counterparts, both before and after being provided with a causal explanation. |
| Mattila and Patterson (2004a) | Independent-interdependent self-construal | Using items from Singelis (1994) | United States, Malaysia, Thailand | Restaurant services | Given the fact that Westerners (vs. Asians) were less sensitive to situational constraints when making attributions, a causal explanation of a service failure could reduce Western consumer's tendency to blame the service provider (i.e., internal attributions) and facilitate more external attributions (i.e., blame situational factors). |

| Wong (2004) | Hofestede's five dimensions | Not measured | United States, Australia, Singapore | Restaurant services | The authors examined the effects of service recovery strategies (compensation and apology) on consumers' post-complaint responses. Compensation improved consumers' evaluations of the service encounter in the three countries but only affected US consumers' repurchase intention and word of mouth behavior. An apology improved satisfaction for Singaporean and Australian consumers but not for US consumers. |
|---|---|---|---|---|---|
| Patterson, Cowley and Prasongsukarn (2006) | Hofestede's individualism vs. collectivism, power distance and uncertainty avoidance | CVSCALE (e.g., Donthu and Yoo 1998) | Australia vs. Thailand | Hotel services | We examined the effects of service attributes on consumers' fairness perceptions. An organization-initiated recovery could enhance perceived interaction justice among consumers of higher (vs. lower) collectivist value orientation. An apology from a service provider of high status increased perceived distributive justice for consumers of higher (vs. lower) power distance value orientation. Having cognitive control over the recovery process enabled a higher level of procedural justice among consumers with higher (vs. lower) uncertainty avoidance value orientation. |

Table 9.1 (Continued)

| Source | Key constructs | Measures of cultural orientation | Samples | Service context | Key findings |
|---|---|---|---|---|---|
| Chan and Wan (2008) | Hofstede's individualism vs. collectivism | Measured independent-interdependent self-construal (Singelies 1994) | United States vs. Hong Kong | Computer repair services | With an outcome failure, US consumers were more dissatisfied than the Chinese consumers while the reverse was true for process failure. US consumers were more likely to complain whereas Chinese consumers were more likely to spread negative comments when dissatisfied. |
| Chan, Wan and Sin (2009) | Concern for face (CFF) and belief in fate (BFF) | Using scales adapted from Cocroft and Ting-Toomey (1994) for measuring CFF and Leung and Bond (2004) for measuring BIF | Asians vs. Americans who lived in Hong Kong | Restaurant services, movie theater and computer repair services | Asian (vs. Western) consumers were characterized by higher CFF and BIF; they were more dissatisfied with social failures than non-social failures. These effects were sensitive to pertinent contextual factors, such as the presence of other consumers and a fate-suggestive brand. |

| Study | Construct | Measurement | Country | Service context | Findings |
|---|---|---|---|---|---|
| Hui, Ho and Wan (2011) | Independent vs. interdependent self-construal | Using items from Singelies (1994) | China and Canada | Computer repair and procurement services | A trusting relationship with the service provider mitigated process failure (e.g., lower switching intention) across both countries and outcome failure in China. It increased (decreased) Canadian (Chinese) consumers' complaint intention. |
| Wan (2013) | CFF and independent vs. interdependent self-construal | Using the Scale developed by Chan and Wan (2009) for measuring CFF and the scale from Singelis (1994) for measuring self-construal | United States and Hong Kong | Restaurant services | In a non-embarrassing failure, Chinese (vs. US) consumers were less likely to complain while for embarrassing failures, Chinese (vs. US) consumers were more likely to complain, switch and spread negative comments. |

industries. Consequently, they may be less likely to complain, switch and spread negative word-of-mouth in this situation. Therefore future research could investigate this possibility.

### The role of observing consumers in service-failure situations

The effects that consumers have in a service setting have long been recognized in the service marketing literature (i.e., the servuction model, Langeard, Bateson, Lovelock and Eiglier, 1981). However, relatively few studies have investigated the effects of other consumers on consumers' service experiences. Earlier research has recognized that the presence of other consumers will influence consumer satisfaction and service evaluations (Brocato, Voorhees and Baker, 2012; Grove and Fisk, 1997). More recently, studies have found that the experience of a particular consumer may influence how the other (observing) consumers evaluate the service – that is, simply observing a service failure that happens to others in the same setting will influence a consumer's attributions and evaluations of the service (Wan, Chan and Su, 2011).

For example, Wan, Chan and Su (2011) found that upon witnessing a service failure, consumers who were prevention-focused (i.e., sensitive to loss vs. non-loss) were more likely to blame the service provider than those who were promotion-focused (i.e., sensitive to gain vs. nongain) when the consumer involved in the service failure was personally similar to them. Given that the literature has noted that Asians are more prevention-focused and Westerners are more promotion-focused (Uskul, Sherman and Fitzgibbon, 2009), it is possible that Asian (vs. Western) consumers will be more likely to blame the service providers when observing a service failure being experienced by a consumer who is similar to them. Apparently, this prediction contradicts previous findings that Asian (vs. Western) consumers are generally less likely to blame service providers (Mattila and Patterson, 2004a). In this regard, it may be worthwhile for future research to look into these ambiguities.

### Consumers' emotional reactions to service failure

This review shows that most of the cross-cultural research previously conducted has focused on examining consumers' cognitive or behavioral responses rather than their emotional responses to service failure. Therefore another opportunity for future research would be to explore consumers' emotional responses, such as regret, to service failure across cultures. Service failures result in unpleasant experiences. However, consumers may feel partly responsible for these experiences when they have a choice to engage in the service encounter. Not only does this lead to dissatisfaction but it also might provoke regret. Regrets arise when consumers imagine how the bad experience might have been avoided had they chosen differently (i.e., counterfactual thinking). Moreover, evidence from cross-cultural research indicates that individualists and collectivists differ in the manner in which they generate counterfactuals (Roese, Hur and Pennington, 1999). This may influence what and how much consumers regret. If this is the case, the effect of choice in post-service-failure situations may vary across cultures.

Chu, Wan and Wyer (2012) looked into this possibility. In the situation they investigated, a consumption failure was preceded by a series of choices. For example, a consumer chooses to eat at restaurant A, then chooses to order dish B and, at the end, finds that the dish tastes very bad. Chu, Wan and Wyer (2012) postulated that exercising choice is a pleasurable process and results in positive feeling. However, when the outcome turns out to be unfavorable, negative reactions such as regret emerge. In situations in which consumers make a sequence of choices, which choice is predominately associated with positive feeling and which is associated with regret may depend on how consumers generate counterfactuals.

Findings from Roese, Hur and Pennington's (1999) study suggest that individualists value achievement and the acquisition of a desirable outcome (i.e., promotion focus). Thus when a promotion goal fails, they tend to mentally undo the later events in the sequence (e.g., not ordering the dish), altering the event that is most sufficient to bring out a positive consequence. In contrast, collectivists are concerned with security and the preservation of status quo (i.e., prevention focus), and they tend to mentally undo the earlier events (e.g., not going to the restaurant in the first place), altering the event that is most necessary for the negative consequence that occurred. Following this logic, Chu, Wan and Wyer (2012) contend that among the individualists (collectivists), choices that occur in the later (earlier) stage tend to be undone mentally and hence provoke more regrets, while earlier (later) choices may elicit positive feeling. In either case, choices have contrasting effects on consumers' reactions. At one point in the sequence regret may predominate, while at another point, positive feeling predominates. Their preliminary work provides initial evidence on the contrasting effects of choice in the collectivist culture. However, the effects of choice in the individualist culture still warrant further investigation.

# References

Aaker, J. L., & Lee, A. (2001) "I" seek pleasures and "we" avoid pains: The role of self-regulatory goals in information processing and persuasion. *Journal of Consumer Research*, 28 (June), 33–49.

Aggarwal, P., & Zhang, M. (2006) The moderating effects of relationship norm salience on consumers' loss aversion. *Journal of Consumer Research*, 33 (3): 413–419.

Bitner, M. J. (1990) Evaluating service encounters: The effects of physical surroundings and employee responses. *Journal of Marketing*, 54 (2): 69–82.

Brocato, E. D., Voorhees, C. M., & Baker, J. (2012) Understanding the influence of cues from other customers in the service experience: A scale development and validation. *Journal of Retailing*, 88 (3): 384–398.

Chan, H., & Wan, L. C. (2008) Consumer responses to service failures: A resource preference model of cultural influences. *Journal of International Marketing*, 16 (1): 72–97.

Chan, H., Wan, L. C., & Sin, L.Y. (2009) The contrasting effects of culture on consumer tolerance: Interpersonal face and impersonal fate. *Journal of Consumer Research*, 36 (2): 292–304.

Choi, S., & Mattila, A.S. (2008) Perceived controllability and service expectations: Influences on customer reactions following service failure. *Journal of Business Research*, 61 (1): 24–30.

Chu, M. Y., Wan, L. C., & Wyer, R. S. (2012) The influence of perceived control in sequential decision-making: A cross-cultural perspective. Paper presented at the *Academy of International Business 2012 Conference*. Xiamen, China.

Cocroft, B.K., & Ting-Toomey, S. (1994) Facework in Japan and the United States. *International Journal of Intercultural Relations*, 1994 (4): 469–506.

Donthu, V., & Yoo, B. (1998) Cultural influences on service quality expectations. *Journal of Service Research*, 1 (2): 178–186.

Folkes, V. S. (1988) Recent attribution research in consumer behavior: A review and new directions. *Journal of Consumer Research*, 14 (4): 548–565.

Goffman, E. (1967) *Interaction Ritual: Essays on Face-to-Face Behavior*. London: Doubleday.

Grönroos, C. (1984) A service quality model and its marketing implications. *European Journal of Marketing*, 18 (4): 36–44.

Grove, S. J., & Fisk, R. P. (1997) The impact of other customers on service experiences: A critical incident examination of "getting along". *Journal of Retailing*, 73 (1): 63–85.

Hirschman, A.O. (1970) *Exit, Voice, and Loyalty: Reponses to Decline in Firms, Organizations and States*. Cambridge: Harvard University Press.

Hofstede, G. (1980) *Culture's Consequences: International Differences in Work-Related Values*. Beverly Hills, CA: Sage Publications.

Hofstede, G. (1991) *Cultures and Organizations: Software of the Mind*. London: McGraw-Hill.

Hui, M. K. & Au, K. (2001) Justice perceptions of complaint-handling: A cross-cultural comparison between PRC and Canadian customers. *Journal of Business Research*, 52 (2): 161–173.

Hui, M. K., Ho, C. K., & Wan, L. C. (2011) Prior relationships and consumer responses to service failures: A cross-cultural study. *Journal of International Marketing*, 19 (1): 59–81.

Hess, R. L. Jr., Ganesan, S., & Klein, N. M.(2003) Service failure and recovery: The impact of relationship factors on customer satisfaction. *Journal of Academy of Marketing Science*, 31 (2): 127–145.

Kalamas, M., Laroche, M., & Makdessian, L. (2008) Reaching the boiling point: Consumers' negative affective reactions to firm-attributed service failures. *Journal of Business Research*, 61 (8): 813–824.

Langeard, E., Bateson, J. E. G., Lovelock, C. H., & Eiglier, P. (1981) *Marketing of Services: New Insights from Consumers and Managers, Report No. 81–104*. Marketing Sciences Institute, Cambridge, MA.

Laroche, M., Ueltschy, L. C., Abe, S., Cleveland, M., & Yannopoulos, P. P. (2004) Service quality perceptions and customer satisfaction: Evaluating the role of culture. *Journal of International Marketing*, 12 (3): 58–85.

Leung, K., & Bond, M. H.(2004) Social axioms: A model of social beliefs in multicultural perspective. In Mark P. Zanna (Ed.), *Advances in Experimental Social Psychology Vol. 36*: 119–197. San Diego, CA: Elsevier.

Liu, R., & McClure, P. (2001) Recognizing cross-cultural differences in consumer complaint behavior and intentions: An empirical examination. *Journal of Consumer Marketing*, 18 (1): 54–75.

Liu, B. S., Furrer, O., & Sudharshan, D. (2001) The relationships between culture and behavioral intentions toward services. *Journal of Service Research*, 4 (2), 118–129.

Markus, H. R., & Kitayama, S. (1991) Culture and the self: Implications for cognition, emotion, and motivation. *Psychological Review*, 98 (2): 224–53.

Mattila, A. S. (2001) The effectiveness of service recovery in a multi-industry setting. *Journal of Services Marketing*, 15 (7): 583–596.

Mattila, A. S., & Patterson, P. G. (2004a) The impact of culture on consumers' perceptions of service recovery efforts. *Journal of Retailing*, 80 (3): 196–206.

Mattila, A. S., & Patterson, P. G. (2004b) Service recovery and fairness perceptions in collectivist and individualist contexts. *Journal of Service Research*, 6 (4): 336–46.

Mittal, V., Huppertz, J. W., & Khare, A. (2008) Customer complaining: The role of tie strength and information control. *Journal of Retailing*, 84 (2): 195–204.

Money, R. B., & Graham, J. L. (1999) Salesperson performance, pay, and job satisfaction: Tests of a model using data collected in the United States and Japan. *Journal of International Business Studies*, 30 (1): 149–172.

Morris, M. W., & Peng, K. (1994) Culture and cause: American and  Chinese attributions for social and physical events. *Journal of Personality and Social Psychology*, 67 (6): 949–971.

Oetzel, J., Ting-Toomey, S., Masumoto, T., Yokochi, Y., Pan, X., Takai, J., & Wilcox, R. (2001) Face and facework in conflict: A cross-cultural comparison of China, Germany, Japan, and the United States. *Communication Monographs*, 68 (24): 235–258.

Oliver, R. L., & DeSarbo, W. S. (1988) Response determinants in satisfaction judgments. *Journal of Consumer Research*, 14 (4): 495–507.

Park, S. H., & Luo, Y. (2001) Guanxi and organizational dynamics: Organizational networking in Chinese firms. *Strategic Management Journal*, 22 (5): 455–477.

Patterson, P. G., Cowley, E., & Prasongsukarn, K. (2006) Service failure recovery: The moderating impact of individual-level cultural value orientation on perception of justice. *International Journal of Research in Marketing*, 23 (3): 263–277.

Roese, N. J., Hur, T., & Pennington, G. L. (1999) Counterfactual thinking and regulatory focus: Implications for action vs. inaction and sufficiency vs. necessity. *Journal of Personality and Social Psychology*, 77 (6): 1109–1120.

Schmitt, B. H., & Pan, Y. (1994) Managing corporate and brand identities in the Asian-Pacific Region. *California Management Review*, 36 (4): 32–48.

Singelis, T. M. (1994) The measurement of independent and interdependent self-construals. *Personality and Social Psychology Bulletin*, 20 (5): 580–591.

Singh, J. (1988) Consumer complaint intentions and behavior: Definitional and taxonomical issues. *Journal of Marketing*, 52 (1): 93–107.

Smith, A. K., Bolton, R. N., & Wagner, J. (1999) A model of customer satisfaction with service encounters involving failure and recovery. *Journal of Marketing Research*, 36 (3): 356–372.

Smith, A. K., & Bolton, R. N. (2003) The effect of customers' emotional responses to service failures on their recovery effort evaluations and satisfaction judgments. *Journal of Academy of Marketing Science*, 31 (1): 5–23.

Tax, S. S., Brown, S. W., & Chandrashekaran, M. (1998) Customer evaluations of service complaint experiences: Implications for relationship marketing. *Journal of Marketing*, 62 (2): 60–76.

Thomas, D. C., Au, K., & Ravlin, E. C. (2003) Cultural variation and the psychological contract. *Journal of Organizational Behavior*, 24 (5): 451–71.

Uskul, A.K., Sherman, D.K., & Fitzgibbon, J., (2009) The cultural congruency effect: culture, regulatory focus, and the effectiveness of gain- vs. loss-framed health Messages. *Journal of Experimental Social Psychology*, 45 (3), 535–541.

Wan, L. C. (2013) Culture's impact on consumer complaining responses to embarrassing service failure. *Journal of Business Research*, 66 (3): 298–305.

Wan, L. C., Chan, E. K., & Su, L. (2011) When will customers care about service failures that happened to strangers? The role of personal similarity and regulatory focus and its implication on service evaluation. *International Journal of Hospitality Management*, 30 (1): 213–220.

Wan, L. C., Hui, M. K., & Wyer, R. S. (2011) The role of relationship norms in responses to service failures. *Journal of Consumer Research*, 38 (2): 260–77.

Weber, E. U., Hsee, C. K., & Sokolowska, L. (1998) What folklore tells us about risk and risk taking: Cross-cultural comparisons of American, German, and Chinese proverbs. *Organizational Behavior and Human Decision Processes*, 75 (2): 170–186.

Weiner, B. (2000) Attributional thoughts about consumer behavior. *Journal of Consumer Research*, 27 (3): 382–387.

Wong, N. Y. (2004) The role of culture in the perception of service recovery. *Journal of Business Research*, 57 (9): 957–963.

Wirtz, J., & Mattila, A. S. (2004) Consumer responses to compensation, speed of recovery and apology after a service failure. *International Journal of Service Industry Management*, 15 (2): 150–166.

Zeithaml, V. A., Parasuraman, A., & Berry, L. L. (1990) *Delivering Quality Service: Balancing Customer Perceptions and Expectations*. New York: Free Press.

# 10
## Self-Discrepancy and Consumer Responses to Counterfeit Products

*Ling Peng, Lisa C. Wan and Patrick S. Poon*

## Introduction

Counterfeiting is the production and sale of a fake product that is seemingly identical to an original brand-name product. International trade in counterfeit goods has shown a steady increase in the new millennium, totaling an estimated €475 billion a year, or nearly 8% of world trade (International Anti-counterfeiting Coalition, 2008). This increase in the buying and selling of counterfeit products continues to gain ground despite global efforts by governments, enforcement agents and intellectual property rights–holders to stop counterfeiting and piracy. The anti-counterfeiting forces seem to be fighting a losing a battle, as consumers often knowingly purchase counterfeits (Nia and Zaichkowsky, 2000). Therefore a clear and actionable understanding of the motivations underlying consumers' purchase of counterfeits is necessary to influence counterfeit consumption behavior (Wilcox, Kim and Sen, 2009).

Academics have examined the problem of counterfeiting from a "supply-side" perspective, examining sources of counterfeit goods and factors such as political, legal and economic infrastructure that may facilitate the practice (Berrell and Wrathall, 2007; Lambkin and Tyndall, 2009). However, it has become clear that this focus on the supply side of the equation is not enough and must be complemented by an equally aggressive attempt to control the demand side of this nebulous market. Getting a handle on what drives a consumer to choose a fake, illegal product is a complex undertaking, as motives vary widely from price and easy access to social acceptability. Ethical orientations, price-quality associations and cultural values are frequently included as determinants of a consumer's propensity to purchase or avoid counterfeit brands (e.g., Phau and Teah, 2009; Chaudhry and Stumpf, 2011; Norum and Cuno, 2011).

There has been a recent research trend among marketing academics to understand what consumer characteristics lead to the purchase of counterfeit brands. Many consumption activities are related to self-definition, and, although it has been widely recognized that self-concept influences consumer thought, emotional experiences, motivation and behavior (Baumeister, 1998), there has been limited research focusing on how consumers' perceived self-concept influences their responses to counterfeit products. A growing body of work has indicated that consumers choose products when their attributes match some aspect of the self (Aaker, 1999; Onkvisit and Shaw, 1987; Zinkhan and Hong, 1991; Claiborne and Sirgy, 1990). Self-concept theory holds that people have a concept of self based on who they think they are (the actual self) and a concept of who they think they would like to be (the ideal self). Most people experience a discrepancy between their actual and ideal selves, but for some consumers this gap is especially large. Higgins et al. (1986) suggest that the greater the magnitude of self-discrepancy possessed by an individual, the more the individual will experience the type of discomfort associated with that self-discrepancy. This study examines whether and how the actual and ideal self-discrepancy influence consumers' attitudes and purchase intentions toward counterfeits. In particular, there are three research objectives: i) to understand the implications and effect of self-discrepancy on consumers' attitudes and purchase intentions toward counterfeits; ii) to highlight the differences across cultures and product categories; and iii) to gain insight into how this effect varies among consumers with different self-monitoring.

Empirical data were collected from respondents in Hong Kong and the United States through an online survey on consumer attitudes and purchase intentions toward counterfeits in the following categories: DVDs/CDs, computer software, brand-name clothes and luxury items. The four product categories were chosen because they are the most common counterfeit purchases, according to the research report conducted by Business Action to Stop Counterfeiting and Privacy (BASCAP) in November 2009, with more than half of consumers reporting that they had bought counterfeit versions of these products. DVDs/CDs and computer software are experience-based products consumed privately while brand-name clothes and luxury items are more symbolic and mostly consumed publicly. Hong Kong and the United States were chosen to represent collectivist and individualist cultural backgrounds, respectively. All of the respondents were aged between 18 and 34 because even though counterfeit purchasers can be found in all age groups, there is a decrease with age in most countries (e.g., 56% of those aged 18–24 compared with 36% of those aged above 50 in the UK, according to the BASCAP research report).

The rest of this chapter is organized as follows. First, the theoretical considerations are discussed and hypotheses proposed. Second, the empirical study design is presented. Next, the research findings are reported and discussed. Finally, the managerial and theoretical implications are highlighted, and directions for further research indicated.

## Theoretical considerations and hypotheses

There are two types of counterfeit product purchased by consumers: deceptive and non-deceptive. Deceptive counterfeiting is when the consumers do not know that what they have purchased is a counterfeit product, whereas non-deceptive purchases of counterfeit products indicate that the consumers willingly buy the counterfeit products (Grossman and Shapiro, 1988). The latter have been referred to as "collaborators" (Cordell, Wongtada and Kieschnick, 1996) and "accomplices" (Tom et al., 1998). This study deals with collaborators who have bought non-deceptive counterfeit products.

### The effect of self-discrepancy

According to self-concept theory, people act in ways that maintain and enhance their self-concept. Consumption is a central part of consumers' everyday lives. People use consumption not only to create and maintain their sense of self but also to locate themselves within society (Elliott, 1994, 1997). Consumption is an important source of symbolic meanings with which a person can create and express their self-concept and identify relations with others.

The self-concept is defined as the cognitive and affective understanding of who a person is and can take two forms: the "actual self" and the "ideal self." The actual self refers to the more realistic appraisal of the qualities that a person does or does not have (i.e., who and what a person thinks they are now), whereas the ideal self is shaped by the imagination of ideals and goals related to what a person aspires to become (Gough, Lazzari and Fioravanti, 1978; Wylie, 1979). This theory is related to psychoanalytic theory in which the actual self is similar to the ego and the ideal self is similar to the superego. In most situations the genuine brands are perceived as more temporally removed (i.e., psychologically distant, not present in an individual's direct experience of reality) from the present due to the high price or lack of availability compared with counterfeits; they may be thought of or constructed but cannot be experienced directly. Hence consumers may alternatively pursue the corresponding counterfeits with a seemingly identical appearance, acceptable quality and lower price characteristics. This may be why the availability and affordability of counterfeits diminish consumers' demand for the genuine brands if they share a strong surface resemblance (Nia and Zaichkowsky, 2000). The indication is that the ideal self is more relevant to genuine brand consumption and the actual self is more relevant to counterfeit brand consumption.

Most people experience a discrepancy between their actual and ideal selves, but for some consumers this gap is especially large. Self-discrepancy theory proposes that the greater the magnitude of self-discrepancy possessed by an individual, the more the individual will experience the type of discomfort associated with that self-discrepancy (Higgins et al., 1986). If the distance between the actual and the ideal self is too great, feelings of unworthiness and inferiority may be promoted (Gough, Fioravanti and Lazzari, 1983). People with large self-discrepancy are vulnerable to dejection from perceived loss of self-fulfillment or esteem and are more likely to engage in personal fantasy and fictional speculations. This study argues that consumers with greater self-discrepancy are more likely to engage in counterfeit consumption as a way of bridging the gap between their actual and ideal selves and to achieve their unfulfilled ambitions for genuine products. By consuming counterfeit products, the consumer is exposed to contradicting gains. Counterfeits represent an image that naturally belongs to their aspirational group (Perez et al., 2010). On the basis of these considerations, the following is hypothesized:

*H1: Self-discrepancy has a positive effect on consumers' attitudes (1a) and purchase intentions (1b) toward counterfeits.*

It is important to note that the self-discrepancy effect may not be equally pronounced for all people and all product categories. It may be stronger for some product categories and people with certain characteristics or predispositions. The next step is to investigate the cross-cultural and cross-category differences in the self-discrepancy effect and determine whether and how self-monitoring moderates this effect.

### Cross-cultural differences in the self-discrepancy effect

Most researchers distinguish between individualist and collectivist cultures (Souiden et al., 2011; Podoshen, Li and Zhang, 2011; Belk, 1988) and the cultural differences appear to be significant. Much of the cross-cultural research has shown that East Asians in collectivist cultures tend to define the self in terms of social relationships, with individual traits tending to be more central to the self as defined by Caucasian Westerners from individualist cultures (Cousins, 1989). Thus East Asians typically possess a better-developed and accessible interdependent self composed of a complex, multifaceted network of associations related to social relationships (vs. personality traits). In contrast, Caucasian Americans typically have a well-developed and accessible independent self due to having many more associative links related to individual traits as opposed to social relationships (Monga and Lau-Gesk, 2007). These differences in self-discrepancy perception emerge because the culture in which a person is reared fosters a specific set of values and thus distinct ways of thinking about the self. In individualistic societies, the meaning of individual goals and achievements is very important while the social fabric and group norms are much looser (Triandis et al., 1988). Belk (1988) states that countries with high individualistic values are motivated to engage in conspicuous consumption due to the consumers' materialism and desire for self-enhancement. In a culture that emphasizes the self and personal interests, an awareness of self-discrepancy might have a great effect on consumption behavior. A collectivist culture, meanwhile, places a strong focus on family and proper manners (Podoshen, Li and Zhang, 2011). Collectivist societies subordinate individual goals in favor of the goals of a few large in-groups (Triandis and Gelfand, 1998). The Asians in collectivist cultures often see their identity as something that is defined in terms of family, professional and social relationships along with the culture, which emphasizes the needs, goals and views of the whole group rather than an individual self (Triandis et al., 1988). The concept of face appears to have a strong influence on purchasing decisions in East Asia. The fear of what others might think if caught with a counterfeit product, which could harm the consumer's image, might have dissuaded East Asians from buying these kinds of product. Therefore the self-discrepancy effect on consumer responses to counterfeits would be more pronounced in individualist societies than in collectivist cultures. We hypothesize the following:

*H2: The self-discrepancy effect on consumer attitudes (2a) and purchase intentions (2b) toward counterfeits is stronger in individualist than in collectivist cultures.*

### Cross-category differences in the self-discrepancy effect

According to the research report from Business Action to Stop Counterfeiting and Privacy (BASCAP) in November 2009, the most common counterfeit purchases are DVDs/CDs, computer software, brand-name clothes and luxury items (e.g., purses, watches, jewelry and leather goods). More than one in two consumers surveyed reported buying counterfeit versions of these products. Among these four product categories, DVDs/CDs and computer software are experience-based, privately consumed products, whereas brand-name clothes and luxury items are symbolic, publicly consumed products. When a product is not consumed or used in the presence of others, there is no public self-presentation (image) to be monitored and regulated for the sake of desired public appearances. As a result, consumers tend to focus more attention on self-discrepancy and thus experience fewer constraints and concerns regarding their counterfeit consumption behavior. In contrast, symbolic products are usually consumed in public to enhance the sense of self-regard (Khalil, 2000). The perceived risk of reputational damage and the associated lack of control over public image can dampen the self-discrepancy effect on counterfeit consumption. Thus the following is hypothesized:

> *H3: The self-discrepancy effect is stronger for privately consumed products than for publicly consumed products.*

### Moderating effect of self-monitoring

Self-monitoring reflects the degree to which a person observes and controls their expressive behavior and self-presentation in accordance with social cues (Gould, 1993; Snyder, 1979). This study investigates the possible moderating effect of self-monitoring due to its apparent theoretical relevance to the self-discrepancy perception. People with strong self-monitoring are very sensitive to the self-images they project in social situations (Snyder, 1985; Snyder and DeBono, 1987). In contrast, weak self-monitors lack either the ability or the desire to regulate their expressive self-presentation. They are less aware of their own expressive behavior and self-image, and less motivated to maintain or enhance it (Snyder and Gangestad, 1986; Hogg, Cox and Keeling, 2000).

There is no doubt that strong self-monitors are more aware of the self-discrepancy than weak self-monitors (Buss, 1980). Strong self-monitors tend to be more socially anxious when they are unable to live up to their positive self-presentation (i.e., aware of the self-discrepancy). This anxiety motivates them to fulfill social expectations (as defined by their ideal self) and worry about the negative public impression they might make if unable to meet them, which results in a more positive attitude and purchase intention toward counterfeits, as counterfeits can help to construct their identity and project an image of genuine brand that they cannot afford. Strong self-monitors are therefore more likely to engage in counterfeit consumption to achieve their unfulfilled ambitions for genuine products while weak self-monitors should be less concerned about the risk of overpromising and failing to meet these promises (Tunnel, 1984). Thus self-monitoring would strengthen the self-discrepancy effect. However, the strong self-monitors' greater sensitivity to the self-image they project in social situations would lead them to have more fear of what others might think if caught with a counterfeit product, which could harm their self-images. In this sense, self-monitoring would weaken the self-discrepancy effect. Given the counteracting factors that determine the effect of self-monitoring on the self-discrepancy effect, self-monitoring may not have a clear effect or, if one of the two major mechanisms (desire to achieve unfulfilled ambitions or fear of damaging image if caught with a counterfeit product) dominates, it may decrease or increase the total self-discrepancy effect. Consequently, no hypotheses are proposed regarding the directionality of the moderating effects of self-monitoring, which leaves the empirical question open to further analysis.

## Empirical research design

To test the hypotheses empirically, an online survey was conducted in the summer of 2012. The sample consisted of 165 US and 166 Hong Kong consumers aged between 18 and 34. The study was limited to young adults because, i) according to Predergast, Leung, and Phau (2002), 78.5% of the people between ages 15 and 29 had purchased pirated products, and counterfeit purchases decrease with age in most countries (BASCAP 2009), and ii) this age group is a new generation characterized by a lot of people using the Internet on a daily basis, which makes it easier and quicker to access them through an online survey.

The online survey collected consumers' attitudes and purchase intentions toward counterfeits from the registered panelists of an online research company. More than 300 respondents aged between 18 and 34 were recruited. The first part of the survey identified the respondents by determining age, gender and ethnicity. Ethnicity was of great importance and therefore, to ensure that respondents answered correctly, the option "other" was offered so that no one would feel that there was no option that suited them. The second part of the survey collected information about the respondents' counterfeit consumption behavior in the previous year and those who had not purchased any counterfeits were screened out. The qualified respondents were then asked about their attitudes and purchase intentions toward counterfeit products in different categories. Attitude was measured on a seven-point scale, bipolarly labeled with "very much dislike" and "very much like." Purchase intention was measured by asking subjects "Suppose that you have become aware of the need to buy a (name of product category), and you can reasonably afford any genuine product of your choice. To what extent do you intend to buy or not intend to buy a counterfeit?" These intentions were measured on a seven-point scale varying from "1 = very unlikely" to "7 = very likely."

Following the practice of Peng, Wong and Wan (2012), respondents were asked to describe themselves from two different points of view – as they actually are and as they would ideally like to be – on a series of semantic differential scales. Only the 12 adjectives (mature vs. youthful, trendy vs. outdated, wild vs. tamed, confident vs. non decisive, feminine vs. masculine, playful vs. dull, sexy vs. not sexy, adventurous vs. conservative, practical vs. not realistic, active vs. low energy, prestigious vs. low standing, and original vs. not original) most relevant to consumption behavior were included in the questionnaire. For self-monitoring, the 13-item empirically validated scale developed by Lennox and Wolfe (1984) was used. The survey ended with a usable sample of 331 respondents, among which 166 were from the United States and 165 from Hong Kong.

## Results and discussion

Some of the respondents' characteristics are highlighted in Table 10.1. No significant differences were detected in terms of respondents' demographic characteristics, such as gender and age.

Table 10.2 reports the mean scores of the respondents' attitudes and purchase intentions toward counterfeits. Standard errors are recorded in parentheses. An examination of Table 10.2 reveals two key points. First, the Hong Kong respondents generally displayed more favorable attitudes and purchase intentions toward counterfeits in all of the product categories compared with the US respondents, but the differences are

*Table 10.1* Age and gender of the respondents

|  | United States | Hong Kong |
| --- | --- | --- |
| Sample size | 165 | 166 |
| Gender |  |  |
| Female | 68.5% | 71.6% |
| Male | 31.5% | 28.4% |
| Age |  |  |
| Less than 20 | 6.7% | 8.4% |
| 20–24 | 35.2% | 35.5% |
| 25–29 | 54.5% | 51.3% |
| 30–34 | 3.6% | 4.8% |

not statistically significant based on the results from independent sample t-tests. Second, among the product categories, the averages show hardly any variation (all paired two-tailed t tests had p values greater than 0.05).

## Self-discrepancy effect

The magnitude of self-discrepancy was calculated by comparing the attributes of the actual self to the corresponding attributes of the ideal self. Following Graeff (1997), Euclidean distance was used to calculate distance scores reflecting the self-discrepancy between the actual and ideal self. No significant difference was observed in the mean self-discrepancy scores between the respondents from both countries (35.3 vs. 33.1, p-value = 0.514). These difference scores were then regressed to the participants' attitudes and purchase intentions toward counterfeit products using SPSS 17.0 across cultures and product categories. Given that consumer responses were measured on seven-point scales where larger values indicated more favorable attitudes and purchase intentions, positive regression estimates indicate the hypothesized positive relationship between self-discrepancy and consumers' attitudes and purchase intentions toward counterfeit products. As the first part of Table 10.3 shows, the parameter estimates of the basic model are reported. The results confirm a strong positive relationship (all of the estimates are significant at the 0.01 level) between actual and ideal self-discrepancy and consumers' attitudes, and purchase intentions toward counterfeits in all four of the product categories and both countries (except consumers' attitudes toward DVDs/CDs and computer software in Hong Kong), suggesting that H1 is generally supported.

*Table 10.2* Comparison of mean scores among four product categories

| Cultures | DVDs/CDs | | Computer software | | Brand-name clothes | | Luxury items | |
|---|---|---|---|---|---|---|---|---|
| | Attitude | PI* | Attitude | PI | Attitude | PI | Attitude | PI |
| United States | 2.96 | 2.73 | 2.88 | 2.67 | 2.98 | 2.84 | 3.04 | 2.79 |
| (Base: 165) | (1.94) | (2.03) | (2.01) | (2.03) | (2.05) | (2.10) | (2.01) | (2.06) |
| Hong Kong | 3.33 | 3.06 | 3.17 | 2.78 | 3.22 | 3.05 | 3.10 | 2.90 |
| (Base: 166) | (1.70) | (1.72) | (1.84) | (1.71) | (1.78) | (1.82) | (1.78) | (1.78) |
| P-value of t-test | .069 | .115 | .172 | .594 | .253 | .327 | .774 | .585 |

*Note*: Seven-point scale is used; standard errors are given in the parentheses. *Purchase intention.

*Table 10.3* Standardized regression estimates

**Perceived self-discrepancy ⇒ responses to counterfeits**

| Basic model | | DVDs/CDs | Computer software | Brand-name clothes | Luxury items |
|---|---|---|---|---|---|
| United States | Attitude | 0.421**(5.922) | 0.384**(5.306) | 0.307**(4.118) | 0.287**(3.820) |
| | PI | 0.456**(6.539) | 0.462**(6.657) | 0.374**(5.146) | 0.391**(5.418) |
| Hong Kong | Attitude | 0.149(1.924) | 0.148(1.915) | 0.249**(3.287) | 0.221**(2.900) |
| | PI | 0.194*(2.537) | 0.254**(3.357) | 0.258**(3.416) | 0.270**(3.595) |
| The effect of self-monitoring | | | | | |
| Attitude among US consumers | Low | 0.538**(5.952) | 0.486**(5.181) | 0.408**(4.169) | 0.411**(4.209) |
| | High | 0.215*(1.894) | 0.248*(2.204) | 0.123(1.065) | 0.114(0.991) |
| PI among US consumers | Low | 0.554**(6.211) | 0.529**(5.820) | 0.469**(4.949) | 0.486**(5.181) |
| | High | 0.300**(2.702) | 0.328**(2.982) | 0.202(1.772) | 0.230*(2.037) |
| Attitude among Hong Kong consumers | Low | 0.076(0.683) | 0.033(0.297) | 0.204(1.873) | 0.177(1.619) |
| | High | 0.235*(2.180) | 0.259*(2.409) | 0.300**(2.832) | 0.282**(2.640) |
| PI among Hong Kong consumers | Low | 0.140(1.272) | 0.227*(2.097) | 0.234*(2.161) | 0.235*(2.179) |
| | High | 0.246*(2.285) | 0.280**(2.626) | 0.288**(2.705) | 0.320**(3.044) |

*Note:* **$np < 0.01$; *$np < 0.05$; figures in brackets are t-values of the estimates.

## Cross-cultural differences in the self-discrepancy effect

To examine the cross-cultural differences in the self-discrepancy effect, an independent sample (United States and Hong Kong) t-test was conducted between the regression estimates. As Table 10.4 shows, the self-discrepancy effect is significantly stronger in the United States than it is in Hong Kong across all of the product categories. Thus H2 is supported.

## Cross-category differences in the self-discrepancy effect

The cross-category differences were investigated using paired sample t-tests between the regression estimates. An interesting finding is that the results for the two countries are different, thus the results for H3 are mixed (see Table 10.5). In the United States, the self-discrepancy effect is remarkably stronger for privately consumed products than for publicly consumed products, suggesting that H3 is supported. In contrast, the findings in Hong Kong display the opposite pattern with the weaker effect detected in privately consumed products than in publicly consumed products, although the effect on purchase intention is not significantly different between computer software and brand-name clothes, suggesting that H3 is not supported. A possible explanation for the case of Hong Kong consumers is their favorable deontological judgment of software piracy and the social benefits they perceive in the copying of creative works (Swinyard et al., 1990). Asians, including people in Hong Kong, consider software piracy ethical and believe that it permits a faster and wider dissemination of knowledge that enhances

*Table 10.4*   Cross-cultural differences in the self-discrepancy effect

|                      | United States (individualism) | Hong Kong (collectivism) |
|----------------------|-------------------------------|--------------------------|
| **Attitude**         |                               |                          |
| DVDs/CDs             | 0.421**                       | 0.149                    |
| Computer software    | 0.384**                       | 0.148                    |
| Brand-name clothes   | 0.307**                       | 0.249                    |
| Luxury items         | 0.287**                       | 0.221                    |
| **Purchase intention** | 0.456**                     | 0.194                    |
| DVDs/CDs             | 0.462**                       | 0.254                    |
| Computer software    | 0.374**                       | 0.258                    |
| Brand-name clothes   | 0.391**                       | 0.270                    |
| Luxury items         |                               |                          |

*Note*: **p < 0.01 in independent sample t-test.

*Table 10.5*  Cross-category differences in the self-discrepancy effect

|  | DVDs/CDs (a) | Computer software (b) | Brand-name clothes (c) | Luxury items (d) |
|---|---|---|---|---|
| **United States** | | | | |
| Attitude | 0.421bcd | 0.384acd | 0.307abd | 0.287abc |
| Purchase intention | 0.456cd | 0.462cd | 0.374ab | 0.391ab |
| **Hong Kong** | | | | |
| Attitude | 0.149cd | 0.148cd | 0.249abd | 0.221abc |
| Purchase intention | 0.194bcd | 0.254ad | 0.258a | 0.270ab |

*Note*: a/b/c/d – significant difference at 90% confidence interval, two-tailed t-test.

society. Thus the purchase and use of pirated CDs/DVDs and unlicensed software is popular among young consumers. This explains why an individual consumer's self-discrepancy has a smaller effect on the consumption of counterfeits in these two product categories. Hong Kong consumers are highly face conscious and prefer to use symbolic products (especially luxury products and name brands) to gain "face," which is often represented by symbols of prestige and reputation gained through the expectation of the impression one makes on others (Podoshen, Li, and Zhang, 2011). Therefore the self-discrepancy effect is stronger for brand-name clothes and luxury items than for DVDs/CDs and computer software.

### The moderation effect of self-monitoring

The measurement scale for self-monitoring adapted from Lennox and Wolfe (1984) shows sufficient reliability with 0.842 for US data and 0.892 for Hong Kong data. First, a median split was performed along the values of self-monitoring (the sum of 13 item scores) to create two subsamples, one with low values of self-monitoring and the other with high values. The basic model was then simultaneously analyzed in both subsamples. The lower part of Table 10.3 shows the parameter estimates for the different subgroups.

The results confirm a moderating effect of self-monitoring on the relationship between self-discrepancy and consumer responses to counterfeits, but the direction of the effect is opposite in the United States and Hong Kong. Self-monitoring weakens the self-discrepancy effect in the United States and strengthens it in Hong Kong. In the United States, the self-discrepancy effect on consumers' attitudes and purchase intentions toward counterfeits was observed to be weaker among strong self-monitors than among weak self-monitors, indicating that fear of damaging the self-image if caught with a counterfeit product dominates. However, in Hong Kong the self-discrepancy effect is stronger among strong self-monitors, indicating that the desire to achieve unfulfilled ambitions through counterfeit consumption dominates. Materialism is more prevalent in individualistic cultures, which leads to conspicuous consumption being more common in individualistic societies (Eastman, Goldsmith and Flynn, 1999). In contrast, Podoshen, Li and Zhang (2011) examine materialism and conspicuous consumption in Chinese youth culture and find that Chinese young adults scored higher in both materialism and conspicuous consumption. The Western, individualistic cultures also affect the collectivistic cultures, which is resulting in the collectivist culture changing (Podoshen, Li and Zhang, 2011).

## Implications and future research

Counterfeiting is an ongoing problem around the world, despite global initiatives and political treaties designed to address the problem. One potential obstacle in effectively managing the issue is that motivations for engaging in the practice are not fully understood. This study is distinctive because it advances the theoretical understanding of consumer responses to counterfeit products by examining how consumers' self-concept and self-discrepancy (between the actual and ideal selves) influence their attitudes and purchase intentions toward counterfeits. Specifically, this study goes beyond the obvious financial motivation for buying cheaper versions of coveted brands to demonstrate that consumers' likelihood of knowingly purchasing counterfeits varies predictably and systematically with the magnitude of self-discrepancy.

These findings support the view that discrepancy between the actual and ideal selves has a positive effect on consumers' attitudes and purchase intentions toward counterfeits. This effect is even more pronounced in individualist cultures than it is in collectivist cultures. As for the cross-category differences, the United States and Hong Kong display opposing patterns with a stronger effect detected in privately consumed products among US consumers and in publicly consumed products among Hong Kong consumers. Furthermore, self-monitoring weakens the self-discrepancy effect in the United States and strengthens it in Hong Kong. This finding can be explained by the coexistence of both positive and negative effects of self-monitoring on the self-discrepancy effect. On the one hand, the awareness of the self-discrepancy can lead to a high level of self-monitoring that favors counterfeits to achieve unfulfilled ambitions for unaffordable genuine products. On the other hand, strong self-monitors would choose to avoid counterfeits due to the fear of what others might think of them if caught with a counterfeit product.

Although this empirical study identifies three important variables – cultural background, product categories and self-monitoring – that can influence the self-discrepancy effect, further research might consider other moderating effects. For example, the product-related context variables, such as the hedonic vs. utilitarian nature of the product, could be examined. In particular, the self-discrepancy effect may be more important for hedonic products and not as important for utilitarian products in which practical functions play a role. In addition, personality traits, such as a need for uniqueness or the perceived risk of counterfeit consumption, may also be relevant. The results of this study also have important implications for marketing managers. Because the self-discrepancy has a positive effect on counterfeit acceptance, the aspirational branding strategies that aim at ideal self-congruence may need to be reconsidered, especially in the privately consumed product categories and individualistic cultures. When the genuine brand is perceived as being out of reach and therefore unreal or not authentic, the ideal brand envisioned may not be attainable. Thus marketing managers should make sure that the brand does not set the ideal so high that consumers distance themselves from the genuine brand.

This study examines the cultural differences (United States vs. Hong Kong) in the self-discrepancy effect. Some would argue that Hong Kong actually represents a hybrid culture of East and West, thus it is not a typical place to represent collectivist culture. Further research might consider replicating the study in mainland China, Japan, Korea or other more typical collectivist countries. However, it is worth noting that the movement toward a global consumer culture indicates that the two cultures are merging and consumers' consumption behavior is quite similar (Belk, 1995). There is a possibility that the reasons for counterfeit consumption differ between individuals but not as much between cultures.

This study's population is limited to young adults aged between 18 and 34, most of whom are university students with similar educations and income backgrounds. Therefore generalizing the results of this study to groups other than this population could create problems and is not recommended. However, the sample provides an opportunity to interpret the results and voice questions that may lead to further research within this unexplored area.

## References

Aaker, J. L. (1999) "The malleable self: The role of self-expression in persuasion", *Journal of Marketing Research*, 36(1), 45–57.

Business Action to Stop Counterfeiting and Privacy (BASCAP) (2009) "Research report on consumer attitudes and perceptions on counterfeiting and piracy", http://www.iccwbo.org/uploadedFiles/BASCAP/Pages/BASCAP-Consumer%20Research%20Report_Final.pdf, date accessed August 14, 2012.

Baumeister, R. (1998) "The self" in *Handbook of Social Psychology* (New York: McGraw-Hill).

Belk, R. (1988) "Possession and the extended self", *Journal of Consumer Research*, 15(2), 139–168.

Belk, R. (1995) "Hyperreality and globalization: Culture in the age of Ronald McDonald", *Journal of International Consumer Marketing*, 8, 23–38.

Berrell, M., & J. Wrathall (2007) "Between Chinese culture and the rule of law", *Management Research News*, 30(1), 57–76.

Buss, A. (1980) *Self-Consciousness and Social Anxiety* (Freeman).

Chaudhry, P., & S. Stumpf (2011) "Consumer complicity with counterfeit products", *Journal of Consumer Marketing*, 28(2), 139–151.

Claiborne, C., & M. Sirgy (1990) "Self-congruity as a model of attitude formation and change: Conceptual review and guide for future research", *Developments in Marketing Science*, Cullowhee, NC: Academy of Marketing Science, 1–7.

Cordell, V., N. Wongtada & R. Kieschnick (1996) "Counterfeit purchase intentions – Role of lawfulness attitudes and product traits as determinants", *Journal of Business Research*, 35, 41–53.

Cousins, S. (1989) "Culture and self-perception in Japan and the United States", *Journal of Personality and Social Psychology*, 56 (January), 124–131.

Eastman, J., R. Goldsmith & L. Flynn (1999) "Status consumption in consumer behavior: Scale development and validation", *Journal of Marketing Theory and Practice*, 7(3), 41–51.

Elliott, R. (1994) "Exploring the symbolic meaning of brands", *British Journal of Management*, 5(1), 13–19.

Elliott, R. (1997) "Existential consumption and irrational desire", *European Journal of Marketing*, 31(3), 285–296.

Gould, S. (1993) "Assessing self-concept discrepancy in consumer behavior: The joint effects of private self-consciousness and self-monitoring", *Advances in Consumer Research*, 20, 419–424.

Graeff, T. (1997) "Consumption situations and the effects of brand image on consumers brand evaluation", *Psychology and Marketing*, 14(1), 49–70.

Gough, H., M. Fioravanti & R. Lazzari (1983) "Some implications of self versus ideal-self congruence on the revised adjective check list", *Journal of Personality and Social Psychology*, 44(6), 1214–1220.

Gough, H., R. Lazzari & M. Fioravanti (1978) "Self versus ideal self: A comparison of five adjective check list indices", *Journal of Consulting and Clinical Psychology*, 46(5), 1085–1091.

Grossman, G., & C. Shapiro (1988) "Counterfeit-product trade", *The American Economic Review*, 78(1), 59–75.

Higgins, T., R. Bond, T. Klein & T. Strauman (1986) "Self-discrepancies and emotional vulnerability: How magnitude, accessibility, and type of discrepancy influences affect", *Journal of Personality and Social Psychology*, 51(1), 5–15.

Hogg, M., A. Cox & K. Keeling (2000) "The impact of self-monitoring on image congruence and product/brand evaluation", *European Journal of Marketing*, 34(5/6), 641–666.

International Anti-counterfeiting Coalition (2008) Facts on Fakes, http://counterfeiting.unicri.it/docs/The%20International%20Anti-Counterfeiting%20Coalition.Facts%20on%20Fakes.pdf, date accessed 14 August 2012.

Khalil, E. (2000) "Symbolic products: Prestige, pride and identity goods", *Theory and Decision*, 49(1), 53–77.

Lambkin, M., & Y. Tyndall (2009) "Brand counterfeiting: A marketing problem that won't go away", *Irish Marketing Review*, 20(1), 35–46.

Lennox, R., & R. Wolfe (1984) "Revision of the self-monitoring scale", *Journal of Personality and Social Psychology*, 46(6), 1349–1364.

Monga, A., & L. Lau-Gesk (2007) "Blending cobrand personalities: An examination of the complex self", *Journal of Marketing Research*, 44(3), 389–400.

Nia, A., & J. Zaichkowsky (2000) "Do counterfeits devalue the ownership of luxury brands", *Journal of Product and Brand Management*, 9(7), 485–497.

Norum, P., & A. Cuno (2011) "Analysis of the demand for counterfeit goods", *Journal of Fashion Marketing and Management*, 15(1), 27–40.

Onkvisit, S., & J. Shaw (1987) "Self-concept and image congruence: Some research and managerial implications", *Journal of Consumer Marketing*, 4(1), 13–23.

Peng, L., A. Wong & L. Wan (2012) "The effects of image congruence and self-monitoring on product evaluations: A comparison between genuine and counterfeit products", *Journal of Global Marketing*, 25(1), 17–28.

Perez, M., R. Castaño & C. Quintanilla (2010) "Constructing identity through the consumption of counterfeit luxury goods", *Qualitative Market Research*, 13(3), 219–235.

Phau, I., & M. Teah (2009) "Devil Wears (Counterfeit) Prada: A Study of antecedents and outcomes of attitudes towards counterfeits of luxury brands", *Journal of Consumer Marketing*, 26(1), 15–27.

Podoshen, J., L. Li & J. Zhang (2011) "Materialism and conspicuous consumption in China: A cross-cultural examination", *International Journal of Consumer Studies*, 35(1), 17–25.

Predergast, G., C. Leung & I. Phau (2002), Understanding consumer demand for non-deceptive pirated brands', *Marketing Intelligence and Planning*, 20(7), 405–416.

Snyder, M. (1979) "Self-monitoring processes", *Advances in Experimental Social Psychology*, 30, 85–125.

Snyder, M., & K. DeBono (1985) "Appeals to image and claims about quality: Understanding the psychology of advertising", *Journal of Personality and Social Psychology*, 49(3), 586–597.

Snyder, M. (1987) *Public Appearances, Private Realities: The Psychology of Self-monitoring* New York, NY : Freeman.

Snyder, M., & S. Gangestad (1986) "On the nature of self-monitoring; Matters of assessment, matters of validity", *Journal of Personality and Social Psychology*, 51(1), 125–139.

Souiden, N., B. M'Saad & F. Pons (2011) "A cross-cultural analysis of consumers" conspicuous consumption of branded fashion accessories', *Journal of International Consumer Marketing*, 23(5), 329–343.

Swinyard, W., R. Heikki & A. Kau (1990) "The morality of software piracy: A cross-cultural analysis", *Journal of Business Ethics*, 9(8), 655–664.

Tom, G., B. Garibaldi, Y. Zeng & J. Pilcher (1998) "Consumer demand for counterfeit goods", *Psychology and Marketing*, 15(5), 405–421.

Triandis, H., & M. Gelfand (1998) "Converging measurement of horizontal and vertical individualism and collectivism", *Journal of Personality and Social Psychology*, 74(1), 118–128.

Triandis, H., R. Bontempo, M. Villareal, M. Asai and N. Lucca (1988) "Individualism and collectivism: Cross-cultural perspectives on self-ingroup relationships", *Journal of Personality and Social Psychology*, 54(2), 323–333.

Tunnel, G. (1984) "The Discrepancy between private and public selves: Public self-consciousness and its correlates", *Journal of Personality Assessment*, 48(5), 549–555.

Wilcox, K., H. Kim & S. Sen (2009) "Why do consumers buy counterfeit luxury brands", *Journal of Marketing Research*, 46(2), 247–259.

Wylie, R. (1979) *The Self-Concept: Theory and Research on Selected Topics*, 2nd edn Lincoln: University of Nebraska Press.

Zinkhan, G., & J. Hong (1991) "Self concept and advertising effectiveness: A conceptual model of congruency conspicuousness, and response mode", *Advances in Consumer Research*, 18, 348–354.

# 11
## Perceptions of Chinese and Indian Brand Personalities in Germany

*Heidi Kreppel and Dirk Holtbrügge*

## Introduction

The past decade has seen an increasing number of companies from emerging markets entering the international marketplace (Aulakh, 2007; Gammeltoft et al., 2010). In particular, many Chinese and Indian companies are going international (Alon et al., 2009; Hansen, 2009). Prominent examples include Haier and Lenovo from China, and Wipro and Infosys from India, all of which have evolved from small start-ups into multinational corporations (MNCs) within a period of less than 20 years (Jinsheng and Ye, 2003; Hamm, 2006; Zhijun, 2006; Kumar, 2009).

When entering foreign markets, many Chinese and Indian MNCs seek to increase their international competitiveness by gaining access to strategic resources and assets, such as advanced technology, established foreign brands, distribution channels and sources of foreign capital (Holtbrügge and Kreppel, 2012). In this attempt, however, they are often confronted by severe challenges. In particular, negative country-of-origin effects impede their acceptance by local consumers and lead to many unsuccessful or even failed market entries (Pappu et al., 2007; Sheth, 2009).

Consequently, a major challenge for Chinese and Indian MNCs is to build a strong and positive brand image. Thus far their success has been measured in manufacturing excellence, low-cost production and economies of scale, but they have not yet successfully built strong brand images. Nargundkar and Bajaj (2002: 71) state that "at best, low-cost services can be an entry point into developed-world markets. But we must leverage the entry to graduate to high value service offerings." Therefore Chinese and Indian MNCs must place more emphasis on marketing and branding to increase their brand image and succeed in international markets (Zeng and Williamson, 2003; Bell, 2008; Wang, 2010).

Several empirical studies reveal that brand image is positively related to sales volume, market share and profitability (Park et al., 1986; Kim et al., 2003; Michell et al., 2001; Smith et al., 2010). Especially among industries in which the technical features of products often converge, it is crucial for companies to set themselves apart from their competitors to meet performance expectations and grow in an increasingly competitive environment. Thus it becomes essential for Chinese and Indian MNCs not only to manufacture, distribute and market their products but also to build strong, positive brand images. According to Buckley and Ghauri (2004), this would enable them to become brand owners – that is, to control design, engineering and marketing and thus increase their value added.

An important prerequisite of brand ownership is to know how the brand is perceived by consumers – that is, which attributes consumers associate with a brand and how these associations differ between various consumer groups. Accordingly, in-depth knowledge of the perceived brand personality helps the company as a brand owner with regard to its marketing strategies in enhancing the effectiveness of its market segmentation and marketing mix decisions (Roncha 2008).

Several studies reveal that the personality of Chinese and Indian brands is influenced to a large degree by negative country-of-origin effects. For example, while Indian brands may be remarkable competitors in the local market, they must work hard to compete in markets outside their home country (Ghodeswar, 2008; Bhardwaj et al., 2010). In a study on the competitiveness of Indian brands, Sheth (2009: 2) concludes that "Indian brand equity will emerge only if we offer better products at lower prices, so that the brand names become globally respected just like Korean brands are doing right now." With reference to the Indian car industry, Natarajan and Thiripurasundari (2010) find that consumers prefer global brands over Indian brands due to superior quality, technological advancements and global reputation. In a study across various product categories (cars, refrigerators, washing machines, televisions, cameras and watches), Kinra (2006) reveals that Indian brands are rated the least positively against foreign brands with regard to technology, quality, status, value for money and credibility. Rao (2001: 460) reports the success of many local brands in India, but concludes that "there are practically no Indian brands that have global or even international name recognition." Lumb and Lall (2006) find products from India to be technically less advanced, more handmade than mass-produced items and projecting a more common rather than exclusive image due to negative country-of-origin effects. Furthermore, Indian products are targeted more at the middle and lower classes than at the upper class. Nargunkhar and Bajaj (2002: 69) affirm that buyers and consumers have a "poor image [...] of India as a country, and of Indian companies. India is perceived as backward, and Indian companies have a non-professional image in terms of almost any parameter known to affect successful marketing."

The situation is similar for Chinese brands. According to a study by Wang and Gao (2010), Chinese brand images are strongly associated with the "Made in China" label, and the negative country-of-origin effect has a significant impact on the perception of Chinese brands among Irish consumers. Liu and Johnson (2005) reveal that Chinese notebook computers are judged according to significantly lower scores than Japanese notebooks, and that these judgments are strongly influenced by a negative country-of-origin effect. Ghazali et al. (2008) conclude that China is ranked far behind developed countries and other developing countries with regard to perceived product quality. The analysis of country-of-origin associations and product evaluations from Aiello et al. (2008) shows that China is ranked lowest in terms of design, prestige and workmanship. Pappu et al. (2007) reveal in a three-country image study that China is rated lowest in terms of country image behind Japan and Malaysia and, accordingly, products from China have a rather unfavorable image. Kreppel and Holtbrügge (2012) demonstrate that the image of Chinese products in Germany is particularly low among older and well-educated consumers.

While several empirical studies demonstrate that Chinese and Indian products are faced with severe country-of-origin effects, little is known about their perceived brand personality – specifically, which characteristics are associated with these brands and which attributes are considered positive or negative. Moreover, the determinants of brand personality and perceptual differences among consumer groups are largely unknown. While studies in other countries have frequently analyzed how the perceived personalities of brands differ among consumers with various demographic, biographic and psychographic backgrounds, little is known of these determinants with regard to Chinese and Indian brands. As previously argued, this knowledge is crucial for market segmentation and the marketing-mix decisions of MNCs from these countries to enhance their success in the international marketplace.

In recent years, a plethora of studies on the internationalization of Chinese and Indian MNCs have been published. These mainly focus on the determinants of outward foreign direct investment (FDI) (e.g., Buckley et al., 2007; Hattari and Rajan, 2010; Berning and Holtbrügge, 2012), location choice (e.g., Makino, Lau and Yeh 2002; Milelli, Hay and Shi 2010) and foreign acquisitions (e.g., Deng, 2009; Rui and Yip 2007; Nayyar, 2008). Other studies deal with the governmental promotion of outward FDI (e.g., Singal and Jain, 2012; Holtbrügge and Berning, 2013) and human resource challenges (e.g., Tung, 2007; Thite, Wilkinson and Shah, 2012). Surprisingly, despite their great relevance, country-of-origin effects and brand personality perceptions have thus far been sparsely addressed in these studies on the internationalization of Chinese and Indian companies.

Based on these considerations, the aim of this study is to analyze how Chinese and Indian brands are perceived by German consumers, and what determinants influence these perceptions. In doing so, the study makes three important contributions: i) it investigates the similarities and differences in the brand personalities of Chinese and Indian brands as they are perceived in Germany; ii) it analyzes which demographic, biographic and psychographic determinants influence the perceived brand personalities of Chinese and Indian brands; and iii) it derives practical implications for Chinese and Indian brands in Germany based on their perceived brand personalities.

The remainder of this chapter is organized as follows. First, the concepts of brand image and brand personality are outlined and Aaker's (1997) brand personality scale is introduced. This scale has proved to be a valid and reliable instrument to investigate how brand perceptions differ among consumers and how they vary in terms of different attributes. Based on this information the research hypotheses are derived. The next section describes the methodology of this study, after which the results are presented and discussed. The chapter concludes with the major contributions and limitations of the study, and some implications for managers and future research.

## Conceptual framework: Brand personality, brand origin and variations in consumer perceptions

As previously argued, building a positive, strong brand image is of crucial importance to Chinese and Indian MNCs that intend to successfully compete on the global stage. In today's highly competitive business environment, brand management is a decisive strategic issue. In this context, it is relevant to know how the brand is perceived by consumers. According to Aaker (1991, 1996), brand associations are anything linked in memory to a brand, including characteristics attributed to it by consumers. These characteristics are described as brand personality. Brand personality refers to human personality traits associated with a brand and, when added to the product's physical attributes and benefits, is defined as "the set of human characteristics associated with a brand" (Aaker, 1997: 347). In this sense, brand personality traits provide emotional value and symbolic meaning that add to, and often become more important than, a product's functional attributes (Aaker, 1997).

To measure brand personality on the basis of human personality traits, Aaker (1997) developed a multidimensional scale that has frequently been applied in international marketing studies. The scale contains 42 personality items, which are grouped into the following dimensions: sincerity, excitement, competence, sophistication and ruggedness. It was tested with a number of product categories and is regarded as a reliable, valid and multidimensional construct that is generalizable across countries (Austin et al., 2003).

Previous studies reveal that the evaluation of brand personalities differs between individuals according to age, gender, education, income and so on (Plummer, 2000; Lee and Rhee, 2008; Geuens et al., 2009; Mulyanegara et al., 2009; Lin, 2010). For example, wealthier individuals are found to put more emphasis on attributes such as "upper class," "unique" and "successful," while individuals with a lower income tend to regard attributes such as "rugged" and "hard-working" as more important. Other studies reveal women to be family-oriented, and perceive attributes such as "feminine" and "honest" as particularly relevant, while men more often value brand characteristics such as "reliable" and "technical." However, previous studies that analyze the influence of these and other individual characteristics on brand personality often lack a sound theoretical explanation for these influences. Instead they are mostly conceptualized as control variables and thus not developed comprehensively.

In this study, it is argued that the effects of individual characteristics on brand perception can be explained from a constructivist perspective. Constructivism stresses that individuals with different demographic, biographic and psychographic backgrounds perceive the various aspects of their environment differently and consequently find different aspects to be important (Berger and Luckmann, 1967; Glasersfeld, 1995). Perceptions usually refer to the process by which external stimuli are selected, organized and interpreted by individuals. In the context of country-of-origin research, the perceptual process could help to explain how consumers evaluate the country-of-origin cue, compared with other cues such as price, quality, design and warranties (Roth and Diamantopoulos, 2009).

The literature on consumer behavior demonstrates that the process of brand perception is influenced by consumers' demographic, biographic and psychographic background (Hoyer and MacInnis, 2006; Schiffman and Kanuk, 2009; Solomon et al., 2010). Such differences in background can lead consumers' attention to specific attributes and may thus result in selective perceptions and evaluations. Selective perception implies that consumers focus on stimuli that relate to their personality and tend to ignore unrelated stimuli. More precisely, they perceive a brand through dimensions that typically capture their own personal background and interpret brand information with regard to their age, experience, education and so on (Suwa, 2003; Sung and Kim, 2010; Cronin and Weingart, 2007). These considerations lead to the following research hypotheses.

## Research hypotheses

As argued above, the basic assumption of this study is that the perceptions of Chinese and Indian brands are strongly influenced by country-of-origin effects. Consumers often do not have profound knowledge (and can even be unaware) of Chinese and Indian brands. They therefore use the country of origin as a surrogate (Bluemelhuber et al., 2007; Balabanis and Diamantopoulos, 2008). While China and India are recognized as emerging economies with high growth rates and high inflows of Western FDI, remarkable differences in the perceptions of the two countries exist (Meredith, 2008; Sheth, 2008; Gupta and Wang, 2009). China is often portrayed as a new economic superpower with both positive and negative consequences for industrialized countries. Moreover, global events such as the Olympic Games in Beijing in 2008 and the Expo in Shanghai in 2010 have attracted public attention. Although both China and India have liberalized their economies, China started this process 12 years earlier and has been able to generate higher growth rates than India. For India, the news coverage is less extensive and refers a great deal to negative issues, such as poverty and environmental disasters. As China receives better and more complex media coverage than India, it is assumed that the images of these countries vary and, consequently, that brands from the two countries will be perceived differently.

The perceptual differences between Chinese and Indian brands have also been revealed in previous empirical studies. For example, Fetscherin and Toncar (2009) analyze consumers' evaluations of Chinese and Indian cars in the United States, based on Aaker's brand personality scale, and reveal that Chinese cars are perceived to be more "daring," "up to date" and "upper class." Moreover, they are considered to be more "intelligent" and "successful." In general, the findings indicate that Chinese cars are perceived as having the potential to be "exciting," "competent" and "sophisticated," which is not the case for cars from India.

With regard to India, Patel (2009) analyzes the brand personality of the newly launched Indian automobile brand Nano by Tata Motors. The study reveals that four out of five brand-personality dimensions are applicable to the Nano brand. These dimensions are "sincerity," "excitement," "competence" and "sophistication." "Ruggedness" was not perceived to be suitable for the personality of the Nano brand. According to a study among Indian consumers by Jin et al. (2006), Indian brands are regarded as "reliable," capable of "good performance," "hand-made" and sold at "reasonable" prices. Simultaneously, they are perceived to be of "poor design," "common," "imitative," "technically backward" and meant for the lower classes. These considerations lead to the following hypothesis:

*H1: The perceived brand personalities of Chinese and Indian brands differ.*

Earlier studies reveal a significant relationship between age and the strength of the country-of-origin effect (Schweiger et al., 1997). Younger consumers tend to show less consumer ethnocentrism, are less affected by country-of-origin cues in their product evaluations and thus hold less rigorous attitudes toward foreign products than older consumers (Dickerson, 1982; Wall and Heslop, 1986). This is also confirmed for brands from emerging countries, as Huang et al. (2008) and Wang and Gao (2010) suggest.

With regard to the underlying theoretical framework, the age-relatedness of brand evaluations can be explained through sources of information used by members of different age groups. Due to a more extensive exposure to new media such as the Internet, social networks and other information platforms with global reach, younger people are often less traditional and tend to exhibit a more liberal attitude toward new products (Jeffres et al., 2004; Lee, 2008; Iske et al., 2008). Furthermore, younger consumers in developed countries experience a liberal and open economy with an abundance of products imported from abroad. Although they might consider brands from emerging countries such as China and India as being of low quality, they may also find them to be more exiting, trendy or cooler than would older consumers (Demirbag et al., 2010). This is in line with research regarding differentiated perceptions of younger and older people due to varied life experience (Bengtson, 1971; Barsalou, 2008), and studies that reveal age's effects on cognition and information processing (Wong et al., 2008; Hertzog et al., 2010). Therefore the following hypothesis is derived:

*H2a: The perceived brand personalities of Chinese and Indian brands are influenced by the consumer's age.*

The influence that the consumer's level of education has on country-of-origin effects has frequently been analyzed in previous studies (Insch and McBride, 2004). Some studies find that higher levels of education are associated with more positive attitudes toward foreign products (Wall et al., 1991; Niss, 1996; Ahmed and d'Astous, 2002). Other studies confirm that people with a higher level of education attach less importance to country-of-origin cues (Festervand et al., 1985; Shrimp and Sharma, 1987; Usunier, 1996; Nijssen and Douglas, 2004; Erdogan and Uzkurt, 2010).

With regard to the underlying theoretical perspective, this phenomenon can be explained by the enhanced cognitive capacities of well-educated individuals (Pressley et al., 1989). Higher levels of education enable individuals to perceive their environment in a more differentiated way and to incorporate various sources of information into cognitive processes. In the context of brand evaluations, enhanced cognitive capacities may reduce the halo effect – that is, the tendency to focus on a single stimulus, such as country-of-origin cues (Yu and Chen, 1993). Therefore the following hypothesis is proposed:

*H2b: The perceived brand personalities of Chinese and Indian brands are influenced by the consumer's level of education.*

Previous research reveals that the perception of foreign countries is also influenced by consumers' international experiences. In particular, the cultural adjustment literature suggests that international experience (e.g., during a private holiday or an occupational overseas assignment) helps individuals to develop a more realistic attitude toward other countries and to build a cosmopolitan mindset (McEvoy and Parker, 1995; Shaffer and Harrison, 1998; Holtbrügge, 2008). Empirical studies emphasize the role of an individual's willingness to create new experiences, particularly while traveling (Black et al., 1992). Other studies argue that previous international experience is an explicit means of augmenting intercultural competence and of creating a multifaceted image of countries (Gregersen et al., 1998; Takeuchi et al., 2005). When individuals travel to foreign countries – even if for a short holiday – they have the opportunity to perceive, process, understand and associate attitudes, customs and norms, and to create more complex images in their mind that reach beyond simple stereotypes (Huang et al., 2005; Takeuchi et al., 2005).

It can be argued that international experience is also relevant when evaluating brands from other countries (Cannon and Yaprak, 2002; Nijssen and Douglas, 2008; Riefler and Diamantopoulos, 2009). For example, it may reduce ethnocentrism and thus decrease the halo effect when evaluating foreign products. From a constructivist perspective, internationally experienced people are argued to develop more differentiated perspectives of other countries and to use more distinct attributes when evaluating products from these countries. According to Watson and Wright (2000), this effect is particularly important when products from culturally distant countries, such as China and India, are evaluated. Therefore the following hypothesis is derived:

*H3a: The perceived brand personalities of Chinese and Indian brands are influenced by the consumer's international experience.*

In the context of this study, it is argued that not experience in other countries in general but experience in China and India in particular may influence an individual's image of brands from these countries. Given the idiosyncrasies of the Chinese and Indian cultures, it is argued that the experience a person has had in other countries may not directly translate when applied to these two countries. This argument is in line with Thomas (2007), who notes that intercultural learning is, to a large extent, culture-bound – that is, attitudes toward a country are mainly influenced by the experience of the individual in and with the particular country and not so much by their international experience in general.

The relevance of country-specific experience in the perception of foreign countries is particularly demonstrated by the cultural adjustment literature. For example, Takeuchi et al. (2005) show that culture-specific international experience has a more positive effect on adjustment than general international experience. A study of Selmer (2002) shows that in the context of US expatriates in Asia, only prior experience in

Asia has a significant influence on their perceived adjustment. This is consistent with the findings of other studies, which show that country-specific international experience has a greater effect on adjustment than overall international experience (Black and Gregersen, 1991; Black et al., 1991). It can be argued that this effect is also relevant to the perception of brands held by other countries, so the following hypothesis is proposed:

> *H3b: The perceived brand personalities of Chinese and Indian brands are influenced by the consumer's experiences in China and India.*

Curiosity has been a widely discussed topic in the marketing literature with regard to consumer attitudes and brand evaluation (Haugtvedt et al., 1992; Hirschmann and Stern, 2001; Schmitt and Lahroodi, 2008). From a constructivist perspective, curiosity refers to an individual's tendency to be open to new ideas, values and experiences, and to consider new stimuli in perceptual processes. Individuals with a large degree of curiosity appreciate the merits of trying new things and are open to new experiences (Le Pine et al., 2000; Kashdan et al., 2004; Schmitt and Lahroodi, 2008). Curious people are inclined to be interested in a range of topics and to focus on the development of many things at once (Menon and Soman, 2002; Reio and Callahan, 2004). Furthermore, curious people are believed to be interested in novelties, such that they make adjustments to existing attitudes and behavior more easily once they have been exposed to new ideas or situations (Stephan, 2009).

In the context of this study, it is argued that China and India are countries with which the majority of consumers might be unfamiliar, and thus are still novel in terms of their recently increased emergence and presence on the global stage. This may also affect the perception of brands from these two countries (Reio and Callahan, 2004; Hu and Tsai, 2009). For example, curious individuals may be more interested in Chinese and Indian products because of their newness. Thus, curiosity may reduce persistent negative attitudes toward these two countries. This leads to the following hypothesis:

> *H4a: The perceived brand personalities of Chinese and Indian brands are influenced by the consumer's level of curiosity.*

Finally, the perceived personalities of Chinese and Indian brands are thought to be influenced by brand awareness. This is defined as a potential buyer's ability to recognize or recall a brand (Aaker 1991; Keller 1993). Several studies reveal a relationship between brand awareness and brand evaluation (Hoyer and Brown, 1990; Cobb-Walgren et al., 1995; Kathuria and Jit, 2009). Brand awareness results mainly from exposure to advertising and other sources of information. Repeated exposure leads to increased brand awareness. Meanwhile, perceived risks tend to decrease (McDonald and Sharp, 2000; Oh, 2000). Other studies show that familiarity leads to a greater affinity for the brand (Janiszewski, 1988; Nelson and McLeod, 2005), and that brand awareness is a first vital step in building a set of associations that are attached to a brand (Stokes, 1985; Rossiter and Percy, 1987; Porter and Claycomb, 1997).

Brand awareness is also assumed to be fundamental in the evaluation of Chinese and Indian brands (Wang and Yang, 2010). Individuals with regular exposure to brands from these two countries may have reflected on their attributes more often. As a consequence, they may have a more positive and differentiated perception of Chinese and Indian brands than individuals with less brand awareness. Thus the following is proposed:

*H4b: The perceived brand personalities of Chinese and Indian brands are influenced by the consumer's awareness of these brands.*

Figure 11.1 summarizes the hypotheses and integrates them into the research model.

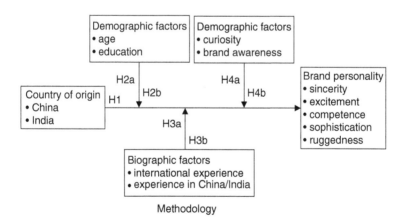

*Figure 11.1* Conceptual framework and research model

## Methodology

### Sample and method

To test the research hypotheses, an empirical study was conducted in Germany between November and December 2008 using a cross-sectional mall-intercept survey. Shopping-mall consumers constitute an adequate sampling universe. Given that they are supposed to have a strong purchase intention and a strong affinity toward purchasing, it may be assumed that they will be willing to answer product-related questions. Furthermore, they are likely to constitute a heterogeneous sample regarding relevant demographic characteristics, which is a major advantage compared with the student samples so often used in country-of-origin studies (Tull and Hawkins, 1990; Liefeld et al., 1996; Pappu et al., 2007).

A questionnaire that covers all aspects of this study was developed based on previous studies. Because the respondents were Germans, questions that were derived from previous studies published in English were translated into German. Afterwards, the questionnaire was back-translated to ensure the reliability and appropriate translation of the items. In a pre-test, the questionnaire was distributed to a sample of 50 individuals and subsequently revised to improve readability and understanding. Because individuals' perceptions of countries' images are known to differ based on their home country, this effect was controlled for by including only German respondents (see also Pappu et al., 2007).

The sample comprised 335 female respondents (51.2%) and 319 male respondents (48.8%). This gender distribution corresponds with the distribution in the German population to a large degree. The age range was from 16 to 75 years with a median of 38.6 years. The age distribution shifted toward the younger population compared with the age distribution in Germany. In particular, the sample consisted of a larger proportion of individuals in the category between 15 and 29 years of age. To control for this effect, an analysis was run using the data of the overrepresented group, weighted according to the real distribution. The results showed no differences compared with the total sample. Therefore the results of the total sample were used to include all of the available information.

In the mall-intercept study, the participants were asked to evaluate the brand personalities of two laptops, one from China and the other from India. Generally, laptops are frequently chosen in country-of-origin studies because the product category is familiar to most respondents.

Moreover, previous studies have demonstrated that the evaluation of laptops involves extensive attribute-based processing in addition to the influence of the product's country of origin (Hong and Wyer, 1989; Page and Herr, 2002; Liu and Johnson, 2005). In contrast with cars, which are also often used as a product category in country-of-origin studies (Fetscherin and Toncar, 2010), Chinese and Indian laptops have been available in Germany for several years.

Another reason for choosing laptops as the product category is that the IT industry is regarded as strategically important in China and India as a main driver of economic growth. Both countries are catching up in this sector, and Chinese and Indian IT MNCs are becoming increasingly competitive in the international marketplace (Gupta and Wang, 2009; Niosi and Tschang, 2009). In recent years, the number of computer brands and models has grown considerably as the gaps in quality, performance and amenities have closed significantly. Although variations in quality and performance still exist, strategies around styling and other intangibles, including the emotional benefits for the customers, provide greater competitive advantages to a computer brand. Consumers are supposed to attach significantly greater importance to brand benefits than to a computer's functional attributes as long as they meet minimum standards (Aaker, 2011). Therefore it is particularly important to build a strong brand image in the industry and to understand how the brand is perceived by various consumer groups.

The participants were randomly assigned to two subsamples: one group to the Chinese brand and the other to the Indian brand. Pre-tests showed that the willingness to evaluate 42 items for two brands was poor, and thus represented a very high drop-out rate. Therefore each respondent was asked to rate either the Chinese or the Indian laptop. Only fully completed questionnaires were included in the study. In the end, 301 respondents evaluated the Chinese laptop and 353 respondents evaluated the Indian laptop.

### Measures

At the beginning of the survey the respondents were shown an identical photo and were informed that the laptop was made in China and carries a Chinese brand name. For the Indian subsample the procedure was analogous. Moreover, the participants received identical technical information about the laptop. Afterwards they were asked to rate the brand personalities of the Chinese and the Indian laptops, respectively, on Aaker's 42-item scale (Aaker, 1997). A seven-point Likert scale was used.

The second part of the survey contained questions in relation to the consumer's demography, biography and psychography. The participants were asked to specify their age in years (Wall et al., 1991; Huang et al., 2008). The level of education was assessed by indicating the highest obtained graduation out of five indicated education levels (Festervand et al., 1985; Shrimp and Sharma, 1987; Wall et al., 1991). For international experience, the total number of travel experiences was assessed (Nijssen and Douglas, 2008). Participants were asked to indicate how many different countries they had visited outside the EU and the length of total time spent abroad (in weeks) for holidays or business reasons (Selmer, 2002; Takeuchi et al., 2005; Huang et al., 2008). Country-specific experience was assessed by indicating the total number of weeks spent in China and India, respectively (Selmer, 2002; Takeuchi et al., 2005). In line with previous studies (Selmer, 2002; Takeuchi et al., 2005; Huang et al., 2008) the participants were also asked to distinguish between private holidays and business travel but provided a very low rate of differentiated answers. Curiosity was assessed on a seven-point Likert scale using three items ("I like to try new things," "I'd rather stick to things that I am familiar with" and "I am interested in new countries and cultures") (Kashdan et al., 2004; Hu and Tsai, 2009; Stephan, 2009). The second item was reverse coded. Cronbach's alpha was 0.643 for the overall sample (0.622 for the China subsample and 0.683 for the India subsample), thus showing sufficient reliability, as suggested by Nunnally (1978). Finally, the respondents were asked if they were aware of brands from China or India. A list of brand labels from the 20 largest Chinese and Indian companies with operations in Germany was presented (Interbrand, 2007, Forbes, 2008) and the product category was mentioned (Aaker, 1991). The respondents had to indicate which brands they knew (Pappu et al., 2007). The arithmetical average of the responses (with $0 = $ "no" and $1 = $ "yes") was calculated and coded as brand awareness.

## Results and discussion

In a first step the reliability and equivalence of the five dimensions of the brand personality scale were assessed. Table 11.1 reveals high scale reliabilities with Cronbach's alphas ranging from 0.796 to $-0.935$ for all five dimensions in both subsamples. This is confirmed by Hotelling's T-squared test. The means of the five dimensions differ significantly at the $p < 0.000$ level.

*Table 11.1*   Reliability and equivalence of brand personality dimensions

| Dimensions | No. of items | Cronbach's alpha | Hotelling's T-squared | F-value | df | p-value |
|---|---|---|---|---|---|---|
| **China** | | | | | | |
| Sincerity | 11 | 0.927 | 244.218 | 23.687 | 10 | 0.000 |
| Excitement | 11 | 0.934 | 379.442 | 36.806 | 10 | 0.000 |
| Competence | 9 | 0.935 | 275.462 | 38.562 | 8 | 0.000 |
| Sophistication | 6 | 0.887 | 214.326 | 42.292 | 5 | 0.000 |
| Ruggedness | 5 | 0.831 | 245.636 | 60.791 | 4 | 0.000 |
| **India** | | | | | | |
| Sincerity | 11 | 0.907 | 283.639 | 27.639 | 10 | 0.000 |
| Excitement | 11 | 0.920 | 273.827 | 26.683 | 10 | 0.000 |
| Competence | 9 | 0.919 | 281.465 | 39.524 | 8 | 0.000 |
| Sophistication | 6 | 0.848 | 234.818 | 46.430 | 5 | 0.000 |
| Ruggedness | 5 | 0.796 | 135.301 | 33.537 | 4 | 0.000 |

*Table 11.2*   Perceptual differences between China and India (means, SD and ANOVA results)

| Dimensions | China (means/SD) | India (means/SD) | F(df) | p |
|---|---|---|---|---|
| Sincerity | 3.2503 (1.229) | 3.3399 (1.111) | 0.957 (1) | 0.328 |
| Excitement | 3.4959 (1.288) | 3.5336 (1.204) | 0.149 (1) | 0.149 |
| Competence | 4.1533 (1.381) | 3.7234 (1.215) | 17.904 (1) | 0.000 |
| Sophistication | 3.1322 (1.279) | 3.0604 (1.170) | 0.560 (1) | 0.454 |
| Ruggedness | 3.8783 (1.320) | 3.4198 (1.218) | 21.236 (1) | 0.000 |

In a second step an ANOVA was conducted to test whether the means of the five dimensions for the two countries were equal (Table 11.2). The results reveal that the Indian laptop was rated higher in "sincerity" and generally supposed to be more "exciting," while the Chinese laptop was regarded as being more "sophisticated," "rugged" and "competent". The differences for "competence" and "ruggedness" are significant at the p < 0.001 level. Generally the arithmetical average of the five dimensions is higher for China (mean = 3.5803) than for India (mean = 3.4155), suggesting that the Chinese brand has a better image than the Indian brand. The difference is significant at the p < 0.1 level, thus confirming H1.

The higher degree of competence and ruggedness attributed to Chinese brands may be explained by the overall image of China as a well-organized, hard-working and highly regulated country. Moreover, the brand personality perceptions reflect the economic success of the country in the last 30 years, which is fundamentally based on the mass production of reliable products and technological achievements. India, in contrast, is regarded as more exotic and different compared to Western countries.

This is also reflected in a closer look at the single items of the brand personality scale. Table 11.3 exhibits the means and standard deviations of all 42 items for the two brands. Moreover, an ANOVA was conducted to test the significance of differences (highlighted in bold letters). The results show that the Chinese laptop is rated as "independent," "contemporary," "reliable," "secure," "hard working," "technical," "corporate," "successful," "confident," "upper class," "Western," "tough" and "rugged". The Indian laptop is perceived to be more "cheerful," "friendly," "trendy," "exciting," "young" and "good looking".

To test for multicollinearity, two-tailed correlations of the independent variables were computed. No correlation was above the 0.40 level, as recommended by Cohen et al. (2003). Moreover, variance inflation factors (VIF) were calculated. All of the VIFs were below 5, indicating no concern for multicollinearity (Cohen et al., 2003).

Two multiple regression analyses were conducted to test H2 to H4. The results are presented in tables 11.4 and 11.5. All of the models are significant at a minimum $p < 0.01$ level. Generally the regression analyses reveal greater explanatory power for the China models ($0.070 < R^2$ adj. $< 0.186$) than for the India models ($0.036 < R^2$ adj. $< 0.080$). The medium-to-low $R^2$ are of little concern here because it was not the purpose of the study to reveal all possible determinants of brand-personality perceptions but to analyze the relevance of demographic, biographic and psychographic determinants. There are obviously other factors that may explain variances in perceived brand personalities, such as personality traits or purchase intentions, but these are not the focus of the study. This is in line with previous studies regarding country-of-origin effects and product evaluations, which often show low $R^2$ values (Thelen et al., 2006; Balabanis and Diamantopoulos, 2008; Ahmed and d'Astous, 2008). One explanation may be that cross-sectional data across individual subjects are prone to yielding weak explanatory relationships (Heimbach et al., 1989).

H2a proposed the significant effects of age on the perceived brand personality. Regression analyses for the Chinese laptop show significant negative age effects on all five dimensions. The older consumers are, the lower they rate the Chinese laptop in terms of "sincerity," "excitement," "competence," "sophistication" and "ruggedness." In the case of the Indian laptop, age has a significant positive effect on "excitement" and "ruggedness" – that is, older consumers have a more positive perception

*Table 11.3* Perceptions of brand personality (means, SD and ANOVA results)

| Dimensions | Items | China | | India | |
|---|---|---|---|---|---|
| | | Mean | SD | mean | SD |
| Sincerity | down-to-earth | 3.71 | 1.533 | 3.58 | 1.528 |
| | family-oriented | 3.17 | 1.524 | 3.25 | 1.505 |
| | small-town | 2.88 | 1.562 | 3.00 | 1.559 |
| | honest | 3.65 | 1.537 | 3.78 | 1.499 |
| | sincere | 3.57 | 1.598 | 3.68 | 1.461 |
| | real | 3.69 | 1.685 | 3.82 | 1.520 |
| | wholesome | 3.08 | 1.639 | 2.91 | 1.463 |
| | original | 3.09 | 1.705 | 2.99 | 1.520 |
| | **cheerful** | **3.11** | **1.667** | **3.41** | **1.738** |
| | sentimental | 2.42 | 1.553 | 2.60 | 1.464 |
| | **friendly** | **3.41** | **1.727** | **3.72** | **1.683** |
| Excitement | daring | 2.85 | 1.625 | 3.04 | 1.502 |
| | **trendy** | **3.52** | **1.662** | **3.98** | **1.716** |
| | **exciting** | **3.07** | **1.678** | **3.38** | **1.616** |
| | spirited | 2.82 | 1.631 | 3.01 | 1.647 |
| | cool | 3.49 | 1.735 | 3.47 | 1.620 |
| | **young** | **3.62** | **1.769** | **3.91** | **1.704** |
| | imaginative | 3.55 | 1.750 | 3.54 | 1.649 |
| | unique | 3.03 | 1.615 | 2.95 | 1.589 |
| | **up-to-date** | **4.23** | **1.632** | **4.01** | **1.688** |
| | **independent** | **3.85** | **1.611** | **3.46** | **1.494** |
| | **contemporary** | **4.41** | **1.537** | **4.11** | **1.513** |
| Competence | **reliable** | **4.17** | **1.679** | **3.61** | **1.408** |
| | **hard working** | **4.01** | **1.749** | **3.63** | **1.541** |
| | **secure** | **4.00** | **1.677** | **3.58** | **1.438** |
| | intelligent | 4.17 | 1.717 | 3.98 | 1.567 |
| | **technical** | **4.87** | **1.532** | **4.43** | **1.626** |
| | **corporate** | **4.49** | **1.661** | **3.92** | **1.665** |
| | **successful** | **4.03** | **1.663** | **3.64** | **1.470** |
| | leader | 3.49 | 1.662 | 2.99 | 1.439 |
| | **confident** | **4.15** | **1.698** | **3.60** | **1.503** |
| Sophistication | **upper class** | **3.99** | **1.666** | **3.41** | **1.468** |
| | glamorous | 2.86 | 1.532 | 2.67 | 1.526 |
| | **good looking** | **3.43** | **1.637** | **3.71** | **1.634** |
| | charming | 3.20 | 1.611 | 3.15 | 1.562 |
| | feminine | 2.54 | 1.550 | 2.54 | 1.557 |
| | smooth | 2.79 | 1.591 | 2.89 | 1.560 |
| Ruggedness | outdoorsy | 2.75 | 1.646 | 2.74 | 1.640 |
| | masculine | 3.73 | 1.874 | 3.24 | 1.766 |
| | **Western** | **4.25** | **1.633** | **3.84** | **1.742** |
| | **tough** | **4.28** | **1.655** | **3.53** | **1.524** |
| | **rugged** | **4.42** | **1.714** | **3.76** | **1.520** |

*Table 11.4*   Regression analysis for China

|  | Sincerity | Excitement | Competence | Sophistication | Ruggedness |
|---|---|---|---|---|---|
| Age | −0.264*** | −0.191** | −0.248*** | −0.192** | −0.160* |
| Education | −0.201** | −0.166* | −0.092 | −0.274*** | −0.188** |
| International Experience | 0.004 | −0.038 | 0.008 | −0.018 | 0.055 |
| Experience in China | −0.003 | 0.057 | −0.050 | 0.043 | −0.073 |
| Curiosity | 0.146* | 0.116† | 0.127* | 0.089 | 0.147* |
| Awareness | 0.154** | 0.154** | 0.316*** | 0.199** | 0.265*** |
| $R^2$ | 0.127 | 0.089 | 0.203 | 0.114 | 0.140 |
| $R^2$ adjusted | 0.109 | 0.070 | 0.186 | 0.096 | 0.122 |
| F | 7.076*** | 4.775*** | 12.386*** | 6.283*** | 7.896*** |

*Note*: n = 301.
* = p < 0.05, ** = p < 0.01 and *** = p < 0.001.

*Table 11.5*   Regression analysis for India

|  | Sincerity | Excitement | Competence | Sophistication | Ruggedness |
|---|---|---|---|---|---|
| Age | 0.069 | 0.201** | 0.052 | 0.079 | 0.162** |
| Education | 0.044 | −0.051 | 0.068 | −0.043 | −0.002 |
| International Experience | −0.030 | −0.058 | 0.004 | 0.004 | 0.027 |
| Experience in India | 0.068 | 0.070 | 0.067 | 0.051 | 0.142 |
| Curiosity | 0.239*** | 0.243*** | 0.218*** | 0.204*** | 0.258*** |
| Awareness | −0.090 | 0.054 | 0.124* | 0.032 | −0.007 |
| $R^2$ | 0.063 | 0.069 | 0.085 | 0.053 | 109 |
| $R^2$ adjusted | 0.046 | 0.080 | 0.069 | 0.036 | 0.093 |
| F | 3.774** | 5.967*** | 5.265** | 3.138** | 6.908*** |

*Note*: n = 353.
* = p < 0.05, ** = p < 0.01 and *** = p < 0.001.

of these two dimensions. The coefficients for the other three dimensions are also positive but not significant. Thus H2a is fully confirmed for China and partially for India.

A possible explanation for the divergent effect of age on the perceptions of products from China and India may be that older individuals still associate China with the former Maoist regime and political oppression, while younger consumers may perceive the country as more positive in terms of its recent tremendous economic success. India, however, had a positive image in the 1960s and 1970s as an exotic tourist destination, hippy attraction and spiritual hotspot, and these perceptions may still influence older individuals' perceptions of the country. Younger people, in contrast, may be more influenced by current media reports about poverty, social differences and natural disasters in India. This negative lens may also affect young consumers' perceptions of Indian brands.

H2b proposed that the consumer's level of education influences the perceived brand personality. Significantly negative effects on "sincerity," "excitement," "sophistication" and "ruggedness" can be assessed in the case of the Chinese laptop. The higher the consumer's level of education, the lower the rating is for these four dimensions of brand personality. One explanation for the negative effect of education is that more highly educated people may pay more attention to negative aspects, such as perceived human rights violations and lack of social and environmental responsibility, which may lead to a more critical view of Chinese products. In contrast, the effect of education is not significant for India. Thus H2b is confirmed for China but not for India.

H3a and H3b proposed the significant effects of international experience and experience in the respective country on the perceived brand personality. No such effects are found, thus H3a and H3b are not confirmed. Neither international experience in general nor experience in China or India in particular have a significant effect on the perceived brand personality. One explanation for this finding may be that the number of countries visited and the length of time spent in China or India might not be relevant. Instead, the purpose (holiday, study or business) and the quality of the experiences (good or bad) during one's stay might influence the evaluation of brand personality. Future studies should consider this aspect and include not only the number and duration of stays but also the evaluation of these stays as an independent variable. It should also distinguish between business and holiday trips, which was not possible in this study due to the small number of responses to this question.

H4a proposed that curiosity would have a significant effect on the dimensions of brand personality. In the case of the Chinese laptop, influences on "sincerity," "excitement," "competence" and "ruggedness" can be found, albeit only at a modest level. In the case of the Indian laptop, curiosity has a highly significant effect on all five dimensions. H4a is therefore supported by the data.

H4b proposed that the perceived brand personality is influenced by brand awareness. Regression analyses for the Chinese brand reveal significant effects on all five dimensions. The more consumers are aware of Chinese brands, the more positively they are perceived. For the Indian laptop, brand awareness only influences the perceived competence. Thus H4b can be confirmed only partially.

## Contributions, limitations and implications

The purpose of this study was to analyze the similarities and differences in the perceived personalities of Chinese and Indian brands, and to explore which demographic, biographic and psychographic determinants influence these perceptions. Based on Aaker's brand personality scale, a mall-intercept study was conducted using a sample of 654 German individuals.

The study extends the literature on country-of-origin effects not only by exploring differences in the perceptions of Chinese and Indian brands in general but also by analyzing on which brand personality dimensions these differences arise. Moreover, demographic, biographic and psychographic factors were included in the research and their effects on brand personality perceptions were examined. The results reveal these factors to have significant influences that have been underestimated in previous research.

A major result of this study is that the personalities of Chinese and Indian brands are perceived differently by German consumers. Chinese brands receive significantly higher values in terms of "competence" and "ruggedness," while Indian brands are mostly perceived as "exiting," "trendy" and "young". The study further reveals that Chinese brands are perceived more positively among younger consumers while the image of Indian brands is better among older consumers. Moreover, education has a negative effect and brand awareness a positive effect on the perception of Chinese brands, while curiosity does increase the perceived image of brands from both countries.

These results lead to various managerial implications. In particular, they may help Chinese and Indian MNCs in their market segmentation and marketing-mix decisions. For example, Chinese MNCs may find it easier to attract younger and less-educated individuals while older consumers may constitute a more suitable target group for Indian MNCs. Moreover, curious individuals may be a more prospective target group from both countries than conservative consumers. Similar recommendations may be derived for branding strategies – that is, for the use of slogans, pictures, communication channels and so on.

This study may also help Chinese and Indian MNCs to obtain a more realistic picture of their image among German consumers. Although the study did not explicitly analyze how Chinese and Indian MNCs view themselves, there is evidence of considerable perceptual gaps (see also Bandyopadhyay and Morais, 2005). While Indian MNCs often present themselves as successful and reliable (Srivastava and Mookerjee, 2004; Ghodeswar, 2008), according to this study, the image of Indian brands in Germany is mostly that of being exiting, trendy and young. Similarly, the brand management of Chinese MNCs often stresses the value of traditions and age (Faure and Fang, 2008; Li, 2008), which may discourage younger consumers as the target group with the most positive brand perception in Germany. This study may therefore help Chinese and Indian MNCs to close potential perception gaps with regard to their brand image in Germany and to more efficiently adapt their branding strategies to local conditions.

This study faces some limitations. First, the method of data collection may raise concern. Although mall-intercept surveys are frequently applied in country-of-origin studies, this method is not without criticism. For example, only mall clients are interviewed and thus the data may be biased toward regional mall shoppers (Bush and Hair, 1985). Moreover, the study includes only German respondents. Therefore it has to be proved whether the results would be similar in other countries or whether they are specific to Germany.

With regard to the measures, it is acknowledged that income levels would have been an interesting variable to include in the study. However, this variable is a sensitive construct in surveys, and is often regarded as intrusive by respondents. Thus questions related to income produce comparatively higher non-response rates or larger measurement error in responses than questions on other topics, especially in a face-to-face method (Tourangeau and Yan, 2007). The pre-test revealed that respondents were reluctant to answer questions related to income. Income was therefore not included in the study.

Furthermore, the results of this study should be interpreted with regard to the product category. Although laptops are frequently chosen in country-of-origin studies and the IT industry is regarded as strategically important in China and India, it is unclear whether the results may be transferred to other product categories. In particular, it would be interesting to include other consumer goods and industrial commodities and services to analyze similarities and differences.

Finally, this study may be limited by the cross-cultural generalizability of Aaker's brand-personality scale. While most previous studies ascribe Aaker's scale a high cross-cultural validity, the results with regard to China and India are ambiguous. For example, Thomas and Sekar (2008) conclude in a study of the Colgate brand in India that ten items of

Aaker's brand-personality scale are not applicable in the Indian setting. For China, Chua and Sung (2010) find that three dimensions of Aaker's scale ("competence," "excitement" and "sophistication") are consistent with those found in the United States, whereas three ("traditionalism," "joyfulness" and "trendiness") carry culture-specific meanings. Similarly, Shengbing and Taihong (2003) reveal five indigenous dimensions of brand personality in China: "benevolence," "wisdom," "courage," "happiness" and "elegance." Thus future studies should analyze whether Aaker's brand-personality scale should be modified to better capture the personalities of Chinese and Indian brands.

## References

Aaker, D. A. (1991) *Managing Brand Equity.* New York: The Free Press.

Aaker, D. A. (1996) *Building Strong Brands.* New York: The Free Press.

Aaker, D. A. (2011) *Brand Relevance: Making Competitors Irrelevant.* San Francisco: Jossey-Bass.

Aaker, J. L. (1997) "Dimensions of brand personality", *Journal of Marketing Research*, XXIV, 347–356.

Ahmed, S. A., & A. d'Astous (2002) "South East Asian consumers perception of country of origin: The case of automobiles and videocassette recorders", *Journal of Asia Pacific Marketing*, I, 19–41.

Ahmed, S. A., & A. d'Astous (2008) "Antecedents, moderators and dimensions of country-of-origin evaluations", *International Marketing Review*, XXV, 75–106.

Aiello, G., R. Donvito, B. Godey, D. Pederzoli, K.-P. Wiedmann, N. Hennings, A. Siebels, P. Chan, J. Tsuchiya, S. Rabino, S. I. Ivanovna, B. Weitz, H. Oh & R. Singh (2008) "An international perspective on luxury brand and country-of-origin effect", *Brand Management*, XVI, 323–337.

Alon, I., J. Chang, M. Fetscherin, C. Lattemann & J. R. McIntyre (eds.) (2009) *China Rules.* New York: Palgrave-McMillan.

Aulakh, P. S. (2007) "Emerging multinationals from developing countries: Motivations, paths and performance", *Journal of International Management*, XIII, 235–240.

Austin, J. R., J. A. Siguaw & A. S. Mattila (2003) "A re-examination of the generalizability of the Aaker brand personality measurement framework", *Journal of Strategic Management*, XI, 77–92.

Balabanis, G., & A. Diamantopoulos (2008) "Brand origin identification by consumers: A classification perspective", *Journal of International Marketing*, XVI, 39–71.

Bandyopadhyay, R., & D. Morais (2005) "Representative dissonance: India's self and Western image", *Annals of Tourism Research*, XXXII, 1006–1021.

Barsalou, L. W. (2008) "Grounded cognition", *Annual Revision of Psychology*, LIX, 617–645.

Bell, S. (2008) *International Brand Management of Chinese Companies. Case Studies on the Chinese Household Appliances and Consumer Electronics Industry Entering US and Western European Markets.* Berlin et al.: Springer.

Bengtson, V. L. (1971) "Inter-age perceptions and the generation gap", *The Gerontologist*, XI, 85–90.

Berger, P. L., & T. Luckmann (1967) *The Social Construction of Reality: A Treatise in the Sociology of Knowledge*. New York: Anchor.

Berning, S., & D. Holtbrügge (2012. "Chinese outward foreign direct investment – A challenge for traditional internationalization theories?" *Journal für Betriebswirtschaft*, LXII, 169–224.

Bhardwaj, V., A. Kumar & Y. K. Kim (2010) "Brand analyses of U.S. global and local brands in india: The case of Levi's", *Journal of Global Marketing*, XXIII, 80–94.

Black, J. S., & H. B. Gregersen (1991) "The other half of the picture: Antecedents of spouse cross-cultural adjustment", *Journal of International Business Studies*, XXII, 461–477.

Black, J. S., & M. E. Mendenhall (1992) *Global Assignments: Successfully Expatriating and Repatriating International Managers*. San Francisco: Jossey-Bass Publishers.

Black, J. S., M. Mendenhall & G. Oddou (1991) "Toward a comprehensive model of expatriate adjustment, an integration of multiple theoretical perspectives", *Academy of Management Review*, XVI, 291–317.

Bluemelhuber, C., L. L. Carter & C. J. Lambe (2007) "Extending the view of brand alliance effects: An integrative examination of the role of country of origin", *International Marketing Review*, XXIV, 427–443.

Buckley, P. J., L. J. Clegg, A. R. Cross, L. Xin, H. Voss & P. Zheng (2007) "The determinants of Chinese outward foreign investment", *Journal of International Business Studies*, XXXVIII, 499–518.

Buckley, P. J., & P. N. Ghauri (2004) "Globalization, economic geography and the strategy of multinational enterprises", *Journal of International Business Studies*, XXXV, 81–98.

Bush, A. J., & J. F. Hair (1985) "An assessment of the mall intercept as a data collection method" *Journal of Marketing Research*, XXII, 158–167.

Cannon, H. M., & A. Yaprak (2002) "Will the real-world citizen please Stand Up! The many faces of cosmopolitan consumer behavior. *Journal of International Marketing*, 10(4), 30–52.

Chua, S. C., & Y. Sung (2010) "Brand personality dimensions in China", *Journal of Marketing Communications*, http://www.informaworld.com/10.1080/13527260903387931, date accessed 6 March 2013.

Cobb-Walgren, C. J., C. A. Ruble & N. Donthu (1995) "Brand equity, Brand preference, and purchase intent", *Journal of Advertising*, XXIV, 25–40.

Cohen, J., P. Cohen, S. G. West & L. S. Aiken (2003) *Applied Multiple Regression/Correlation Analysis for the Behavioral Sciences*. Mahwan: Lawrence Erlbaum.

Cronin, M. A., & L. R. Weingart (2007) "Representational gaps, information processing, and conflict in functionally diverse teams", *Academy of Management Review*, XXXII, 761–773.

Demirbag, M., S. Sahadev & K. Mellahi (2010) "Country image and consumer preference for emerging economy products: The moderating role of consumer materialism", *International Marketing Review*, XXVII, 141–163.

Deng, P. (2009) "Why do Chinese firms tend to acquire strategic assets in international expansion?" *Journal of World Business*, ILIV, 74–84.

Dickerson, K. G. (1982) "Imported vs. US-produced apparel: Consumer views and buying patterns", *Home Economic Research Journal*, X, 241–252.

Erdogan, B. Z., & C. Ukurt (2010) "Effects of ethnocentric tendency on consumers" perception of product attributes for foreign and domestic products', *Cross Cultural Management*, XVII, 393–406.

Faure, G. O., & T. Fang (2008) "Changing Chinese values: Keeping up with paradoxes", *International Business Review*, XVII, 194–207.

Festervand, T. A., J. A. Lumpkin & W. Lundstrom (1985) "Consumers perceptions of imports: An update and extension", *Akron Business and Economic Review*, XVI, 31–36.

Fetscherin, M., & M. Toncar (2009) "Country of origin effects on U.S. consumers" brand personality perception of automobiles from China and India', *Multinational Business Review*, XVII, 111–127.

Fetscherin, M., & M. Toncar (2010) "The effects of the country of brand and the country of manufacturing of automobiles", *International Marketing Review*, XXVII, 164–178.

Forbes (2008) Forbes Global 2000, www.forbes.com, date accessed 15 October 2008.

Gammeltoft, P., H. Barnard & A. Madhok (2010) "Emerging multinationals, emerging theory: Macro- and micro-level perspectives", *Journal of International Management*, XVI, 95–101.

Geuens, M., B. Weijters & K. de Wul (2009) "A new measure of brand personality", *International Journal of Research in Marketing*, XXVI, 97–107.

Ghazali, M. M., S. Othman, A. Z. Yahya & M. S. Ibrahim (2008) "Products and country of origin effects: The Malaysian consumer perception", *International Review of Business Research Papers*, IV, 91–102.

Ghodeswar, B. M. (2008) "Building brand identity in competitive markets: A conceptual model", *Journal of Product & Brand Management*, XVII, 4–12.

Gregersen, H. B., A. J. Morrison & J. S. Black (1998) "Developing leaders for the global frontier", *Sloan Management Review*, XL, 21–32.

Gupta, A. K., & H. Wang (2009) *Getting China and India Right: Strategies for Leveraging the World's Fastest Growing Economies for Global Advantage*. San Francisco: Jossey-Bass.

Hamm, S. (2006) *Bangalore Tiger: How Indian Tech Upstart Wipro is Rewriting the Rules of Global Competition*. New York et al.: McGraw-Hill.

Hansen, M. W. (2009) "The rise of Indian multinationals: Explaining outward foreign direct investment from India" in R. Kumar & M. Patibandla (eds.) *Institutional Dynamics and the Evolution of the Indian Economy*. New York: Palgrave-McMillan.

Hattari, R., & R. S. Rajan (2010) "India as a source of outward foreign direct investment", *Oxford Development Studies*, XXXVIII, 497–518.

Haugtvedt, C. P., R. E. Petty & J. T. Cacioppo (1992) "Need for cognition and advertising: Understanding the role of personality variables in consumer behavior", *Journal of Consumer Psychology*, I, 239–260.

Heimbach, A. E., J. K. Johansson & D. MacLachlan (1989) "Product familiarity, information processing, and country-of-irigin cues", *Advances in Consumer Research*, XVI, 460–467.

Hertzog, C., S. M. Sinclair & J. Dunlosky (2010) "Age differences in the monitoring of learning: Cross-sectional evidence of spared resolution across the Adult Life Span", *Developmental Psychology*, XLVI, 939–948.

Hirschmann, E. C., & B. B. Stern (2001) "Do consumers" genes influence their behavior? Findings on novelty seeking and compulsive consumption", *Advances in Consumer Research*, XXVIII, 403–410.

Holtbrügge, D. (ed.) (2008) *Cultural Adjustment of Expatriates. Theoretical Concepts and Empirical Studies*. München-Mering: Hamp.

Holtbrügge, D., & S. Berning (2013) "How relevant is government support for Chinese outward foreign direct investment? – A Literature Review", in: C. C. Julian, Z. U. Ahmed & J. Xu (eds.) *Research Handbook on the Globalization of Chinese Firms*. Cheltenham: Edward Elgar (in press).

Holtbrügge, D., & H. Kreppel (2012) "Determinants of outward foreign direct investment from BRIC countries. An explorative study", *International Journal of Emerging Markets*, VII, 4–30.

Hong, S. T., & R. S. Wyer Jr. (1989) "Effects of country-of-origin and product-attribute information on product evaluation: An information processing perspective", *Journal of Consumer Research*, XVI, 175–187.

Hoyer, W. D., & S. P. Brown (1990) "Effects of brand awareness on choice for a common, repeat-purchase product", *Journal of Consumer Research*, XVII, 141–158.

Hoyer, W. D., & D. J. MacInnis (2006) *Consumer Behavior*, 4th edn. Mason: South-Western.

Hu, A. W., & W. M. Tsai (2009) "An empirical study of an enjoyment-based response hierarchy model of watching MDTV on the move", *Journal of Consumer Marketing*, XXVI, 66–77.

Huang, T. J., S. C. Chi & J. J. Lawler (2005) "The relationship between expatriates" personality traits and their adjustment to international assignments', *Journal of Human Resource Management*, XVI, 1656–1670.

Huang, Y. A., I. Phau, C. Lin, H. J. Chung & K. H. Lin (2008) "Allocentrism and consumer ethnocentrism: The effects of social identity on purchase intentions", *Social Behaviour and Personality*, VI, 1097–1110.

Insch, G. S., & J. B. McBride (2004) "The impact of country-of-origin cues on consumer perceptions of product quality: A binational test of the decomposed country-of-origin construct", *Journal of Business Research*, LVII, 256–265.

Interbrand (2007) *The Best Chinese Brands 2007*. Beijing: Interbrand Publication.

Iske, S., A. Klein, N. Kutscher & H. U. Otto (2008) "Young people's internet use and its significance for informal education and social participation", *Technology, Pedagogy and Education*, XVII, 131–141.

Janiszewski, C. (1988) "Preconscious processing effects: The independence of attitude formation and conscious "thought, *Journal of Consumer Research*, XV, 199–209.

Jeffres, L. W., D. J. Atkin, C. C. Bracken & K. A. Neuendorf (2004) "Cosmopoliteness in the internet age", *Journal of Computer-Mediated Communication*, X, http://onlinelibrary.wiley.com/doi/10.1111/j.1083-6101.2004.tb00227.x/full, date accessed 10 March 2013.

Jin, Z., B. Chansarkar & N. M. Kondap (2006) "Brand origin in an emerging market: Perception of Indian consumers", *Asia Pacific Journal of Marketing*, XVIII, 283–302.

Jinsheng, J., & S. Xian Ye (2003) *The Haier Way. The Making of a Chinese Business Leader and a Global Brand*. Dumont: Homa & Sekey Books.

Kashdan, T. B., P. Rose & F. D. Fincham (2004) "Curiosity and exploration: Facilitating positive subjective experiences and personal growth opportunities", *Journal of Personality Assessment*, LXXXII, 291–305.

Kathuria, L. M., & B. Jit (2009) "An empirical study on brand awareness and the factors influencing brand loyalty towards hair shampoos", *IUP Journal of Brand Management*, VI, 122–133.

Keller, K. L. (1993) "Conceptualizing, measuring and managing customer-based brand equity", *Journal of Marketing*, LVII, 1–22.

Kim, H. B., W. G. Kim & A. A. Jeong (2003) "The effect of consumer-based brand equity on firms' financial performance", *Journal of Consumer Marketing*, XX, 335–352.

Kinra, N. (2006) "The effect of country-of-origin on foreign brand names in the indian market", *Marketing Intelligence and Planning*, XXIV, 15–30.

Kreppel, H., & D. Holtbrügge (2012), The perceived attractiveness of Chinese products by German consumers. A socio-psychological approach', *Journal of Global Marketing*, XXV, 79–99.

Kumar, N. (2009) *India's Global Powerhouses: How They Are Taking on the World*. Boston: Harvard Business School Press.

Lee, E. J., & E. Y. Rhee (2008) "Conceptual framework of within-category brand personality based on consumers" perception (WCBP-CP): The Case of Men's Apparel Category in South Korea', *Brand Management*, XV, 465–489.

Lee, L. (2008) "The impact of young people's internet use on class boundaries and life trajectories", *Sociology*, XLII, 137–154.

LePine, J. A., J. A. Colquitt & A. Erez (2000) "Adaptability to changing task contexts: Effects of general cognitive ability, conscientiousness, and openness to experience", *Personnel Psychology*, LIII, 563–593.

Li, H. (2008) "Branding Chinese products. between nationalism and transnationalism", *International Journal of Communication*, II, 1125–1163.

Liefield, J. P., L. Heslop, N. Papadopoulos & M. Wall (1996) "Dutch consumer use of intrinsic, country-of-origin, and price cues in product evaluation and choice", *Journal of International Consumer Marketing*, IX, 57–81.

Lin, L. Y. (2010) "The relationship of consumer personality trait, brand personality and brand loyalty: An empirical study of toys and video games buyers" *Journal of Product and Brand Management*, XIX, 4–17.

Liu, S. S., & K. D. Johnson (2005) "The automatic country-of-origin effects on brand judgments", *Journal of Advertising*, XXXIV, 87–97.

Lumb, R., & V. Lall (2006) "Perception of the quality of products made in India by consumers from the United States. A longitudinal analysis", *Indian Journal of Economics and Business*, V, 47–60.

Makino, S., C.-M. Lau & R.-S. Yeh (2002) "Asset exploitation versus asset-seeking: Implications for location choice of foreign direct investment form newly industrialized economies", *Journal of International Business Studies*, XXXIII, 403–421.

McDonald, E. K., & B. M. Sharp (2000) "Brand awareness effects on consumer decision making for a common, repeat purchase product: A replication", *Journal of Business Research*, XLVIII, 5–15.

McEvoy, G. M., & B. Parker (1995) "Expatriate adjustment: Causes and consequences" in J. Selmer (ed.) *Expatriate Management: New Ideas for International Business*. Westport: Quorum Books.

Menon, S., & D. Soman (2002) "Managing the power of curiosity for effective web advertising strategies", *Journal of Advertising*, XXXI, 1–14.

Meredith, R. (2008) *The Elephant and the Dragon: The Rise of India and China and What it Means for All of Us*. New York: W.W. Norton & Company.

Michell, P., J. King & J. Reast (2001) "Brand Values Related to Industrial Products", *Industrial Marketing Management*, XXX, 415–425.

Milelli, C., F. Hay & Y. Shi (2010) "Chinese and Indian firms in Europe: Characteristics, impacts and policy implications", *International Journal of Emerging Markets*, V, 377–397.

Mulyanegara, R. C., Y. Tsarenko & A. Anderson (2009) "The big five and brand personality: Investigating the impact of consumer personality on preferences towards particular brand personality", *Journal of Brand Management*, XVI, 234–247.

Nargundhar, R., & C. Bajaj (2002) "International marketing strategy for Indian companies: Value, image and other issues", *ICFAI Journal of Marketing*, I, 67–73.

Nayyar, D. (2008) "The internationalisation of firms from India: Investment, mergers and acquisitions", *Oxford Development Studies*, XXXVI, 111–131.

Nelson, M. R., L. E. McLeod (2005) "Adolescent brand consciousness and product placements: Awareness, liking, and perceived effects on self and others", *International Journal of Consumer Studies*, XXIX, 515–528.

Nijssen, E. J., & S. P. Douglas (2004) "Examining the animosity model in a country with a high level of foreign trade", *International Journal of Research in Marketing*, XXI, 23–38.

Nijssen, E. J., & S. P. Douglas (2008) "Consumer world-mindedness, Social mindedness and store image", *Journal of International Marketing*, XVI, 84–107.

Niosi, J., & F. T. Tschang (2009) "The strategies of Chinese and Indian software multinationals: Implications for internationalization theory", *Industrial and Corporate Change*, XVIII, 269–294.

Niss, H. (1996) "Country of origin marketing over the product life cycle: A danish case study", *European Journal of Marketing*, XXX, 6–22.

Nunnally, J. (1978) *Psychometric Theory*, 2nd edn. New York et al.: McGraw-Hill.

Oh, H. (2000) "The effect of brand class, Brand awareness, and price on customer value and behavorial intentions", *Journal of Hospitality and Tourism Research*, XXIV, 136–162.

Page, C., & P. M. Herr (2002) "An investigation of the processes by which product design and brand strength interact to determine initial affect and quality judgments", *Journal of Consumer Psychology*, XII, 133–147.

Pappu, R., P. G. Quester & R. W. Cooksey (2007) "Country image and consumer-based brand equity: Relationships and implications for international marketing", *Journal of International Business Studies*, XXXVIII, 726–745.

Park, C. W., B. J. Jaworski D. J. MacInnis (1986) "Strategic brand concept: Image management", *Journal of Marketing*, L, 135–145.

Patel, V. (2009) "Measuring brand personality: An empirical study", *Prerana*, I, 59–67.

Porter, S. S., & C. Claycomb (1997) "The influence of brand recognition on retail store image", *Journal of Product and Brand Management*, VI, 373–387.

Plummer, J. T. (2000) "How personality makes a "difference, *Journal of Advertising Research*, XL, 79–84.

Pressley, M., J. G. Borkwski & W. Schneider (1989) "Good information processing: What it is and how education can promote it", *International Journal of Educational Research*, XIII, 857–867.

Rao, S. L. (2001) "Indian companies in an open economy", *Economic and Political Weekly*, XXXVI, 457–461.

Reio, T. G. Jr., & J. L. Callahan (2004) "Affect, curiosity, and socialization-related learning: A path analysis of antecedents to job performance", *Journal of Business and Psychology*, XIX, 3–22.

Riefler, P., & A. Diamantopoulos (2009) "Consumer cosmopolitanism: Review and replication of the CYMYC scale", *Journal of Business Research*, LXII, 407–419.

Roncha, A. (2008) "Nordic brands towards a design-oriented concept", *Journal of Brand Management*, XVI, 21–29.

Rossiter, J. R., & L. Percy (1987) *Advertising and Promotion Management*. Boston: McGraw-Hill.

Roth, K. P., & A. Diamantopoulos (2009) "Advancing the country image construct", *Journal of Business Research*, LXII, 726–740.

Rui, H., & G. S. Yip (2008) "Foreign acquisitions by Chinese firms: A Strategic intent perspective", *Journal of World Business*, XLIII, 213–226.

Schiffman, L., & L. Kanuk (2009) *Consumer Behavior*, 10th ed. Harlow: Prentice Hall.

Schmitt, F. F., & R. Lahroodi (2008) "The epistemic value of curiosity", *Educational Theory*, LVIII, 125–148.

Schweiger, G., T. Otter & A. Strebinger (1997) "The influence of country of origin and brand on product evaluation and the implications Thereof for location decisions", *CEMS Business Review*, II, 5–26.

Selmer, J. (2002) "Practice makes perfect? International experience and expatriate adjustment", *Management International Review*, XLII, 71–87.

Shaffer, M. A., & D. A. Harrison (1998) "Expatriates" psychological withdrawal from international assignments: Work, nonwork, and family influences', *Personnel Psychology*, LI, 87–118.

Shengbing, H., & L. Taihong (2003) "Dimensions of brand personality in China", *Nankai Business Review*, I, DOI: cnki: ISSN: 1008–3448.0.2003-01-001, date accessed 10 March 2013.

Sheth, J. N. (2008) *Chindia Rising. How China and India Will Benefit Your Business*. New York et al.: McGraw-Hill.

Sheth, J. N. (2009) "Making india globally competitive", *Vikalpa*, XXIX, 1–9.

Shimp, T. A., & S. Sharma (1987) "Consumer ethnocentrism: Construction and validation for the CETSCALE", *Journal of Marketing Research*, XXIV, 280–289.

Singal, A., & A. K. Jain (2012) "Outward FDI trends from India: Emerging MNCs and strategic issues", *International Journal of Emerging Markets*, VII, 443–456.

Smith, K. T., M. Smith, & K. Wang (2010) "Does brand management of corporate reputation translate into higher market value?", *Journal of Strategic Marketing*, XVIII, 201–221.

Solomon, M. R., G. Bamossy, S. Askegaard & M. K. Hogg (2010). *Consumer Behaviour. A European Perspective.* 4th ed., Harlow: Prentice Hall.

Srivastava, N. V., & A. Mookerjee (2004) "Determinants of brand equity for banking business application software products", *International Journal of Technology Management*, XXVIII, 128–138.

Stephan, Y. (2009) "Openness to experience and active older adults' life satisfaction: A trait and facet-level analysis", *Personality and Individual Differences*, XLVII, 637–661.

Stokes, R. C. (1985) "The effect of price, package design, and brand familiarity on perceived quality" in J. Jacoby, & J. C. Olson (eds.) *Perceived Quality.* Lexington: Lexington Books, 64–79.

Sung, Y., & J. Kim (2010) "Effect of brand personality on brand trust and brand effect", *Psychology and Marketing*, XXVII, 639–661.

Suwa, M. (2003) "Constructive perception: Coordinating perception and conception toward acts of problem-finding in a creative experience", *Japanese Psychological Research*, XLV, 221–234.

Takeuchi, R., P.E. Tesluk, S. Yun, & D. Lepak (2005) "An integrative view of international experience", *Academy of Management Journal.* XLVIII, 85–100.

Thelen, S., J.B. Ford, & E. D. Honeycutt (2006) "Assessing Russian Consumers' Imported versus Domestic Product Bias", *Thunderbird International Business Review*, XLVIII, 687–704.

Thomas, B. J., & P. C. Sekar (2008) "Measurement and validity of jennifer Aaker's brand personality scale", *Vikalpa*, XXXIII, 49–61.

Thiripurasundari, U., & P. Natarajan (2010) "Local brand vs. global brand syndrome – A study with reference to indian car industry", *Advances in Management*, III, 41–46.

Thite, M., A. Wilkinson & D. Shah (2012) "Internationalization and HRM strategies across subsidiaries in multinational corporations from emerging economies. A conceptual framework", *Journal of World Business*, XLVII, 251–258.

Thomas, A. (2007) "Intercultural training methods are culture specific: Culture assimilator as an example" in T. Schmalzer, G. Apfelthaler, K. Hansen & R. Singh (eds.) *Intercultural Communication Competence.* Macmillan India: Delhi, pp. 5–21.

Tourangeau, R., & T. Yan (2007) "Sensitive questions in surveys", *Psychological Bulletin*, CXXXIII, 859–883.

Tung, R. L. (2007) "The human resource challenge to outward foreign direct investment aspirations from emerging economies: The case of "China, *International Journal of Human Resource Management*, XVIII, 868–889.

Tull, D. S., & D. I. Hawkins (1990) *Marketing Research: Measurement and Method* New York, NY: Macmillan.

Usunier, J. C. (1996) *Marketing across Cultures.* 2nd edn Prentice Hall: London.

Von Glasersfeld, E. (1995) *Radical Constructivism: A Way of Knowing and Learning* London: Falmer Press.

Wall, M., & L. A. Heslop (1986) "Consumer attitudes toward Canadia-made versus imported products", *Journal of the Academy of Marketing Science*, XIV, 27–36.

Wall, M., J. Liefield & L. A. Heslop (1991) "Impact of country-of-origin cues on consumer judgments in multi-cue situations: A covariance analysis", *Journal of the Academy of Marketing Science*, XIX, 105–113.

Wang, J. (2010) *Brand New China: Advertising, Media, and Commercial Culture.* Boston: Harvard University Press.

Wang, X., & Y. Gao (2010) "Irish consumers' perception of Chinese band how to improve the 'Made in China' image", *Journal of Asia Business Studies*, IV, 80–85.

Wang, X., & Z. Yang (2010) "The effect of brand credibility on consumers" brand purchase intention in emerging economies. The moderating role of brand awareness and brand image', *Journal of Global Marketing*, XXIII, 177–188.

Watson, J. J., & K. Wright (2000) "Consumer ethnocentrism and attitudes towards domestic and foreign products", *European Journal of Marketing*, XXXIV, 1149–1466.

Wong, M., E. Gardner, W. Lang & L. Coulon (2008) "Generational differences in personality and motivation. Do they exist and what are the implications for the workplace?", *Journal of Managerial Psychology*, XXIII, 878–890.

Yu, C. M. J., & C. N. Chen (1993) "A research note on country-of-origin in industrial settings" in N. Papadopoulos & L. A. Heslop (eds.) *Product Country Images: Impact and Role in International Marketing.* New York: International Business Press, pp. 245–254.

Zeng, M., & P.J. Williamson (2003) "The hidden dragons", *Harvard Business Review*, VXXXI, 92–99.

Zhijun, L. (2006) *The Lenovo Affair: The Growth of China's Computer Giant and Its Takeover of IBM-PC.* New York et al.: Wiley.

# Index

Printed and bound in Great Britain by
CPI Group (UK) Ltd, Croydon, CR0 4YY